Born in Carshalton, Surrey, Kevin Hall spent his childhood in Bath, Somerset. He attended the City of Bath Grammar School, then moved to Isleworth to study at Borough Road Teacher Training College. He settled in Hounslow with his wife, Lindsey, where they raised a family, and he taught for 38 years in two local boys' secondary schools.

Kevin Michael Hall

SCHOOL SHIT

Dear Simon and Sophie,

A generation behind me, but both great mates.

Best wishes,

Kevin

7th Nov. 2017

AUSTIN MACAULEY PUBLISHERS™

LONDON • CAMBRIDGE • NEW YORK • SHARJAH

A CIP catalogue record for this title is available from the British Library.

ISBN 9781786935397 (Paperback)
ISBN 9781786935403 (Hardback)
ISBN 9781786935410 (E-Book)
www.austinmacauley.com

First Published (2017)
Austin Macauley Publishers Ltd.
25 Canada Square
Canary Wharf
London
E14 5LQ

Dedication

To Lindsey, who propped me up when I flagged over four decades in education and encouraged me to write, and to Rocco, my grandson, in the hope that his unique talents won't be overlooked in the machinery of the state school system.

Acknowledgements

The best times as a teacher are those when one is lucky enough to be an integral part of a vibrant and talented team. I am indebted to the best team mates with whom I worked for over a decade: Paul, Rosella, Verna and Patty.

The contributions of Anita Spillane and Jo Thompson were invaluable, enlightening me as to the unique benefits of home education.

Contents

Preface

It was my initial intention to write about the ups and downs of my lengthy teaching career in secondary education. However, the more I wrote the more I found that I was becoming critical of my own part in the educational process. I then moved on to focusing on what I considered to be the flaws in state education provision and, logically, felt that it would be irresponsible of me not to make suggestions for improvements.

Teaching methodology has not kept pace with changes that have taken place in the ways that children in the 11 to 18 age group now access and assimilate information. The ease and speed with which they handle current technology leaves most teachers floundering in their wake. Schools patronise young people in ways that cannot be allowed to continue. They need to be given more freedom and space to develop, with new pedagogical structures that foster individuality, initiative and creativity. The days of children spending lessons crammed into rooms thirty at a time for five days a week are passé. Genuine choice should be offered that takes into account personal talents and specialisms.

Whenever one reads about changes proposed to the secondary curriculum, the emphasis is always on the compulsory elements. Rarely does anyone get excited, for example, about what could be offered at key stage 4 over and above Science, English, Mathematics, Geography or History, and a modern language, as prescribed in an early educational sound bite from the Conservative administration elected in May 2015.

I survived as a teacher thanks to my wife and my sense of fun. Teaching isn't child's play, and I never overlooked the fact that children have to be given every encouragement and opportunity to succeed academically. However, human intercourse works best when the serious is complemented occasionally by the humorous. In this book, I hope to sustain the reader's interest by maintaining a similar balance.

I also write with the intention of paying tribute to all those young people with whom I shared the most rewarding moments of my career. Children crave to be taught by teachers who are passionate about their subjects and their teaching. In return, they can inspire teachers with their appetite for learning, openness and warmth. Their good humour sustained me through the good times and the bad. I have tried to recall and include as many examples of children's wit, wisdom and mischief as possible. Those who were never lucky enough to teach should not be denied an insight into the wonders of a unique vocation.

Why 'School Shit'?

The everyday language spoken by teenagers, amongst whom I spent thirty-eight years in two schools, can be a torment for teachers. Being an English specialist, I probably cringed more than most at the linguistic excesses that beset me. I had no option but to come to terms with the informal language that was in common usage the moment pupils left the classroom. I would be prepared to admit that much of the 'street' language proved tiresome for this teacher of advancing years. However, there were odd occasions when the vernacular, as spoken by lively adolescents, was incisively direct and entertaining. There was one speech habit I found engagingly succinct, particularly at times when my frustrations with the job got the better of me.

Well before I retired in 2010 from my role as assistant headteacher in the west London boys' secondary school where I'd enjoyed good relationships with staff and students, I'd picked up on the widespread teenagers' habit of concluding utterances with the word 'shit' when conversing on any matter. The term was included habitually in the everyday speech of many of the boys I taught, though rarely with the conscious intention to offend adults. It was merely conversational etiquette. They would refer, for example, to 'homework shit', or the 'university shit' they had to get their heads around when applying for higher education. The addition of this one word perfectly sums up the often tedious aspect of essential and unavoidable tasks that occupy so much of a teacher's time on a day-to-day basis. I still smile whenever I hear the expression: there are occasions when one has to accept that coarse language can get right to the nub of the matter.

I remember appending the word to a comment myself once when explaining to a sixth-form group that I hadn't had time to watch a film on television that they had recommended because I was doing 'marking shit'. They almost fell off their chairs with merriment.

To summarise, 'School Shit' is the ideal title for this book. It brings home to me the best and the worst aspects of teaching: the enjoyment of interacting with young people, the best part of the job for me, and the ever-present tedium of onerous administrative duties, the worst aspect of teaching by far.

1. Background and Education

Until the age of sixteen, I lived on an estate of single-storey, two-bedroomed prefabricated bungalows just outside of Bath. Not the ideal accommodation for my parents and their four children. I was the oldest child and probably the keenest member of the family to move into a proper house made of bricks, like those most of my school friends inhabited. I felt it somehow degrading that, should it be necessary, I could get into the 'house' with a tin opener if I ever forgot my key. I aspired to stairs, tiles on the roof and drawers and cupboards made of wood. I grew to hate the shabby 'prefabs' and blame growing up in them for contributing to my feelings of social inferiority that took decades to shake off.

I enjoyed the social and sporting aspects of the primary and secondary schools I attended in Bath, but the older I became the less I enjoyed being taught. I was not an academic but, at best, a 'slogger' who achieved a fair degree of success in school examinations in the 1960s by dint of sheer bloody-mindedness. I wanted to be as 'brainy' as my peers. I also never wanted to give any of my more disagreeable teachers the pleasure of thinking that, even though I looked to be from the other side of the tracks, I was destined for educational failure. I was highly competitive in all things, a quality I disguised fairly successfully by adopting a shy and reserved personality.

My primary school was a small church school at the top of one of the hills just outside of the city. As a child, I used to wonder why the area had the unusual name of Odd Down. Years later I did some research and discovered that there had once been an asylum on the site of St Martin's Hospital, just over the way from my estate. I remember as a child that I had a tendency to notice the detail of my environment that friends generally overlooked. I was seven years of age when my lovely teacher, Miss Holmes, set the class a writing topic: My Journey to School. I passed my book in along with everyone else's and, not long afterwards, she was praising me effusively to the rest of the class. I was surprised that she'd attached any importance to my mentioning in my account the fact that one of the houses that I passed as I approached the Post Office at Noad's Corner had a stone plaque on the wall on which was written 'On this site stood thatched cottage'. Just a small detail to me, but apparently big news to Miss Holmes.

The following year I was taught by Miss Collier, an aged lady with a bun, a shawl and immense capacities for patience and kindness. I remember her complimenting me constantly on my art work and the stories I wrote for her. Children's clothing made by Ladybird was very popular in the late 1950s, and Miss Collier set us the task of writing a story explaining how the ladybird got its spots. I'd forgotten all about my story when, a few weeks later, I found myself the centre of attention in assembly. I was presented with a certificate and two Ladybird shirts for winning the essay-writing competition set by the company. I grew even fonder of Miss Collier as a result of this first taste of literary success.

My final term in her class provided me with yet another public accolade. The Bath and District school sports day, at which all primary schools were represented, was held at the Recreation Ground, and Miss Collier had picked me for the sack race. I considered this a huge privilege, even more so when she released me to practise on the school field during lesson time. It must have seemed strange to passers-by on their way to the shops seeing a lone little boy in a sack hopping along on a narrow strip of grass just within the school grounds. Come the big day, I won my qualifying race and, in the final, narrowly beat the favourite, a boy even smaller than me who was able to run freely inside his sack. Eventually losing his balance, he fell a few yards from the line and I was able to overtake him. I can still hear the din that accompanied my success. What glory! First in the sack race!

In the year before taking the 11-plus examination, Mr Hurley, a strict but fair-minded older gentleman, set my class written tests in ten subject areas and awarded marks out of twenty for each. I was amazed when he finally announced to the class that my score of 171 marks out of 200 (I still have my report book) put me in first place, particularly as several members of the class regularly and gleefully pointed out to me, 'Your ass is hanging out of your trousers!' It was true that the grey material of the seat of my shorts had frayed to nothing on both sides, revealing the white lining beneath. Money to replace worn-out clothes was always difficult to find at home and, although I didn't want to attach too much significance to the matter, I never felt that I looked smart enough to be smart.

By this time I was reading fiction assiduously. Books and football were my two passions. Reading provided me with exercise for the brain and football exercise for the body. Television wasn't yet an entertainment option. There were few television sets on my estate, and my parents certainly couldn't afford one. My first experience of watching television was at the house of a friend whose parents were the first in the street to own a set. I wasn't inside his house, but standing on a dustbin with another friend beneath the kitchen window. This tricky balancing act enabled us to look through the door from the kitchen into the living room and at the television in the corner. But fiction books provided me with more than enough entertainment until we eventually had a set at home. The *Jennings* and *William* books were wonderful reads, appealing to my love of silliness. When they ran out I even tried *Billy Bunter*, although I found these a little inaccessible.

Incidentally, at the time of writing in the spring of 2015, it seems surreally ironic to read that the Conservative Party promises to ensure that all pupils will leave primary school in the future knowing their times tables, up to twelve times, and be able to read a novel. These two aims were par for the course for me and my schoolmates over fifty years ago when I left primary school.

The kindest thing to say about most of the boys' grammar school teachers who taught me from age eleven at the top of Beechen Cliff was that they generally lacked charisma and weren't that keen on the company of children. There were two exceptions for me. An English teacher, Tony Lawdham, gave me the nickname 'Harry'. He seemed genuinely interested in my efforts to impress him with my humorous stories. I can still picture him leaning nonchalantly against the window ledge at the front of the class, his comb-over wriggling forward untidily over his high forehead, and a raucous burst of laughter erupting from his pigeon chest as he reads aloud a snatch of silliness from my exercise book. He once asked the class to write a story that had to include an odd assortment of words, including 'oasis', 'donkey' and 'doughnut'… his sense of humour getting the better of him again. In my story, a man lost in the desert, dying of thirst and hunger, eventually meets a nomad on his camel and pleads, "Please, can you give me something to eat? Just a doughnut!" It's strange the ephemera one's memory retains.

Another Tony, Tony Pembroke, introduced me to rugby at age eleven. Youthful, handsome, and endlessly patient, he taught me how to perfect a screw kick. He openly praised those who showed ability, including me. This was a novel experience and I fed on it.

English lessons and rugby meant everything to me from then on. These two characters remain fixed in my memory and were role models for me when I became a teacher. I wanted to demonstrate to children that I could both laugh uninhibitedly with them and inspire them.

The rest of my secondary school teachers weren't a patch on the two Tonys. I was never lazy, but my desire to do my very best academically in all areas faltered during the seven years I spent there. Looking through my old school reports, I notice that the word 'promise' appears more often than the word 'success'. I did fairly well at O-Level, but my A-Level results were disappointing.

Several of the teachers I found to be uninspiring, and their lessons were terminally turgid. I don't want to suggest that they were all middle-aged miseries, but there were a few genuinely distressed souls. An apparently unhappily married French teacher introduced himself to my first-form (Year 7) class as Mr L., living at 'Stalag Luft 3' in Weston Village. My Latin teacher, a ferocious hard-drinking Welshman, enjoyed slippering any member of the class who didn't laugh loudly enough at his jokes. Even worse, my Chemistry teacher made me the butt of most of his sarcasm for five years after I innocently drew a soda syphon on the chalkboard in response to his asking the class if anyone knew how a syphon worked. I can still remember the sense of pride I felt at having drawn the soft drink dispenser in perfect proportion – then the humiliation.

Mr B. initially gave me hope in Geography: he was a younger man, tall, slim, square-jawed, dark-haired and handsome. He looked as though he should be donning goggles and flying jacket instead of gown and mortar board, and hurtling down a runway in a Spitfire to urgent cries of 'Scramble! Scramble!' However, I soon found out that his nickname was 'Banger' and that he stood no nonsense whatsoever. He was a violent man and could be terrifying if crossed. His classroom was silent and lifeless, lesson after lesson spent copying notes off the blackboard. He slippered boys regularly and without compassion. Looking back on those days, I often wonder if he ended his career feeling proud that 'Banger' had been the nickname by which pupils had referred to him.

It's often said that children learn best if they have inspirational teachers. In my case, my greatest educational achievement during the years of compulsory schooling was passing O-Level Chemistry, out of unadulterated contempt for Mr R. Teachers who inspire this reaction can do serious damage to the developing character of an impressionable adolescent. I had no interest in his subject because this man loathed anyone who wasn't a scientific genius. I, in turn, disliked every moment I spent in his science lab.

In my last year as a student in his class, he made it known to the rest of the boys that I would fail my O-Level abysmally. This pronouncement seemed to give him some degree of pleasure. I decided that I would wipe the smirk permanently off his face by secretly reading the course text book through twice from cover to cover as my revision before the GCE examination. As a result, I not only passed but achieved a good enough grade to qualify for the A-Level course in his subject. I cannot convey the pleasure I experienced when, on returning to school to sign on for the sixth form, I returned for the last time to the science block, searched him out, and tossed the text book on to the table at which he was seated without a word. Revenge is a dish best served cold.

My best experiences as a grammar-school student, other than English lessons or being involved in sporting activities, were when teachers provided opportunities for me to have a completely free hand to work on topics of my own choosing. I chose *The Story of Flight*, a thrilling journey for my Form 1 science project. On this occasion, my work wasn't thrown straight in the bin, but I was criticised for producing it on paper of inferior quality. This wasn't my fault as there was never any writing paper at home because you couldn't eat it. I spent six weeks in Form 2 History lessons researching *Henry V and the French Wars*, a wonderful experience involving the preparation of an inordinately long essay for one of such tender years, with detailed maps and accompanying battle plans.

An enterprising trainee English teacher set my Year 10 group a whole-term's homework on the reading of at least three novels by one writer, and the production of an accompanying critical essay. I chose Graham Greene, for no particular reason that I remember, and discovered the book that switched me on to reading serious stuff – the wondrous *The Quiet American*. I can still remember standing at the front of the classroom telling everyone enthusiastically why they should forget Biggles and move up a few literary notches.

The high point of my A-Level Geography course involved the requirement to produce a piece of examination coursework of my own choosing. I opted to complete a local study on 'The changing pattern of industry in Norton Radstock'. I was so pleased with my efforts that I still have the dog-eared assignment today. As I was a 'mod' at the time, I had a battered old Lambretta scooter that enabled me to travel around the small towns and villages of the Norton-Radstock area.

I arranged appointments and conducted interviews with numerous industrialists. These included Mr J. H. Harwood, Secretary of the National Coal Board for the Bristol and Somerset Coalfield; Mr M. W. Gay, Under-Manager of the Kilmersdon Colliery; Mr Hobbs, Personnel Manager at Dent Allcroft, a glove-making company; and Mr Perret, a foreman at the Somervale Joinery Works. That was my most adventurous experience of inquiry-based learning and I loved it. I felt very adult and was determined to give a good account of myself. If Banger had told me during a lesson that the coal seams at Stratton-on-the–Fosse were difficult to mine because they were almost vertical, I would have consigned the information to some remote part of the 90% of my brain that I didn't use. But because J. H. Harwood had told me that blasting seams there with explosives regularly caused coal to rain down on traffic, I'll never forget it.

Despite producing a good piece of coursework, I failed Geography A-Level. I revised regional geography for my first examination when I should have been preparing for the physical geography paper. That's the excuse I always offer, but the likely truth is that I'd studied a subject for two years that held little interest for me other than my project. I'd opted for the course as a filler to make up my three subjects. I'd also chosen French to complete my three A-Levels, not because I was a fluent linguist but because there was a literature component to the course. The introduction to Balzac was a real eye-opener for me, my imagination fired by the story of an ambitious young man discovering the sordid ways of the world in *Le Père Goriot*.

When I eventually found myself standing at the front of a classroom ten years later, I didn't know as much about children as I would have liked, but I knew that I would never use physical or psychological bullying in my teaching. My prime aim was to make my classroom a happy one, where pupils would never feel bored, threatened or unfairly treated. The value of independent inquiry was also high on my list of educational priorities.

I consider myself fortunate that I inherited two important qualities from my parents. My mother, Brenda, possessed the application gene that I am eternally grateful she passed on to me. A hospital worker and then a shop assistant in a department store in Bath, she had the ability to beaver away uncomplaining at any task, particularly if it involved helping others. From my father, an engineering fitter by trade, I gained his Celtic I'm-as-bloody-good-as-any-of-you gene, that stood me in good stead in both sporting and professional capacities. Handsome, distant and secretive, he drove away forever from my family in his Hillman Husky a few months after I left for London to start my Certificate in Education at Borough Road College. The eldest of four children, I subsequently carried a burden of guilt for leaving behind me in Bath my mother, my two sisters, Julie and Michelle, and my brother, Christopher. They'd relied on me in all manner of ways as a steadying family influence. Without me around, their lives became tougher, whereas mine opened out in all manner of exciting directions.

Moving to London for my three-year course moulded me into the resilient, quietly confident person I am now. My family was waving me off from a sleepy Bath Spa railway station one minute, and a few hours later I found myself in the terrifying sprawl of the west London suburbs. I struggled with a serious shock to my system as I made my way from Paddington across London to my first digs off the Great West Road in Heston. My general anxiety was compounded by the screaming of passenger jets flying low overhead every few minutes on their way in and out of Heathrow.

It was ironic that I should end up in Greater London. One of my English teachers, who had moved to Bath from London, had once darkly warned my O-Level English group, his Zapata moustache quivering, 'Whatever you do, don't move to the London suburbs to live – it's soul-destroying.' I've subsequently discovered that the alternative of remaining a resident on the outskirts of Bath would have proved a greater risk to my soul. My experience has been that one is unlikely to become emotionally, intellectually, or spiritually complacent in the hustle and bustle of Greater London's cosmopolitan life.

I certainly missed my family, and was keenly aware of how much they missed me as a result of my father's sudden departure. I also regretted losing easy access to the countryside from Bath. Accustoming myself to my sense of dislocation and the pressing claustrophobia of suburbia took me several months. Nevertheless, I gradually came to terms with being a small fish in a huge ocean, a process that knocked much of the superciliousness out of my character.

I had enjoyed the safety and predictability of growing up in the beautiful city of Bath. Living in west London, by contrast, opened up a complex new canvas before me. My persona underwent shock therapy as I was, by turns, thrilled and disturbed by the novelty of my new world. Living and studying within a genuinely multi-racial environment did wonders for developing my maturity. Life was full of excitement and incident, a vast range of opportunities available, of which I could not possibly have conceived.

I came out at the end of my three-year course with a Certificate in Education and a desire to live a useful life. I applied for a teaching post in Hounslow, with the stated desire on my application form to have the opportunity to 'work with the less able'. I was fortunate enough to land a job immediately, working at a boys' comprehensive in Isleworth. Although I taught in boys' comprehensives until my retirement, this was not because I am an advocate of single-sex education. I tried at various stages in my career to gain a position in a co-educational school, but was either not called for interview or unsuccessful if I got that far.

I did myself no favours at interview for two reasons: first, I found it unbecoming to sit with a fixed grin spouting the latest educational jargon with any conviction; and, second, I didn't see why I should re-state aloud what I had already included in my lengthy letter of application simply because my interviewers hadn't had the courtesy to read it. My sixth-form form tutor, Mr Corrick, had once written of me in an end-of-year report, 'He does not suffer fools gladly.' It never occurred to me when I read his assessment that this quality would have such a bearing on my future employment prospects.

Things didn't turn out as badly as they might have regarding my desire for co-educational experience because I subsequently found myself able to teach mixed groups at A-Level, thanks to the policy of the sharing of sixth-form students in consortium arrangements with three other local secondary schools.

In 1986, I put in a successful application for a year's secondment to convert my teaching certificate into a degree, and subsequently gained a First in Education with English. The most rewarding component of the course was *Tragedy*, with Zak Leader the course lecturer. Being of an essentially saturnine disposition in my private life, my wife has since found endless mirth reminding me of the aptness that I was once, and still am in her eyes, a tragic student. She has never been prepared to accept my argument that what she perceives as an essential pessimism in my make-up is merely realism in disguise. There have to be some Eeyores in the world, and I'm not ashamed to admit that I'm one of them. What's wrong with being constantly prepared for the wheels to come off your life in the blink of an eye?

I was destined to teach boys and never had a problem with my lot. Here lies the explanation for the repeated use of the pronouns 'he', 'his' and 'him' in this book, so I ask you now not to take offence at this stylistic feature.

2. Career Overview

Since retiring as a secondary school English teacher seven years ago, I've had plenty of time to appraise my career in detail. Looking at my involvement in the machinery of state education from a distance has clarified matters for me. You may think that frequent and objective self-analysis would occur as a matter of course throughout one's employment, whatever the job. But such a process was alien to me. When I was in my mid-thirties, a colleague once asked me, 'What job are you aiming to be doing in five years' time?' My immediate reply was, 'Teaching English.' I hadn't thought beyond simply doing the job I'd been doing so far because I enjoyed it and believed I was good at it. 'But you can't do the same thing for the next thirty years,' he added. I stopped and thought about this comment for a few minutes, and then carried on teaching.

Having found a worthwhile and rewarding way to earn a living, I didn't want to think much beyond the classroom in which I was teaching. The idea that I feared the prospect of chasing professional advancement was a criticism that one could try levelling at me, but the politicking and horse-trading inherent in being a go-getter had no appeal. I'm honest enough to admit that, when things are going well, I am inclined to let my life drift quietly along, where others might be ceaselessly looking for the main chance to 'get on'. To be fair to myself, even if I had been ambitious professionally, my home life was so emotionally and physically demanding once my wife and I started a family that I prioritised domestic demands over career aspirations – if I ever had any.

My wife, Lindsey, and I had a severely handicapped child to look after and we both put her needs before our own. Coupled with this commitment, there are other relevant details about my early life that may explain why I remained so determined to put my handicapped family before any ideas I may have had about wanting to climb the education ladder.

My childhood had been unusual, a good training ground for life's unpredictability. Coming from a background where domestic strife was a regular occurrence, I developed a strong sense of self-preservation, despite being constantly anxious. As the eldest of four, I tried my best to protect my younger brother and two sisters from the distress arising from parental discord. My father found the demands of looking after a wife and four children frustrating in the extreme, given his predilections for gambling, drinking and a weakness for the opposite sex. He was very close with his weekly wage, my mother never knowing how much he earned from one year to the next. When serious arguments between the two of them occurred, he sometimes found it difficult to control his temper.

Years later, I would confide with teaching groups that my childhood home was one where weekend violence was not an uncommon occurrence. Referencing my own childhood experiences was a strategy I used if I ever discovered any of the children I taught came from similar backgrounds. Without causing embarrassment by referring to them directly in class or openly acknowledging their plight, I hoped that those suffering in silence, as I had done, would gain some reassurance from hearing a teacher making the admission that he'd had direct experience of domestic violence.

As a child, I struggled with the notion that I was inferior to my peers because I came from an unsettled family background. I knew that the neighbours could hear what was taking place in our tin home and always assumed that my family was talked about. When I became a teacher, I wanted children I taught who were in the same predicament to know that this childhood cross is one that many have to bear, but that one day it would be lifted from the shoulders of those unlucky enough to experience that anguish. I understood first hand that a child is unable to see an end to what seems a constant and endless torment. I felt it a duty to attempt to reassure those I taught that, whatever distress they daily suffered, a day would eventually arrive when that pain would stop.

I decided early in adulthood that my main ambition in life was to create a fulfilling family life of my own. I'd felt cheated of the strife-free childhood that most of my school friends had taken for granted, but I could find consolation in bringing up children of my own in a loving family environment.

However, achieving my goal of contentment in family life proved to be far more of a personal challenge than I could ever have imagined. Our first daughter was born with serious congenital heart defects. Her condition took a yet more dramatic turn for the worse when she suffered major brain damage as a result of haemorrhaging after an operation at sixteen months. For the rest of her life, she could do little more than eat, drink, and smile. We loved Keeley dearly, and managed to look after her at home throughout her eighteen years of life. I fed and washed her every morning before she went off to the special school she attended. When I got home from work in the evening, I gave her tea, cuddles and put her to bed. I did this throughout her life and would not have given up the daily contact with her for the world.

When she died aged eighteen, I was forty-four years old. The profound sense of loss I experienced made the responsibilities of teaching a struggle for me. For the following five years, my demanding but rewarding career seemed to require much more of an effort to maintain the same level of enjoyment. I remember once snapping at Paul, an English colleague and friend for no justifiable reason. His reaction was to ask aloud the question, "When are we going to get the old Kev back?"

My wife and second daughter, Lucy, three years younger than Keeley, needed me to get them through the difficult years that followed just as much as I needed them. Losing a child is one of the most painful blows one can ever be dealt, leaving a wound to a parent's psyche that never heals. Physically and mentally impaired as she was, Keeley was as dear to us as any child could be. The emphasis on the unity of the family remained sacrosanct. For Lindsey and me, providing a secure home environment for Lucy and the encouragement for her to find her own place in the world were also all-consuming priorities. Where Keeley had been gentle and passive, Lucy was a fireball of fun and energy with very different but equally important needs. The efforts required to keep my home life on track militated against any notions of becoming a thrusting careerist. I enjoyed the occasional compliment on a job well done, but did not anticipate such recognition setting me up for promotion.

A drama teacher friend, commenting on my professional preference for sitting on the sidelines of school affairs described me as being a 'war correspondent'. I demonstrated little interest in internal politics that could be divisive in the staff room, and preferred to leave it to others to compete for promotion. The epithet applied to me was not intended as a compliment. Mike wanted me to recognise the fact that others perceived me as being morally neutral when it came to commenting on school developments and initiatives, and avoiding involvement in staff association issues that were considered important. In other words, I didn't like to get my hands 'dirty' and was a 'yes man' in the eyes of the school's management team. I was certainly conscientious, but surprised at the implied criticism.

I have to admit to being relieved at avoiding the *sturm und drang* that ambitious colleagues suffered in their efforts to move onwards and upwards in the teaching game. There was enough storm and stress for me to deal with at home, without putting myself in the bear pit of school politicking. During periods when my elder daughter was ill, it was often well after midnight before she could be left to go off to sleep. At such times, when I eventually fell into bed myself, I remember celebrating the achievement of us all having survived another day as a family together before falling asleep. Keeley was my touchstone: if she were well, the world was well.

Despite the difficulties and heartaches my family suffered collectively during Keeley's life, I took no more than a week off work in my entire career for personal sickness. Working hard was therapeutic for me, and my commitment to all aspects of school life remained intact. When Keeley was nine years old, I applied for a year's secondment to take a year off teaching in order to study and convert my teaching certificate to a degree qualification. I was prompted to do this merely because I wanted to ensure job security when teaching became a degree profession. I hadn't suddenly caught the promotion bug. I worked best in the early hours of the morning and succeeded in gaining a First. Fear of wasting the money the education authority had invested in me and the possibility of even failing the course brought out the best in me. Subsequent elevations over the years to head of English, head of sixth form and assistant head came about as a result of the headteacher asking me if I would do him a favour and be good enough to apply for the posts. I had no aching personal desire to put myself forward for the positions, but found myself elevated to each of them in turn.

In all my years as a teacher, there was no possibility that I would take for granted how fortunate I was to have such an enjoyable and rewarding job, but I could never have allowed myself to put my career before family considerations. I'm a single-minded person, a paradoxical consequence of a tough childhood. I was fond of trying to convince my students that personal suffering can make one more able to cope with life's vicissitudes, but their reactions invariably suggested they thought I was a baton short of a relay team. I envisaged my life mapped out for me: I had to be strong enough both to protect and provide for my family and to give everything I could to keep my job. Growing up in relative poverty had made me respect the fact that I was financially on to a good thing having a job for life, as teaching then seemed to me. However, just as there were unforeseen crises in Keeley's health that had a serious negative impact on family life, so there were educational developments that marred my enjoyment of life at the chalk face.

***

Gaining a degree in my secondment year gave me the extra sense of employment security I needed, but it also put me in the frame for the head of English post that subsequently became vacant. I accepted the job, with some hesitation, aware that I would now have to get my hands dirty.

I had two overriding concerns at this development in my career. The first was that I would be expected to demonstrate leadership to my departmental team, several of them experienced senior teachers with management roles. My only experience of leadership so far had been when I was made captain of my primary school football team, though we did only lose one match and ended up top of the league. There was hope. I also had the National Curriculum to worry about – a worthy teaching tool for the diffident, but generally perceived to be an unwarranted imposition for the 'gifted and talented' teacher. My friend Paul once asked me if I could explain the distinction between the adjectives 'gifted' and 'talented' because nobody had yet been able to offer him a satisfactory explanation.

I decided from the outset that I wouldn't be foolish enough to disregard the recently-introduced statutory regulations, but I would try to protect my department from their worst time-intensive excesses. Thus, I prepared myself for a future filled with hour upon tedious hour compiling assessment tools, record-keeping forms and essential forward-planning documentation. I took the decision to do the bulk of this administrative work myself as I wanted my departmental colleagues to retain their enthusiasm for teaching English at whatever cost. A happy department becomes a happy 'family'. Maintaining the delicate balance between dutifully following top-down autocratic legislation and educating children intelligently is a major challenge for the thinking teacher.

In my new and elevated position, I found myself preoccupied with others' expectations of what I should be doing; the levels at which I should be performing in various capacities; the mounting stacks of documentation required to prove that my department was functioning effectively; and constantly having to meet pressing deadlines. I regularly felt drained and worn down by these responsibilities, but I'd known from the outset that this would be the case. I'd realised that I had been made a head of department in a core subject area at one of the most difficult periods in the history of state education.

The watchwords of the new educational age were: 'If it moves, assess it. If it's taught, document it.' The culture of state education seemed to become one in which teachers were being driven admin mad. A long-term effect of this crass policy of implementing a system that is geared towards generating an ever-increasing teacher workload is teacher burn-out. It's the reason many young people leave the profession within six years. To mark the thirty-year anniversary of the national curriculum, 50,000 teachers left the profession between November 2013 and November 2014.

To add to the tribulations of the state workforce that remains, the concept of teaching effectiveness is now synonymous with an analytical overview of the examination performance of one's students, and not much else. The news in late 2015 that the government intended to reintroduce testing for seven-year-olds reinforced my belief that the general direction of education in this country would continue to be assessment-driven, a scenario unlikely to improve the attractiveness of teaching as a profession. The drive for baseline assessment of four-year-old children in England is a logical concomitant of the government's blinkered mindset. Children's wellbeing and emotional health are of subordinate importance, although school prospectuses boldly claim otherwise.

My apologies if I appear to be ranting, but I retain the belief that teaching can once again become a fulfilling vocation for the whole profession, not just those in isolated pockets of sanity. In retrospect, I'm able to recall with fondness my rewarding interaction with children over four decades, despite the huge amount of time I devoted to covering my back with myriad paper trails.

Now that the imperative to comply with educational initiatives and school policy has been permanently removed from my existence, I realise how weighed down I had become by professional servility and pedagogical tedium. The longer I taught, the more I felt the external pressure from all sides to rein in my unique and colourful (in my eyes) teaching persona that took several years to cultivate, and to march to the tune of professional conformity.

The emphasis shifted in my day-to-day work to the extent that in the second half of my thirty-eight year career, I spent far more time on paperwork than teaching in the classroom. When I use the term 'paperwork', I am, of course, referring to virtual paper, the sort provided on a screen by Microsoft Word that never runs out. I wasn't an exception in the staff room: the majority of my colleagues agreed that they were in the same situation. You can't move in the job now for burgeoning piles of record sheets and documents to complete.

Every dogma has its day in the teaching business. Around every corner is a new assessment tool, essential data recording requirement or compulsory national directive to negotiate, involving laborious daily sessions bent over a laptop. The advent of the personal computer never fulfilled the early promise of making the job of teaching easier; it made the profession slaves to the keypad.

On my first day at the school where I taught for the last thirty three years in the job, I was heartened to see a snooker table at one end of the staff room. Male and female members of staff played during their few free lessons and at lunch time. I only played the odd game as calculating angles had never been one of my strengths, but the sturdy old table was a comforting presence.

That end of the staff room when I left three decades later was fitted out with half a dozen PC terminals, the snooker table a distant memory for the very few. At any time of the day, there would be a line of hunched and twitching seated figures, silently tapping out essential data. Quite right too, you may be thinking. My feeling is that when the snooker table went out of the door, so did the warmth of the staff-room community. I've visited London offices of all kinds in my various capacities as a teacher over the past ten years and seen pin-ball machines, table football machines, table-tennis tables and all sorts for employees' recreational use during down time. Perhaps the idea of creating a sense of staff cohesion is coming back into fashion in more enlightened institutions. Working hard and playing hard encourage healthy competitive juices. I am in no doubt that a happy staff is a productive staff. Much as I'm aware of opening myself up to ridicule for promoting a concept as unquantifiable as happiness, I stand by this conviction.

Over the years I noticed that fewer and fewer teachers were spending time in the staff room at morning break and lunch time. The demands of the job became all-consuming, requiring individuals constantly to feed the school's computer network with information whenever there was a spare moment. Its voracious appetite was insatiable. There is minimal down time now in secondary schools. After the sounding of the bell to end the final lesson, the staff room would be empty. But the car park would still be full for another hour and a half or more. This was the signal for teachers to log on to the school's intranet for daily data time.

There was a decline in after-school activities for pupils, but a corresponding increase in laptop activity for teachers. For a few years I enjoyed a Friday after-school game of five-a-side football in the sports hall with a group of colleagues. Even that activity eventually folded, owing to a requirement to divert surplus energy into the school's computer grid. When I asked those teaching in schools locally and in other parts of the country about their working conditions, I discovered that the grass was just as parched everywhere else.

I was a bit of an imposter in my various leadership capacities. My strengths were my ability to inspire children to enjoy the learning process and to encourage them to progress in my subject area. I was most certainly not a conventional leader, but more of a loner. My high boredom threshold and capacity for beavering away in solitary on 'essential' administrative work did much to release my departmental colleagues to do what they were so good at – teaching as opposed to assessing. I was thankful that I always had such a talented (or gifted?) group of teachers in my department.

On the final day of my career, I underwent a formal lesson observation. At the death, so to speak, my teaching ability was formally assessed. Strange, perhaps, but I retired at a time when the school was in the middle of a lesson observation programme. I was graded by one of the deputy heads as 'Outstanding', as I had hoped. I write this not to brag, but to give extra clout to any criticisms I make here of formal teaching methodology in state schools. I don't believe that people in glass houses should run the risk of throwing stones.

Despite the pleasure I took in inspiring children to learn, legions of education police of various political and ideological persuasions had coerced me into 1) producing reams of what I considered to be often irrelevant and sometimes nonsensical information as a matter of course; 2) being complicit in reducing my subject to a knack list called listeracy (sorry 'literacy'); 3) focusing to an unhealthy extent on assessment at the expense of my teaching; and 4) placing too great a priority on examination results and league-table positions. When teachers are subjected to such pressures, the most important element of the teaching equation – the child – may become an afterthought. The more time I devoted to chasing the best examination results possible, the less time I had for the individual needs of the children in my classes. Whenever I found myself becoming impatient and irritable in the classroom, I usually needed to look no further than myself to find the cause.

At any time in an academic year I would be expected to state exactly, to any data hound who asked me, the percentage of my Year 9 students who would be expected to achieve Level 5 and above in the English SAT, and the percentage of GCSE students who would be achieving a grade C or above in English, with supplementary data on the proportion of borderline candidates in each examination who could also be expected to reach the critical levels with additional coaching. Examination coaching is a major industry in secondary schools, particularly in the core subjects of English, Mathematics and Science. The revision book industry has now gone stratospheric.

My purposes in writing about secondary education at this late stage in my life are twofold. I feel obliged to pass on engaging insights relating to those interesting experiences I still cherish. I also feel compelled to articulate, as convincingly as I can, suggestions for changes to secondary education that I believe to be essential.

3. From Innocence to Experience

Being naïve, keen, inexperienced and a country bumpkin in the big city resulted in some embarrassing moments in the early days of my career. Before turning into a reasonably confident, though socially diffident, classroom practitioner, I was most definitely a yokel in the smoke.

One incident involved me trying just a little too hard to make the best possible impression on my first headteacher, Mr G. He was a genial man, short of stature, who rarely raised his voice beyond much more than a whisper. His deputy-head, Mr H., on the other hand, was a bluff, no-nonsense Yorkshireman, the head's terrifying enforcer. His ferocious bark terrified teachers as well as pupils. His smoking habit finally caught up with him in the last few years of his career, rendering his vocal cords virtually useless. In his prime, any student sent to him knew that he would be in for the roughest of rides. Besides receiving stinging verbal rebukes, recalcitrants might also leave his office smarting from physical wounds inflicted by his cane. Corporal punishment was still the ultimate deterrent for dealing with serious misbehaviour in the early 1970s when I started teaching.

I apologise for interrupting myself here to make a few observations on punishing children. The world has moved on and corporal punishment is now perceived as an educational aberration consigned to the past. Sanctions of a different kind are now in place, but they may appear to play into the hands of 'problem pupils'. For example, issuing the punishment of a week's exclusion for a serious misdemeanour was, as I came to discover, sometimes greeted with a smile of satisfaction from the disruptive student in question. In such a case, the pupil concerned may have welcomed having a week off school, but his parents, both possibly in full-time employment, would not necessarily have felt the same way.

I have a problem with the concept of punishment. I encountered many in the profession who spent an inordinate amount of their time devising a range of punishments for various levels of misbehaviour. Wherever possible, I avoided chastising children. If a child told me that he had forgotten to do his homework, the most common offence, I would be in a quandary. The majority of those who couldn't meet homework demands invariably came from backgrounds where parents provided no encouragement or space for them to work at home. I should have been focusing my attention on these parents. I avoided punishing by organising homework sessions after school or at lunch time. These arrangements were intended as a way around a problem. All of the important work I asked my students to complete, particularly at GCSE level, was set as homework. There was little possibility that this work would have been of any merit if it became the product of a detention. It was important for those I taught to perceive the homework I set as worthy of serious application, and for them to see me as sympathetic and supportive, as opposed to indifferent and inflexible.

My personal experience of the ultimate school punishment, the cane, had taught me the futility of making enemies of children by treating them in an inhumane manner.

41

There was also another counter-productive aspect of corporal punishment: a few bruises across the backside were not the only imprints that the cane, slipper, or ruler left behind. Receiving physical punishment represented a badge of courage to be worn with pride by many of my secondary school peers.

My sadistic Latin teacher regularly offered a choice of punishment if anyone misbehaved in his lessons: stay behind for an hour's detention or take a caning. Those boys who sought a reputation for toughness amongst their peers cheerfully accepted the cane, in the knowledge that their prestige amongst the student ranks would be significantly enhanced. There were even those who bragged about 'wearing out' a teacher, by forcing him to exert himself unduly. As vice-captain of the Colts XV, I once took up the offer of being thrashed without a second's thought, in the knowledge that the best possible boost for my reputation would be to demonstrate publicly that I could 'take it' from 'Bricky' (the Latin teacher's nickname). The alternative he offered me was to come into school for a half-day detention during half term. My offence? I failed to hand in homework on time.

I was firm in my handling of boys, when the need arose. I was also intuitively aware that the moment I singled out anyone for a formal punishment, I was at risk of 'losing' a student. I regularly pre-empted the need to do so thanks to the teaching style I cultivated. Defusing potential crises or confrontation through the use of humour or melodramatic outbursts of mock anger became an integral technique of my teaching style from very early on. I could switch the volume and tone of my voice in an instant from friendly and quietly spoken to a fire-cracker effect that would make most of the class jump visibly. Inwardly I would be smiling at the ruse, but I achieved the desired result of making the children alert, attentive and co-operative, without singling out any individual for humiliation. Since retiring, I met a young man I'd taught twenty years previously who summed up his memories of my teaching with the words, 'You were fair and funny, but you could have a filthy temper.' He was right on the first two points but, fortunately, had never twigged that my 'filthy temper' was all part of the act.

Any victim of physical or verbal violence is inclined to develop an aversion to the perpetrator, as was certainly the case with me. 'Bricky' did a good job as regards boosting my standing amongst my peers, but the first chance I got I dropped Latin in order to avoid further contact with him. The excessive punitive treatment he indulged in was something he enjoyed but I didn't. He wanted to be feared, but he was also despised. From the perspective of one who went on to become an English teacher, dropping Latin at fourteen years of age is a decision that I have since come to regret.

Getting back to the story about the very start of my teaching career, whenever I recall the first occasion that I put my head above the staff room parapet, I squirm to think that I could have been so green. I had been in post only a few months when the call went up at a staff meeting for a volunteer to take over minute-taking duties at future meetings. I saw this as an opportunity to make my mark and raised my arm. As no one else thought the responsibility worth a light, I was duly given the job. The complete lack of interest from my colleagues should have been a warning.

I knew nothing about the protocols for recording, producing and disseminating minutes. However, Mr G. clearly believed that I did, so assured had I appeared when I

43

offered my services. I subsequently realised that one of my failings is that I can give a convincingly passable impression of appearing to be in control when, in reality, I'm well out of my depth. At the first meeting I scribbled away in my notebook, jotting down most of the staff contributions verbatim.

This was in the days before personal computers, when teachers waged constant battles first thing every morning with their colleagues to have access to one of the school's two Banda machines, or spirit duplicators as they were called. From a prepared master copy of text, usually handwritten, hundreds more could be produced by fixing it to a large metal drum, pouring half a gallon of neat alcohol into a reservoir and then cranking a handle one revolution for each copy needed. Some of the male teachers would see using the machine as an opportunity to demonstrate their prodigious forearm and bicep power by turning the handle as swiftly as possible. Others would take their time, intent instead on inhaling the intoxicating fumes that issued from the machine. The whiff of alcohol stayed with the pile of duplicated sheets for a good while after they had been produced. Whenever I distributed fresh copies to a class, it was a source of amusement to watch the boys as they sniffed the papers extravagantly to savour the heady aroma. The older boys could always be relied upon to trot out their ready quips: 'You just come from the pub, sir?'… 'Bit early in the day even for you, ain't it, sir?'… and so on.

There was one duplicator in the staff room and another in the main office. From eight o'clock every morning, teachers would rush into the staff room armed with spirit masters, make a beeline for the copier and join the impatient queue. Happy days! Little did we know what awaited us a few years down the line – thirty hours a week hunched over PCs, preparing reams of absolutely essential educational materials. No sane educationist could have predicted such a scenario.

But I digress. I had sheets of staff-meeting copy and spent many hours two-finger typing the minutes on to numerous spirit-master sheets. I eventually completed the task and, before the start of school, posted copies into staff pigeon holes. I left one with the head's secretary. During my first lesson of the day, a pupil knocked on the door of my classroom, entered and handed me a note from Mr G., asking me to come to his office at the earliest opportunity.

I anticipated fulsome praise for a job thoroughly well done and hurried to his office at morning break. Mr H. was in the corridor outside the head's office and he raised his eyebrows at my approach – nothing else. Something was up!

I was au fait with the expression 'incandescent with rage', but I'd never been the target of a person in the grip of this condition. He rose from his chair behind his expansive desk and pushed towards me a copy of my minutes. 'Is this some kind of joke?' he asked, giving me the glare that I would soon be trying so hard to perfect. He clearly wasn't himself. The fact that he was my normally mild-mannered boss was a serious cause for alarm, but there was an element of novelty to his choler. I wondered if I were about to be sacked.

I should mention that I'd innocently set out my minutes so that the document closely resembled a play script. I'd taken the trouble to include as many word-for-word contributions from those present at the meeting as I could. It was my genuine belief that my thoroughness would impress everyone who bothered to read the record. It didn't take the head long to make me realise that everyone on the staff would think me a complete idiot. As Mr G. had spoken at length on all of the topics discussed, his contributions dominated every page. After the initial tirade on the subject of what on earth I thought I'd been doing, he proceeded to itemise, through gritted teeth, denials that he had actually said this, that or most of the other. Despite the fact that I was in some disagreement with his observations, I decided that the wise course in this situation would be to 'button it', as my father used to say. He also put me right with handy pointers as to exactly what I should do if I wanted to continue as minutes' secretary. After apologising profusely, I was allowed to leave, having assured him that I knew exactly what was required of me in future.

Following his clear instructions, I rushed to the staff room and retrieved as many of the duplicated sheets from the staff pigeon holes as I could. That evening, I spent a few more hours producing the minutes in the correct format. After a fretful night's sleep, I delivered a copy directly to the head the next morning and awaited his verdict. By lunch-time I discovered that he was happy for me to circulate the revised version and, more was the pity, to continue in my role as minutes secretary. I vowed that I would be circumspect in the extreme before volunteering again for any additional responsibility.

I don't know if word had got around that I was soft in the head, but I found myself at the end of my second term up for another dose of public embarrassment. This time it was in connection with my taking part in the annual end-of-season Staff XI versus Boys 1st XI football fixture. I no longer possessed much in the way of footballing skill, having switched to playing rugby at secondary school, but what I lacked in ability I tried to make up for in enthusiasm. Once again, this character trait was at risk of setting me up for a fall. I think I must have inherited the dodgy 'dipstick gene' from some numbskull in my genealogical tree.

The day of the match arrived, to be played on the upper-school football pitch at four p.m. I was teaching at the time in the lower school, separated from the main school site by a busy road. Two other members of the team, both like me young and relatively new to the job and the school, received a message during the morning from Mr G., the Head of PE who taught across the road. A god in mortal form, he was universally lauded for consistently producing football and cricket teams par excellence throughout the school. A great socialiser, his department regularly celebrated its sporting successes at one local hostelry or another. Wherever they assembled for post-victory celebrations, it was taken as read that it would end in beers, lots of them.

My lower-school colleagues and I were instructed to change into our football kit as quickly as possible at lunch time and to hurry across to the main school for the staff team photograph. There was talk of the photograph featuring in the local newspaper. The Head of PE's word was law and there was no chance that any of us would risk being late. Minutes after the lunch bell had sounded, all three of us hurriedly changed into the match kit that had been sent over to us. With untied boot laces trailing, I hurried after them across the zebra crossing so as not to miss the photo shoot.

As I followed my young colleagues through the car park towards the main door, I happened to glance up and saw a group of teachers looking from a first-floor window, pointing and laughing at the two ahead of me. My caution radar suddenly kicked in, putting me on urgent alert. I suspected all was not as it seemed. Coming to a halt, I watched as my team mates continued through the main entrance and turned left into the school hall. Raucous laughter echoed from within the building. It sounded as though the entire school was in a state of hysteria.

Turning on my heel, I returned to the sanctuary of my lower-school classroom. Whatever ridicule my fellow footballers were being subjected to, I didn't want to be included.

I subsequently found out that the PE Department had hatched the April Fool plot. There was no photograph being taken, and I suddenly grasped the reason for the garishly-coloured kit that had been sent over to us. The two unsuspecting staff footballers had walked straight into a cauldron of ridicule that I had freakishly managed to avoid. I hadn't realised the date and, even if I had, I was inexperienced in the ways of the school world. I had no idea that schools celebrated the day so enthusiastically. From that day on, however, I always went about my daily round exercising great caution if I ever found myself at work on April the first.

In the first ten years or so of my teaching, parents were there in the background but were just part of the distant school scenery. Accountability wasn't a big thing back then, most parents happy to be kept in the dark as to what actually went on at their children's school. I had a few notable experiences that required me to reassess my complacent attitude towards them.

The parents of one thirteen-year-old pupil objected to the head of the English department reading the novel *The Ghost of Thomas Kempe* by Penelope Lively to the class. The novel's main character is a boy who accidentally releases the spirit of a seventeenth-century sorcerer when his family moves into an old cottage. Mr M. was apparently peddling black magic when he should have been teaching English, and

I was one of his apprentices because I also enjoyed using the novel as a class reader. The headteacher got involved and arrangements were made for the boy to be withdrawn from the classroom whenever the book was being read to the class. The story created a momentary wave of incredulity at a subsequent department meeting. This event was my first taste of parent power.

A few years later, I found myself teaching the same student in my GCSE class, and this time his parents refused to allow him to study *Macbeth*, putting forward the same objection that I was promoting Satanism. On this occasion he was withdrawn from classes and given one-to-one tuition studying an alternative Shakespeare play that would have no disturbing effect whatsoever on his pubescent emotional turmoil – *Romeo and Juliet* (!). The idea that my teaching Shakespeare could be interpreted as causing irreparable psychological damage to immature minds had never occurred to me. Eccentric as I considered the parents' objection to be, perhaps I was wrong. There may well be a need in the future for every school to include a warning in its prospectus in the interests of health and safety: 'Warning! The study of literature (particularly Shakespeare's plays) may seriously damage your child's psychological state.' In the litigatory age in which we find ourselves, parental sensibilities of all kinds have to be respected.

Another episode that alerted me to the idiosyncrasies of parenting concerned a Year 9 pupil who smelled of human excrement. I'd always been aware that sharing my teaching space with a classful of sweaty teenage boys could be uncomfortable. The acrid smell of teenage sweat, particularly as temperatures rose in the summer months, could be almost overpowering, but I'd never experienced anything of this nature. The pungent smell stayed in the room long after the pupil had gone. The rest of the class was too embarrassed ever to pass comment on the smell and had as little to do with him as possible.

In the short time that I taught him, he sat alone at the back of the class. Even from that distance, I was in a nauseous state whenever he was in the room. The special needs department informed me that they were aware of this case of neglect and that steps were being taken to encourage his parents to deal with the situation. I felt totally helpless. Much as I believed that I personally should do something immediately to put a stop to this poor boy's desperate situation, I found it difficult to approach him, literally, owing to his repellent odour. Had I managed to talk to him, how would I have broached such a delicate matter? This was one situation where I was relieved I could put my trust in someone else to find a solution.

There was one aspect of teaching with which I constantly struggled: significant numbers of teachers were essentially indifferent to the performance of any but those who demonstrated an aptitude for their subject. The longer I taught, the more I saw all teachers as belonging to one of two groups, those who are sympathetic to all children in their care and those who are antipathetic to a sizeable minority. The latter may have the charm to pass themselves off as child-friendly, but their efforts tend to be directed towards the extrinsic rewards of professional advancement and a higher salary. Talk to anyone about their school experiences, and they will refer to teachers they recall as being either 'all right' or those they 'hated'. Children ascertain very quickly if they are in the presence of a professional with a genuine concern for their progress, or a charlatan on an ego trip.

My fear is that those professionals who are motivated by personal advancement are the ones who achieve positions of authority and influence in education. Thus, the best may find themselves dancing to the tune of the mediocre in schools. Going as far back as my first teaching experience in 1971, I remember reading a poem of such exceptional depth, written by a young adolescent, that I showed it to the head of department. The poem's focus on the pain and anxiety of facing the prospect of adulthood was raw and powerful in its use of language. The response of the head of English was, 'Are you going to deal with him or do you want me to?' He assumed that I had shown him the poem because I considered it disgraceful and wanted the boy punished. I couldn't conceive even then how such a man could have risen to any position of prominence in a school.

4. Cycling in the New Forest

The extra-curricular aspects of a teaching career are often memorable. This was certainly the case with one particular school activity in which I took part. Indeed, writing this chapter proved to be the most enjoyable by a country mile.

***

One of the highlights of the school year, for me and most of the students, was the annual Activities Week, which took place towards the end of the Summer Term. It was perceived by the boys as a week off school, but the teachers I worked with didn't see it that way at all. It was an opportunity to teach boys 'lessons for life'. With Years 10 to 13 on study leave, the timetable was suspended for the rest of the school and students chose from a list of alternative activities, many off-site and some of them residential experiences. In addition to day trips to London museums, art galleries and historical sites, there were camping excursions and, my favourite, the Year 9 cycling trip to the New Forest. The education authority had bought an old village school building and grounds on the outskirts of the forest in Godshill, for use by borough schools. It was known as The Lodge and it provided children with the opportunity to experience a totally contrasting environment from the west London suburbs. I opted to help out with this activity for ten years or so and enjoyed every minute.

Barry was the trip organiser and I was his second-in-command. Each year he booked five days at the site, from which we set off on daily rides to Brockenhurst, Salisbury, and the area around Fordingbridge. He did all the administration, completing reams of risk-assessment forms, publicising the event amongst Year 9 boys, and getting interested parents into school to talk to them about all aspects of the trip. The caretaker and I drove a minibus each from west London to Godshill, one with the teachers and fifteen or so boys who had selected the week of cycling, and the other transporting the bikes. Allyson was another staff regular who, like me, was diminutive in stature but a strong cyclist. She owned an expensive lightweight machine and could leave most of the cycle party trailing in her wake when she hit the gas.

The lodge itself offered spartan accommodation, with a few armchairs and a temperamental television in the lounge, metal-framed bunk beds in the four bedroom areas and a basic kitchen. This was where I spent much of my time when I wasn't cycling, supervising and making sure that nobody was electrocuted or burnt to a crisp. The room was dominated by an enormous antiquated electric cooker, with two huge hot plates that took an age to heat up and an oven door that required a certain knack and considerable strength to open it. There was a fridge freezer, a bulky Formica-topped table and a sink with a double drainer. One grisly task I undertook on a daily basis was to clear the outside drain cover that became blocked with huge quantities of food waste. The boys never quite got the hang of clearing what they didn't eat off their plates into the waste bin.

The lodge had a small playground area to the side, ideal for a spare-time kickabout with a football. However, the elderly residents of the detached house next door had ensured that :No ball games' signs had been installed by our education authority. They didn't want their silent existence to be disturbed by the sounds of children playing, even if it was only very occasionally when the lodge was hired by school parties. They used the argument of "not scaring our expensive horses with your noise" as their objection to ball games. As the 'playground' was no longer for playing in, our group spent most of the time, when not cycling, inside the building. The first important lesson for life for our students: Children should not be seen and not heard in parochial England.

When taking groups of children on residential trips, the routine of daily checks has to be established. Our party comprised fourteen year olds, the majority of whom clearly never did much around the house. We couldn't even assume that they had showered or eaten breakfast to start the day. If they didn't shower, the daily five-pound note provided by their parents was withheld. We were used to all the excuses boys came up with to avoid preparing meals for themselves. One answered that he'd already eaten a Mars bar in bed when I questioned why he wasn't bothering about breakfast. On returning to the lodge after a day's cycling, we would take the group to the local supermarket to buy the items needed for their evening meal. It usually took us a few days to dissuade them from filling their baskets entirely with carbohydrates and carbonated drinks. Lesson for Life 2: Fast food is not always healthy food.

Organising the boys to cook their own hot meal each evening was an important element of the residential trip. Without fail, we encountered initial resistance. The favourite option on the first trip to the local shop was pot noodle, with crisps and chocolate to follow. On the second day most of them realised that cycling in excess of thirty five miles a day required more substantial sustenance: most of them started to pool their money and cooked in pairs or small groups. Left to themselves, it was amazing how much initiative they demonstrated. However, there was a lot for them to learn in a short space of time. Some were attracted by the picture on a packet of fajitas, which they bought with great enthusiasm, not realising that they also needed to buy meat and other ingredients before they could start preparing the meal.

We staff members took it in turns to cook for each other, but often wished that we could share what some of the boys were serving up. My speciality of bangers and mash was poor fare compared to some of the dishes that began to appear in our busy kitchen – casseroles, mixed grills, and even risottos. Had we tried to teach the groups how to prepare each of these meals, I'm sure there would have been only half-hearted interest. Left to themselves, their imaginations ran wild. There were times, however, when whole meals went badly wrong and had to be consigned to the waste bin. Lesson for Life 3: Failure often precedes success.

There was no dishwasher, like the at home, so washing up afterwards was another hurdle to be overcome. Organising rotas worked to a degree, but teenagers' standards of cleanliness never quite measured up to mine, so I nominated myself as the late-night-kitchen-tidy-upper-in-chief.

The daily bike check was also essential, as some of the cycles were so unroadworthy that they needed a rebuild before they could be trusted on the New Forest roads. Fortunately there was a holiday camp just down the hill with a cycle hire shop, where we could buy spares and, in extreme case, hire bikes. Prior to setting off each day, Barry would reinforce the fact that the many steep hills in the area required the boys to apply their brakes when going downhill. As they were accustomed to cycling around on flat London roads, their bikes either weren't equipped with effective brakes or they were unaccustomed to using them. Consequently, there was regular maintenance work to guard against accidents.

My responsibility on the road was to ride along at the back of the line of cyclists as tail-end-Charlie. I would make sure that stragglers were never left behind and I fixed breakdowns, everything from flat tyres to chains coming off or breaking. We did our best to keep everyone in the saddle for as long as possible, but we weren't slave drivers. I ensured that whenever a boy dismounted on a steep ascent I was on hand to accompany him. The week in the New Forest had to be enjoyable for all, whatever one's cycling ability. I can't recall how many times I reminded myself as we set off along straight roads cutting across the forest on peaceful sunny mornings: 'I'm being paid to do this.'

Country lanes present few problems, but the few main roads we travelled could be hazardous. On one occasion we even made a trip across to the Isle of Wight. It was a wet morning as our group approached Lymington, and we had to negotiate a tight left-hand bend on a narrow section of road. Suddenly I noticed that one of our party a few places ahead of me had somehow shifted his backside off his saddle – it was resting on the offside wing of a Ford Fiesta.

I'm keenly attuned to the potential dangers that face cyclists, and my instinctive reaction to a boy abandoning good road sense would be to shout an admonitory comment. On this occasion fear made me dumb. The slightest distraction might cause the boy to end up under the car's wheels. In my mind I saw him being crushed, having mistaken the bonnet of a car for his saddle. I imagined the headlines on the front pages of the tabloids: 'Teachers take tearaways on terror trip'. My reputation, job, career and pension were all suddenly in the balance, just like Taranjeet's bum. Slowly, he seemed to become aware that he was no longer fully attached to his bike and he shifted his body back into the correct cycling posture. A rush of relief hit me and I congratulated him on having returned safely to his saddle. In my book, it's always better to avoid censure if a compliment can be paid instead.

When we had all arrived safely at the ferry point, I asked how he'd managed to mistake the wing of a reasonably-priced car for his saddle. He looked at me as if I were having a hallucinatory attack. I pointed out that I'd seen him taking time out on the bonnet of a hatchback whilst the rest of the group had been cycling carefully down the main road to the ferry point as instructed.

"What you talking about, sir?" he queried. "I wasn't hitchin' no lift."

I had to accept his claims that he had been blissfully unaware of the incident, but I still have my doubts.

I remember one boy, Ricky, as being the most laid-back cyclist we ever took to the New Forest. Quietly confident in his own cycling ability and equally quietly spoken, everything was a breeze for him... until the day he came adrift from his bike, hurtled across the road and ended up in a ditch along the Rhinefield Ornamental Drive.

I was only a few bike lengths away from him when it happened, as we freewheeled down a gentle gradient, tall Douglas firs towering either side of us. Although it was a dry day, loose gravel had been washed into the road from a previous heavy downpour. I saw Ricky's handlebars twitch slightly, causing him instinctively to apply his brakes as his bike took a course to the crown of the road. The effect of this reflex action was that his front wheel locked. He sailed over his handlebars and tumbled diagonally across the road, for all the world like a trained stuntman performing one of the more difficult operations from his repertoire. His progress was arrested when he dropped into a ditch on the other side of the road.

I gave the call to the boys ahead of me to stop and pass the word on that there had been an accident. I dismounted, dropped my bike in a heap, and ran to investigate. I was certain that 'cool' Ricky had suffered serious injury, or worse. He was face up, eyes closed and motionless as I approached him. Barry was soon approaching the scene, having told the rest of the party to park up by the roadside. His strained features suggested that he feared the worst when he saw Ricky's inert form.

'Is he all right?' he called.

'He hasn't moved yet,' I answered. I struggled to suppress a growing feeling that he was no longer of this world.

'Ricky! You all right, mate?' Barry inquired uncertainly as we stood over him.

We knew all about recovery positions, mouth to mouth and heart massage, but we held back until we'd made a preliminary assessment. My jaw dropped as Ricky suddenly opened his eyes, hauled himself slowly out of the ditch and started to brush himself off.

'You had us worried there, Ricky. What happened?' Barry asked, much relieved.

'Hit a bump and came off,' he stated casually.

I thanked God that there had been no traffic on the road when he'd lost control, and that cycle helmets were compulsory. Ricky stretched himself off languidly, checked his helmet and searched for his bike.

'You're good to go then?' asked Barry, trying hard to sound his usual nonchalant self. 'Your bike seems all right too,' he laughed, as he pulled it off the road towards the kerb.

Miraculously his bike was undamaged and in full working order. Ricky mounted up, took his place in the line and we continued our journey. Boys exchanged quizzical looks at each other, clearly as surprised as we were that there'd be no need for the emergency services. The gods of the road were certainly smiling down on us that day. Lesson for Life 4: Avoid unnecessary fuss.

Another near disaster occurred a few years later when Jack also took a header over his handlebars. Once again we were fortunate that there was no traffic on the quiet country lane as we descended through dark woods on our way to Salisbury. On this occasion, we were free-wheeling down a steep incline, dabbing our breaks constantly. Jack was an extrovert character with a big future as a golfer. After performing a perfect somersault over his handlebars just ahead of me, he landed heavily on his shoulder. My immediate fears were twofold: 1) he had possibly sustained multiple fractures, and 2) his golfing dreams may have come to a premature end. This stretch of road was completely covered by overhanging tree branches, making it difficult to see clearly the damage he'd suffered.

Jack wasn't quite the cool customer that Ricky had been. He really did moan and groan aloud, lying crumpled at the side of the road. As I took a closer look, I realised that he did have good reason to complain as there was damage to his clothing and extensive grazing of his arms. Unable to stand, he had to be carried to a point of safety on a grass verge.

Barry then arrived, after receiving news of the accident at the head of the line, followed by Allyson. One by one, the rest of the pack arrived on the scene. We agreed that this was definitely a case for calling an ambulance, and used the school-issue mobile phone to call emergency services and contact the school with the details of the incident. Despite being at least five miles from the nearest village, an ambulance arrived within twenty minutes from Salisbury District Hospital.

We'd decided that I should accompany Jack in the ambulance, and we were relieved when the hugely accommodating crew said that they would also take our bikes in the back of the vehicle. I spent the rest of the day with Jack at the hospital, feeling rather self-conscious in my cycling gear. My relief when we discovered that there were no breaks was immense. He'd suffered extensive bruising but, we were assured, his golf swing would be unimpaired. Barry is still in touch with Jack, who can never apologise enough for his carelessness whenever they recall the incident.

The road for the trio of teachers was unerringly wonderful. We were all totally absorbed by the workings of our cycles, our daily progress through the beauty and tranquillity of the forest, and the vagaries of the weather conditions. The trick was to get the students to share this experience by the end of the week. Barry's favourite ride was to Salisbury because there was an especially picturesque straight section of road, just before we met the A46. Here the interlacing trees create a leafy tunnel, and cycling along this half-mile stretch offers an almost transcendental experience. It was at its best in full sunshine, when rays of light flickered through the foliage to create a magical effect. Photographs we took of cyclists disappearing in the distance down the tunnel still take my breath away. Lesson for Life 5: Life is enriched immeasurably if one takes the time to enjoy the beauty of the natural world. This is one lesson that few bother to teach children.

Having a sweet tooth and a particular interest in pastries, the Brockenhurst run was always special for me. My favourite patisserie in the world can be found here and it produces a cherry Danish pastry par excellence. After two hours or so in the saddle, I would pedal with renewed vigour across the water splash at the entrance to the village, in the knowledge that heaven awaited a hundred yards up the road. After locking up our bikes in the nearby car park, we would head back to the high street looking for a spot of lunch. If I were lucky, there would be a tray of oven-fresh pastries in the little shop waiting to be plundered. This was the one occasion on the trip when I eschewed sensible eating. Every year I shamelessly handed over whatever I was required to pay for my regulation three pastries. Seated outside at the tables and chairs in the warm midday sun, I ate them one by one in full view of everyone. Absolute bliss! If I did feel a hint of guilt, I quickly dismissed it in the knowledge that the twenty-mile journey back to Godshill, for the most part against a strong wind, would burn up all of the calories I was consuming and more. Lesson for Life 6: Teachers are only human.

As the boys assessed their physical endurance at the end of each day of exhausting cycling, they were more than happy to pore over Barry's ordnance survey maps of the forest. It became an early evening routine for them to brush up on their map work, taking it in turns to present detailed explanations of the routes we had taken to the rest of the group. It was gratifying to witness them identifying the symbols for cycle trails, gradients steeper than 1 in 5, cattle grids and churches with or without spires. It was fun for them to decode the secret language of these maps that explained every detail of the wonderful environment to which they had been transported. This was authentic education, children learning not for examinations or house points but for themselves. These debriefing sessions also required them to highlight each day's 'good bits' and 'bad bits', other than the 'uphills' (bad) and 'downhills' (good). There was so much that they wanted to talk about, rather than watch television. Lesson for Life 7: Television isn't as much fun as real life.

One destination that couldn't fail to excite their grey matter was the Anglo-Saxon church of St Mary in Breamore, north of Godshill, with its square central tower. After struggling to grasp the concept that people had been using this very building as a place of worship for almost seven hundred years, the boys then set about trying to decipher the strange old English inscriptions on the wall-mounted plaques, marking the resting places of family lines down through the centuries.

The nearby farm museum was another attraction that offered a unique educational experience, featuring artefacts that captured the sights, sounds and smells of farm work through the ages. The Rockbourne Roman Villa Museum, only a short cycle ride further on, was also a fascinating stop. Some of our cyclists thought we were joking when we said that the Romans invented central heating, until they saw for themselves the remains of the clay pipe work for the villa's hypocaust. Lesson for Life 8: Seeing is believing.

The display of the pottery jar containing over 7,000 Roman coins that had been hidden on the site over seventeen hundred years ago suggested to the more imaginative members of our group a surprise raid by Saxon invaders. Their imaginations filled with images of a terrifying night attack by axe-wielding marauders whilst the villa's inhabitants were sound asleep. How could a community be living peacefully in the South Downs for four or five hundred years and be wiped out in the blink of an eye? They really did want to know.

Despite the fact that the cycle week was slotted in at the end of the summer term, we often experienced cloudbursts that drenched us. The emergency procedure then was to stop at the nearest café or snack bar for a warm drink and a chance to dry out. My worry was that a large party of sodden adolescents turning up unexpectedly would not be welcomed by the proprietors. However, as soon as they realised that they were not dealing with a bunch of mischievous London teenagers but a group of polite young men from the capital, they couldn't do enough for them. Boys with reputations for being uncooperative and temperamental turned on the style that they often suppressed in the school setting, transforming themselves into young men of the world with good manners and charm to spare. Glowing with pride, I would settle myself quietly in a corner with a cup of tea and enjoy observing the good-natured goings-on around me as the staff provided hot refreshment and did their best to dry out wet clothing. The job of being an effective teacher involves more than simply gaining good examination results. Lesson for Life 9: Respect others and they'll reciprocate.

On the Thursday evening before returning to school the following day, Barry always booked a table as a surprise for the students in the restaurant of the public house a hundred yards up the road from the lodge. The place assumed legendary status for every group we took to Godshill because its name was, to them, hilariously unbelievable: The Fighting Cocks. By this time many of them playfully claimed to be so saddle-weary that they never wanted to ride a bike again, so a slap-up meal together, which they didn't have to prepare themselves, was a blessed relief. The locals made us very welcome and the landlord was only too pleased to have the custom of such a large group. The food was exceptional and the mood celebratory as we exchanged notes on the many memorable moments of the week. They relished the hill challenges, cycling through storms, the sheer exhilaration of speeding along through some of the most beautiful scenery in the country, and the camaraderie of the road.

The most important Lesson for Life (10) I felt I could ever teach any child was: Hang in there. Life is so much more rewarding if one can simply keep going, whatever obstacles one has to confront. A boy once asked me when I'd cycled up a long steep incline, 'How do you manage to keep going without getting off and walking?' I explained that I focused on counting in my head to take my mind off any pain my body might be experiencing. I told him that by the time I'd counted one hundred pushes on the pedals, I believed I'd be at the top of the hill. 'But what if you counted to a hundred and still hadn't got to the top?' he asked. The obvious reply was, 'I'd count another hundred.' Just to reinforce my point, after the gruelling forty-mile day trip to Brockenhurst and back, I would quickly change into my running gear on our return to the lodge and issue an invitation to any of the boys who had crashed out on beds and sofas, 'Anybody fancy a five-mile run to Fordingbridge and back?' Nobody ever took up my challenge.

Down through the years, Barry, Allyson and I have bumped into a number of our cyclists in adult life. Many have confided to us that the New Forest trip was the best time in their secondary school lives. Learning lessons for life on challenging residential trips is completely different from learning in the classroom. Being responsible for personal hygiene, feeding oneself, budgeting for a week, plotting a route on a map, and maintaining one's bike in a roadworthy condition are invaluable learning experiences.

Returning to school, daily routines such as issuing reprimands for lateness or not wearing correct uniform all seemed rather pointless.

5. Philanthropy

Schools play an essential part in encouraging the philanthropic impulse in children. It's a necessary counter to those social influences that focus on and promote self-interest. This statement may sound trite, but we live in a world where philanthropy is a relatively small-scale operation. Press reports that in 2015 48% of the world's wealth was owned by one per cent of the population would suggest that taking, or grasping, is still more fashionable than giving. Unfortunately, the amount of money raised by charities to alleviate the sufferings of those in need is a drop in the ocean compared to the huge amount of wealth amassed by the seriously rich.

The excessively wealthy (i.e. those who succumb to the twin temptations of 1) megalomania and 2) lining their own pockets big-time) rely heavily on governments and schools to be their own and society's conscience, with regard to preserving that most endangered of species – charity. The government does its bit in a small way when the nation is flush, but for the past decade chancellors have spent much of their time devising new wheezes to justify securing the treasury's purse strings ever more tightly. Much as any prime minister might wish to relieve the plight of the homeless at a stroke, nothing will happen without the say-so of those with the real power behind the throne – the oligarchs and plutocrats who have the clout to dictate the course of entire economies.

There are powerful financial forces at work in the business world, about which I know little, that largely dictate the course of every important aspect of society. This being the status quo, it is even more important for the individual to be able to learn what it is to be charitable.

The contribution made to society by those engaged in charitable work is valuable in moral as well as material terms. I have always been in favour of developing people's charity muscles. Being a city dweller, I have the greatest respect for organisations working to alleviate the distress of the homeless, particularly the Salvation Army. The idea of having to live on the streets is one that I find distressing in the extreme.

My late father-in-law, a civil servant, regularly criticised me for involving myself in charitable enterprises organised at school. His logic was that society's ills were so self-evident that politicians should be addressing them before undertaking any other costly projects; for example, Concorde, the arms race, space exploration and the Channel Tunnel. He believed that teachers should be teaching and not raising funds for causes that were the state's responsibility. He retained to his dying day the conviction that governments waste money and speculate irresponsibly in a host of ways because they know they can rely on the voluntary work of compassionate members of the public to fill financial gaps. I continued to endorse charity work, despite any sympathy I might have had with regard to his arguments. I held on to the belief that, if I helped to raise funds for specific charities, they would be certain to receive some of the money they needed. In the real world, treasury money is difficult to acquire, however deserving the cause.

I have to be honest and admit that I do resent government officials who withhold money, raised through taxation, to fund services (including schools) adequately. Equally, I cannot sympathise with those dismissive of charity workers who have decided to take decisive action to guarantee targeted financial support for the needy. This attitude conveniently absolves those subscribers of any responsibility actively to demonstrate their compassion for humanity. Feeling compassion for the less fortunate is a quality that all children must retain, if born with it, or learn. I don't consider paying income tax to be an act of charity. It is abhorrent to think that there are those amongst the very wealthy who seek specialist advice on the avoidance of paying tax on their earnings and/or accumulated wealth.

I spent a career promoting philanthropy with the full support of my family. My last school had a strong PTA that organised an annual summer fair, and my wife and I used to help out by providing hot food for those who came along on the big day. We were Mr and Mrs Barbecue every year for a dozen years or more. Those smoke-shrouded hours in the summer sun raised a useful total annually, but put me off ever barbecuing at home. My wife complained bitterly that if I could cook five hundred bangers and burgers for the school, I could do two each for us in the back garden when the sun came out. But no! A line has to be drawn in the sand for the sake of one's own sanity. When a soldier returned home from the front, the last thing he wanted to do was dig a trench in the garden. Alas, the summer fair is no more. I can only imagine that the burgeoning list of administrative duties required of schools and their governors has inevitably resulted in casualties.

I remember assembling at Greenwich with my daughter on a bright spring morning in 2012 as we prepared to run our first London marathon for Shooting Star CHASE, a charity for children with life-limiting illnesses. Lucy had dedicated her participation in the event to her sister, Keeley, who had died at age eighteen. Unsure as to how best to raise a significant amount in sponsorship, I contacted my old school for help. Euan, the headteacher agreed that the school would get behind us, and Gwyn, a senior teacher and good friend spread the word amongst the pupils. Several hundred pounds were raised by children I had once taught. We were given a huge lift on the day of the run by the presence at twenty-three miles of a large group of parents whose children would benefit from the money raised.

Three years later, when my great-niece, Harmonie, lost all her limbs as a result of contracting meningitis, my daughter, Ross, her partner, and I all ran the 2015 London Marathon in aid of the Meningitis Research Campaign and raised £5,200.

Compassion is one motive for getting involved in fund-raising events. However, the very word 'compassion' is fast becoming a pejorative term in the hard-nosed twenty-first century. For cynics, it's the emotion that motivates so-called 'do-gooders'. This description is inimical to me. It's an unfeeling term (intentional use of *transferred epithet*) used to imply that those who get involved with a charity only do so to make themselves feel 'good'.

Thankfully, there are many who simply find themselves having to act in order to cope with feelings of helplessness when tragedy strikes either those close to home or in the wider world. It's easy to pass responsibility on to others when a funding crisis comes to the public's attention. This is the reflex of the self-righteous who would prefer not to act directly for the good of humankind.

The Charity Walk

For twenty years the secondary boys' school where I taught organised an annual 25-mile sponsored walk in aid of a local charity selected by the students themselves. The pleasurable memories I have of my participation in this event alone confirmed my belief that working with young people can be enormously beneficial for one's own character.

The school's Charities Committee, comprising sixth-form students, PTA members and staff, spent weeks preparing the route, organising checkpoints and enlisting walkers, not only from my school but also those from other secondary schools within the authority. One of my colleagues in the English department, Verna, was the staff liaison and brains behind successive walks. I have a guilty confession: I still have a video-cassette recording of the 1988 walk that she loaned me. I even have an old VCR on which to play it.

On the Sunday of the walk in late March, there would be up to 2,000 students blazing a trail from Isleworth to Chiswick, Roehampton, Richmond Park, Kingston, Hampton Court, Teddington and back to Isleworth. Most of those who started the course finished it. This was fund raising on an epic scale, with tens of thousands of pounds being raised for numerous causes.

Such an event couldn't happen now because health and safety considerations wouldn't permit it. There were only three rules for those taking part as far as I can remember: No litter. No stereos. No shouting. It was impossible for anyone to get lost or come to any harm because there were hundreds of volunteers along the route. Refreshments were constantly available so nobody ever collapsed from thirst or malnutrition. The hotdog tent at Hampton Court, set up and run by parents, was always a welcome sight as leg-weary teenagers dragged themselves along the towpath.

Despite the difficulties of my domestic situation, I took part each year. Lindsey and I were caring for our severely handicapped child at home and, in order that I wasn't absent from home for a full day, where I was needed at weekends, I ran the walk. My elder daughter, Keeley, was born with a heart condition and suffered extensive brain damage at sixteen months when she haemorrhaged after the first of what was planned to be a series of operations. She lost her sight, all power of movement and had to learn to eat and drink again. We took her home after she had recovered physically from the operation, naïvely believing that she would make a miraculous mental recovery in the security of her own home. She made no significant progress, other than regaining the ability to smile, and was never operated on again. She died of pneumonia just after her eighteenth birthday. To us, Keeley was different but we loved her no less than Lucy, our second daughter who, thankfully, was healthy in every respect.

I desperately wanted to be a part of Walk Day, but I felt guilty about leaving my wife for a whole day to do all of the heavy lifting involved in caring for Keeley. As I was in the habit of jogging a few miles two or three times a week, I decided that I would gradually increase my distances so that I could run the walk in four and a half hours or so, as opposed to walking it in a day.

I'd been doing this for a few years when Scope, a charity working with disabled people and their families, contacted the school. They knew about the annual fund-raising walk and wanted to know if John Conteh, former World Light Heavyweight Boxing Champion and one of their star supporters, could run the event with teachers and students as a practice run-out for the London Marathon. I was approached by the school's charities committee and invited to accompany John around the course. What could I do but accept such an offer! A sixth former, Stephen Tibber, also courageously decided to join us.

It's difficult to describe the awkwardness and anxiety I felt when introduced to John on the morning of the event. I had watched this man on television performing at the highest level in his sport on the world stage. I consider boxing to be the toughest of all sports, and here was this gladiator of the ring thanking me for accommodating him. Although he was no longer boxing professionally, he was still a superb physical specimen. We were the same age, thirty three years old, and I thought myself fairly fit at the time, but he was in exceptional condition. Initially, I couldn't help but feel overawed by his presence. But I soon discovered that I had no need to feel this way: he was so unassuming and amicable. His Liverpool accent was as strong as his physique, and I struggled to understand him at times. I also struggled to keep up with him once we set off. I'm sure that I held John and Stephen back, having a much shorter stride than the two six-footers, but they never complained.

John spoke at length about the importance of family life and the joy of finding a replacement for his boxing career – education. He was studying for a degree and taking it very seriously. He explained that boxing was, in his opinion, the most disciplined of all sports, and he'd found that discipline to be a transferrable ability that was invaluable in his studies.

He was excellent company during the run, chatting freely for the first eighteen miles or so. But with half a dozen miles to go, I was in trouble trying to keep pace with him. At this stage he would probably have been experiencing difficulties caused by running with those of slower pace, but he couldn't run on as he didn't know the route. I continued but was struggling with each step. It was at this point that I realised why John had become a world champion in his field and I was a mere mortal. He demonstrated an iron will: the closer we got to the finish, the faster he wanted to run. I felt guilty about the situation, but he couldn't have been more gracious.

He thanked us profusely at the end, causing me further embarrassment. It was a unique experience in my life, running with a sporting household name, one who taught me the importance of identifying one's personal strengths and exploiting them to the full. Although I was a qualified teacher, I only had a Certificate in Education. I had faith in my ability as a teacher but, in a profession where everybody coming into the job now had a degree, I felt that I ought to follow suit. I decided, therefore, that I would take a lesson from John Conteh: if he was studying for a degree, so would I. I applied for a year's secondment to convert my certificate into a full degree and was successful in my application. A little over two years after running twenty-five miles with John Conteh, I was the proud possessor of a degree certificate. The man had been my inspiration, although he never knew it.

Looking back at footage of the 1988 Walk, I smile at the big quiffs, shellsuits, and the enormous mobile phones used by the staff and student supervisors. What I recall most vividly were the lengths to which people were prepared to go to tap into the vast reserves of enthusiasm that young people possess to look beyond themselves. An enterprise of this size couldn't take place nowadays, but one can still rely on young people's capacity for self-sacrifice, the readiness to give up their time and energy to come to the aid of those needing help.

Red Nose Day

Fund raising has subsequently become more organised in schools, with activities planned in school calendars to benefit local, national and international charities. A member of staff takes on the onerous responsibility of coordinating a school's charities schedule, and is responsible for ensuring the success of this vital area of school life.

Red Nose Day subsequently replaced the 'Walk' at my last school in terms of the sheer numbers of students actively involved on one day in the year. In place of the single 25-mile enterprise organised by older students, numerous smaller-scale fund-raising initiatives devised by boys of all ages took place. During lunch or break time, I could buy a home-made cake at the library cake sale, try to beat the goalie in the school playground, or guess the number of sweets in a jar. The fund-raising spirit was infectious, with staff getting into the spirit of things in their own unique ways. Beard-shaving stunts, staff versus boys basketball, and five-a-side football challenges were very popular. Three female members of staff even dressed in full boys' school uniform and, with collection tins in hand, did a lunch-time tour of the school to boost takings. The act of supporting charitable causes was equated with fun, and the whole school was carried along by the momentum of the project.

Harvest Challenge

The Harvest Challenge was another major charitable event, involving the collection of non-perishable food items by pupils for the benefit of the older, less well-off residents in the borough. I still have photographs of the temporary collection point for all the tins and boxes – the school stage – piled high with everything from beef stew to baked beans.

Volunteers from Years 10 and 11 organised the parcelling up of contributions in bright yellow plastic containers and the deliveries in the school minibus to various distribution points. There was an old people's luncheon club near Heathrow airport, an organisation for homeless people in Richmond, and a café meeting place for the residents of a well-known Hounslow high-rise complex. Children annually brought into school enough food to fill in excess of a hundred food parcels, and these donations were always gratefully received by needy individuals and families.

***

Billions may be flowing into the capital to buy up the city's exclusive properties, but in soup-kitchen London there are increasing numbers of people who are struggling to survive. I now find myself resident in the fourth most deprived borough in greater London. The charitable work undertaken in schools is a great example of children's capacity for selflessness, a quality that many of them will, thankfully, carry with them into adult life.

6. The News

My second headteacher asked me to produce a fortnightly four-page school newsletter in 1982. I found myself still doing the job twenty-eight years later. The head made the helpful point that he was offering me the unpaid additional responsibility because I was "spending too much time marking" and needed another string to my bow. Presumably he thought that concentrating on teaching commitments was simply a case of me fiddling about. Needless to say, I carried on marking as I always had done and found myself even more snowed under with work. The main reasons for the longevity of my newsletter-writing tenure were twofold. One, over-worked teachers tend to maintain body and soul by applying the barge-pole principle when presented with the offer of certain additional voluntary responsibilities, and nobody could ever be persuaded to take the job from me. Two, being able to spell and punctuate reasonably well, I became a victim of my own competence. The main attraction of the job was that it entailed scope for creativity and freedom, and I genuinely enjoyed the responsibility in a masochistic kind of way.

This was in the days before home computers. If I asked someone to write an article for inclusion in the newsletter, that's what they had to do. There was no easily-correctible Word software and no email. People had to put pen to paper and produce a neat draft of three hundred words – neither an easy nor a speedy task. I had to get used to buttering people up, chasing them up, begging even, for a worthy contribution. Almost overnight I became the teacher one would least like to bump into around the school. My popularity went into reverse. Colleagues and pupils would see me coming along the corridor and duck into a classroom, an office or the loo in order to avoid having to confront me and apologise for failing to meet a copy deadline. Fortunately, being a Capricorn, I had limitless patience and a boundless capacity for grovelling subservience in the pursuit of my goals. These qualities set me in good stead for the next three decades. Where possible, I would prevent embarrassment with staff and students by writing as much of the newsletter content myself as possible. Consequently I had to become a roving reporter, in addition to my teaching commitments. All this and no extra money for my pains.

I always kept in mind that very few people have both the time and the confidence to produce a detailed written account of a newsworthy activity or event. There were those who made it clear to me, in the friendliest manner possible, that I would be wasting my time if I asked them for an article. One member of the science faculty who never produced a single word, despite my pleas, argued that he found writing a shopping list difficult. He had little interest in literature of any kind. I recall him bragging that he had never read or seen a performance of a Shakespeare play. I soon resorted to asking for a bullet-point list of the main details of an activity from those too modest or over-worked to pen an account themselves. This they were happier to do in order to promote extra-curricular activities that they had taken the trouble to organise. The one advantage of having to write the bulk of the text myself was that the periodical quickly acquired a distinctive house style, namely the enthusiastic promotion of all aspects of school life.

Most students were cautious about being published in the News. The idea of their name appearing beneath the title of an article that everyone in the school would read was too intimidating a prospect to entertain. Before the days of social networking, when self-promotion became the vogue, I found teenagers to be generally modest, unassuming and secretive. The school had boys winning national honours in various areas who categorically wanted to keep their achievements out of the public domain. Facebook changed all that, sometimes with disastrous consequences.

I was always aware that some young people had the potential to be spiteful towards their peers, which could explain why the majority didn't want to appear in print. The fear that one might be laying oneself open to scorn and ridicule for being uniquely talented or unnaturally keen about a particular interest was a constant in the teenage mindset. Fear of the admonition 'boff' was ever present.

Looking at the lives young people lead in the twenty-first century, there are two significant developments that I could not have foreseen in the early 1980s. First, there is the profound psychological switch to embracing the concept of online self-aggrandisement. It seems that many teenagers nowadays are happy to let it all hang out – sometimes literally. This is not simply a case of disclosing one's personal activities school-wide but, potentially, nationwide. Second, I couldn't have imagined that I would hear, all too often, reports in the media of teenage suicides, as a direct consequence of online bullying. Towards the end of my time as a teacher, I regularly discussed with my teaching groups the need for discretion when they updated their personal accounts with commentary, still images or video footage. Children in primary schools can easily open personal online accounts, despite the regulatory guideline that networking sites are only for those aged thirteen and over. The dangers to them of daily interaction with the virtual realities offered by the internet are many.

Having collected a dozen or more handwritten articles for the school newspaper, I would correct them clearly in red ink and pass them on to a volunteer parent who kindly typed them up in columns, newspaper style. The cutting and pasting job, using Letraset for titles and headlines, usually took five hours per issue. The fumes from the Cow Gum glue I used for cutting and pasting gave me a headache that I took with me to bed and woke up with. The viscous spirit-based adhesive was knockout. It was rather messy too, any residue left on the paper being difficult to remove. The best method was to rub it in a circular manner with your fingertip until it formed a small 'bogie' that could be picked off the paper. What you did with it after that was up to you.

On cut-and-paste evenings, I'd sit myself at the dining table surrounded by typed copy that I had to juggle to fit on to four A4 sheets. I'd always fancied myself at being good at drawing, and I enjoyed the simple pleasure of producing illustrations to improve the appearance of the News. I'd start at around seven p.m. after the evening meal and seeing the children off to bed. The little portable television in its red plastic case would be in the corner of the room to keep me company. I particularly associate programmes such as 'Rising Damp', 'Bless This House', 'The Sweeney' and Hammer horror films with my late-night sedentary labours. My wife would bring me a final mug of tea at about eight and then leave me to it. I knew that when she turned in at about ten thirty, I'd still have another couple of hours to go.

In the early days when editions came off the press and were distributed around the school, I entertained the thought that one or two colleagues might compliment me on the final product. However, this rarely happened. I eventually told myself that the apparent lack of interest must be the result of staff being snowed under with their own responsibilities; the idea of commenting in any way on the newsletter presumably didn't occur to them. The only regular feedback that came my way was the pointing out of minor mistakes that I'd made, for example the occasional misspelling of a pupil's name. I found that I could overlook the critical apathy because I eventually concluded that I was doing the work for myself. If I were happy with the modest publication, that was enough for me.

From my experience, teachers are reluctant to praise each other. Indeed, I think they get by generally with little or no praise at all from anyone. Children weren't in the habit of leaving my classroom with an effusive, 'Sir, you were smokin' today!' And when parents came to open evenings, they were more likely to start proceedings with, 'My Johnny's exercise book hasn't been marked for two weeks.' I desperately hoped to hear something expansively gushing and uplifting to the soul such as, 'My son thinks your teaching is the mutt's!' The best that could be expected, however, was usually a bleated, 'My son quite likes English.'

For the average teacher struggling to cope with an impossible workload, the avoidance of professional criticism has become the new praise. Newcomers to the job may still experience, as I did, the reality that teachers are expected to praise children constantly but receive none themselves. I once told one of my headteachers that I thought he was doing a great job in his tireless efforts to improve the school. His stunned and speechless reaction indicated that he, like me, was unaccustomed to receiving praise from any quarter.

I've kept a copy of almost every edition of the News that I produced. Deep down I'm proud of the work that I put in over three decades to highlight some of the best work of my school in the classroom and beyond. Re-reading them has been particularly instructive. I was appalled by some of the plays on words in the headlines I used. Occasionally I managed to miss the unintentional humour in some of those I came up with, as in the case of a report about a cricket match between teachers and sixth-form leavers that I entitled 'Staff beat boys'. I particularly enjoyed reliving events from the period before the national curriculum and assessment really applied a stranglehold on school life. In the first ten years of the newsletter, between 1982 and 1992, teachers still devoted a huge amount of goodwill to activities that are not so common in schools nowadays.

I was impressed by the range of extra-curricular activities that staff readily organised, some of them decidedly challenging. The nannification of state education is tightening its grip on all aspects of school life. For example, reams of health-and-safety forms must be completed before a teacher can take a child beyond the school gates during the school day. One of the questions that brought out the devil in me regarding the set of forms that were required asked me to produce a list of the precautions I would take to protect the children in my care: a) during the journeys to and from event locations and b) throughout the organised activity. Every fibre of my being urged me to respond to *a)* with the reassurance that my party of students would walk in single file, chain-linked by the ankle, and that I would carry a lion tamer's chair and lash to keep the group under total control at all times.

Over a quarter of a century ago, one of our lower-sixth boys parachuted solo out of a plane in aid of the Heart Transplant Trust. The local education authority was even involved in organising the jump at Cranfield's London Skydiving Centre. The parachutist, Duncan, found the experience so thrilling that, on landing, he immediately went and paid a second full fee of £17 to jump again five hours later. Had our strict health-and-safety policy been in place then, what would one have written in answer to *b)*? Possibly: 'A thick covering of goose down will be spread over the landing area in order to eliminate any possibility of bruising to the student's nether regions on landing.' In 1990 Duncan raised £214 for the Heart Transplant Trust. I wouldn't imagine that a student request to undertake a fund-raising challenge of this sort would get past a headteacher's secretary today.

On the subject of skydiving, three teachers, including the then head of school, also parachuted from 2,000 feet in aid of Greenpeace in 1983. There was the promise of extra sponsorship riding on this jump as one schoolboy donor pledged double the amount he'd promised if the head's parachute didn't open. One can't help but think that a politically sensitive initiative of this nature might nowadays seriously dent one's promotion prospects. Greenpeace was prepared to go to considerable and often dangerous lengths at this time to raise awareness of the threats to our environment. Some quarters of the Establishment had serious reservations about the organisation and its more extreme escapades.

There was a period when the local environment excited great interest amongst the school population. Shortly after the

82

publication of the sky-diving accounts, Kim, a biology teacher, came forward with an article about the efforts of one of her teaching groups to save the *hairy-lipped snail*, a resident of the nearby marshes. Then she wrote about her efforts to provide the correct nutrition and treatment necessary to ensure the survival of ten ducklings that had hatched in the school's conservation area. When they subsequently died of botulism, Form 3A went into mourning. But there was a happy ending of sorts for the pupils. Seven of another ten ducklings to hatch in the school grounds survived after being fed a special mash, prepared by the science department, and receiving treatment for a thyroid condition. The headline I used for that story was 'Ducking Out' Appalling! I still don't see any connection with the article.

Gradually students began to open up with offerings when the News became established and they felt secure in the knowledge that anything they contributed would be presented seriously. Andrew, in Year 11, wrote about the 1957 Ford Anglia 100E that he had bought for £10, and the restoration work that he had carried out with a view to a total rebuild. Andrew was one of the most modest and unassuming boys in my form group at the time, and I could never have imagined that he would have had the drive (pun apologies) to take on what he termed his 'big challenge'. Another unusual feature came from a Year 7 pupil who wrote about his collection of 'really cute' pet tarantulas. Lucifer, his Highland Black, was the favourite of his brood. His pets, he reassured readers, were not rough to the touch as one might imagine, but 'velvety smooth'. I must remember to check that detail next time I'm handling one. The highlight of the account was the description of a tarantula moulting.

At the dawn of personal computing, one student volunteered to contribute a column on the topic. July 1984 saw the opening of the school's first ever computer room, with the installation of five BBC Micros. A few months later there was a buzz around the school as two Spectrum ZX 48k machines were added. From small acorns... In fact, the Acorn Electron, a more affordable version of the BBC Micro, became one of the most popular computers of its time. Excitement increased two years later when the mighty Commodore 64 appeared, at a bargain price of £50. The first party of our pupils ever to go to an Earl's Court PC Show in 1988 reported that the only computers on show were Amigas and Ataris.

The excitement amongst staff when two rooms full of PCs with internet connection first became available for timetabled lessons was tempered by an important consideration. Intense competition amongst staff to book the rooms for their classes meant that one was seldom able to use the facilities, and certainly not with any regularity. A decade later, mechanisms had to be introduced to prevent children from accessing porn during lessons. I remember being warned when I first used one of the rooms to remain on my feet at all times and to move constantly around the banks of computers as I taught in order to check what was on the screens. If you were a real amateur in the computing stakes and didn't know then that one touch of a button could quickly reduce a screen page, you were on a hiding to nothing. Pupils seemed to learn PC wrinkles much more quickly than their teachers.

The History department submitted to me regular accounts during the 1980s of trips made by A-Level students to The Commons for Prime Minister's Question Time. The subsequent write-ups usually reflected a sense of students feeling let down as opposed to uplifted by the experience. The focus on the behaviour of MPs tended to be of greater interest to them than the content of the debates; for example, 'MPs lounged about with their feet on the benches in front of them until they were called to order.' Another commented, 'The issue that excited fits of screaming and laughing amongst MPs was immigration.' The fact that Enoch Powell was present at the time presumably wouldn't have helped matters. After visiting Westminster on June 20th 1985, Tim, one of the most astute sixth formers I ever taught, was moved to observe: 'The exchanges between Margaret Thatcher, David Owen, Neil Kinnock, Nigel Lawson, Roy Hattersley and the like weren't as bitter and unruly as I have heard on the radio, but there were still crying out and loud laughter from both sides of the House.'

If MPs never quite matched up to our boys' expectations of how politicians should conduct themselves on such occasions, one character certainly did excite their admiration. When Arthur Scargill was a guest speaker at Central Hall in January 1986, one student stated that he and his fellow students 'were impressed by the hostility of the questions directed towards him by the audience and by his skill as a powerful orator to answer them.' It was a pity that Question Time trips fizzled out after that heady period in the 1980s.

One particularly successful activity organised by the History department in 1991, a few years after the introduction of the National Curriculum, involved students listening to the memories of invited guest Ralph Fuller, a First World War veteran. The most interesting details of his experiences, as far as the boys were concerned, didn't focus on his war-time recollections but his education. He revealed that in ten years of schooling he didn't take a single examination and was never asked to complete homework. The only certificate he ever received was his treasured Good Conduct Certificate. For some reason, Shakespeare comes to mind: 'Something is rotten in the state of Denmark.'

In 1987, the first party of our students arrived at a high school in Baltimore on a newly-established school exchange. It was a real coup for Tony, the head at the time. The thirteen boys lucky enough to make the first trip across the Atlantic had a wonderful experience. When the Americans arrived on these shores for the return visit, it was gratifying to read their assessments of life in the UK. One discovered that American television offered 'a great number of poor quality programmes', whilst another was of the opinion that 'the British are aeons ahead of us in musical taste'. On a darker note, it was at this time that I heard the satanic acronym 'SAT' for the first time. One of the young Americans mentioned it to me in casual conversation. Little did I know the shadow that these three letters would cast over the rest of my career.

Trawling through the back issues of the News, I uncovered many examples of children's acute powers of observation. Perhaps the most telling truism of all those I unearthed was the stark observation, 'Beefeaters are extraordinarily grumpy.' The transparency of children, who have yet to learn the art of discretion, is also always heart-warming, as in the case of the twelve year old who wrote the following after a school visit to Paris, 'We visited the Arc de Triomphe, the Eiffel Tower and Burger King.' Ah, saving the best for last. It's important that the teachers of the future have a clear idea of where children's priorities lie.

Finally, I include what I consider to be the most interesting pupil suggestion that I ever published: 'Students should be able to write their own reports.' The more I think about this one, the more sense it seems to make.

7. Why Teach?

It's difficult to justify fully to myself that teaching was such a pleasurable and fulfilling occupation when I reflect on the pressures of the job. Now into my seventh year of retirement, I'm still woken by a recurring nightmare that I can't shake off.

I have to hurry from the staff room to teach a lesson but, despite my efforts to reach the classroom, I'm delayed at every turn. When I do eventually make it, standing outside the classroom at the head of a line of gleeful pupils is the last headteacher I worked for, looking irritably at his watch. He stood a foot taller than me, making the dream even more disturbing. At this point I find my conscious self trying to interrupt my subconscious torment with the message, 'Don't panic. This is your regular nightmare. Wake up now!' And I do just that every time, waking in a sweat, heart pounding.

I also find myself planning English lessons in my sleep. Very recently I spent most of the night preparing an exercise to highlight why the English language is so difficult to learn. It involved me compiling a list of words all ending with the same 'eez' sound, but spelt differently on each occasion: bees, breeze, cheese, disease, frieze, keys, peas, quays, reprise… I'm told some people dream about sex.

The job has gone away but a residue of the constant anxiety that came with it hasn't. My teaching career should never have been so stressful, but burgeoning levels of top-down governmental interference over thirty years made life for ordinary classroom teachers frustrating in so many respects. The intolerable workload alone makes teaching a challenging career choice, such that only the truly committed and masochistic professional can cope with it long term. For many it's become a 'five-year job' option. Teaching also became a despised profession, the general public duped into believing the lie that teachers mainly comprised obstructive and incompetent Marxists.

Lying half-awake in the early hours, I curse the education secretaries that I loathed almost as much as they appeared to despise state-school teachers: Sir Keith Joseph, Kenneth Baker, Michael Gove, at al. Michael Gove's arrival on the education scene was only seven months before I retired, but in that short time I judged him to hold teachers and academics in greater contempt than any of his predecessors ever had. As we move towards 2020, I consider that his contribution to the teacher shortfall crisis has been significant. With the able support of his chief inspector of schools, Sir Michael Wilshaw, he oversaw what I considered to be an essentially bullying educational culture. It's small wonder that almost ten per cent of England's teaching force left the state sector between November 2013 and November 2014.

Teaching is not, therefore, the most fashionable long-term career choice. DfE television advertising campaigns rightfully draw attention to the wonders of a teaching career, but overlook the immense weight of imposed drudgery. In 2015 a 'national scandal' broke that four out of ten teachers leave the profession within five years of completing their training. The cause of this scandal? It depends whom you ask. The chief of school inspectors recently blamed indiscipline in the classroom. This stock response is an attack on teachers, the implication being that they are 'allowing' children to misbehave.

Teachers have always had to contend with pupil behaviour issues but, it could be argued, trainees are no longer receiving adequate training to deal with the testing disciplinary situations they encounter. From this perspective, teacher providers and school induction staff must be at fault. In financial terms, teacher wastage is reported to have cost the nation a billion pounds between 2011 and 2016. Teacher union leaders argue that the cause of such large numbers of young teachers leaving the profession is the huge burden of administration for which they weren't prepared.

Much as I'm reluctant to beat an old drum, I do believe that teachers were better prepared for the classroom under the system operating in days of yore, whereby new recruits were prepared for the job in discrete teacher-training institutions. Local education authority advisers then visited teachers regularly in the first year of their school placement to check on progress and offer a range of support strategies, should they be needed.

The one-year PGCE course, currently undertaken by graduates choosing to teach, comprises teaching practice in the main, with a modicum of theory thrown in. Hard-pressed teachers within schools provide additional support and prepare detailed performance reports. This money-saving system places an even greater burden on those already shouldering a significant workload.

I was responsible for the induction of beginner teachers in the final decade of my career. It was a responsibility that I enjoyed, and I like to think that I focused on the positive aspects of teaching, despite the concerns I had about teacher workload that were colouring the job for me. Now that the shortage of teachers has become an acute problem, something more considered than a knee-jerk reaction is required. The views of chief inspectors and union representatives are important, but there is an even bigger picture: our education system requires major surgery, not a few sticking plasters. When schools are in better health, teachers will be more likely to remain in post for longer than five years.

Teachers

One answer to this chapter's title question is: teachers. Speaking from my experience of secondary schools, I believe teachers generally to be an exceptional group of people. There will be bad apples, as in all walks of life, but a more reasonable, measured and civil group of people you couldn't wish to meet. I can still recall the collective despair that filled my staff room at break time on the day that Bush and Blair invaded Iraq.

There is always the tiny minority to avoid whose heads have been swayed by DfE arguments to transform children's education into an activity more akin to a military training programme. But one is unlikely to bump into members of this zealous group too often in the staff room because they tend to hide themselves away in their management offices. My thinking about such professional gold-diggers who will espouse any educational psycho-babble in order to move up the professional ladder was, and still is, that a little knowledge can be a dangerous thing.

Teachers tend to share the desired qualities of patience, compassion, and self-sacrifice. In thirty-eight years I only worked with one teacher who had a genuinely vicious streak, the sort that Pink Floyd famously sang about – a teacher with behavioural difficulties. This individual was a callous self-obsessed bully who patronised pupils and scorned those colleagues weak enough to allow that person to do so.

A school staff room is a civilised, expletive-free environment. I've experienced staff-room cliques, but they've never been of the ferocious variety. The negative stereotyping of teachers in the media over the years has been undeserved. From 'Carry on Teacher' to 'Please, Sir' and 'Waterloo Road', the public has been presented with a succession of eccentrics, lovesick fruit loops and emotional wrecks. If schools were full of such oddballs, prospectuses would have to come with health warnings attached.

Children

Another answer to the above question is: the students. A career working with children will always be stimulating in the extreme, and can be as fulfilling as one wants it to be. If you aspire to teach, you may be surprised to hear that your charges will be interested in you as a person. Most of them will want to get on with you, perhaps even like you. Although you will be programmed to resist the temptation to 'like' them, they will generally want a) a quiet life, b) to be as successful in your subject area as possible, and, therefore, c) to get on with you. A smile and an encouraging word go a long way with children. There will be dark days when smiling may require the utmost effort, but get rid of those scowls and flash the pearly whites whatever mood you're in. 'Eyes and teeth!' as Eric, a teaching friend, used to say to me. The ideal scenario for getting on with students is in one-to-one exchanges, where inhibition about saying something that could be interpreted as 'sucking up' to the teacher won't be an obstacle.

It takes time for a class collectively to relax with a new teacher. There will be the initial teething troubles, involving behavioural adjustments of all class members as they assess and respond to the teacher's classroom standards, peculiarities of temperament, and application of adolescent perceptions of fairness. In all things, it's vital to keep the concept of fairness to the forefront of one's mind.

Some elements within secondary teaching groups will spend an initial period of time mulling over the question, 'How far can I push this one?' The teacher, by the same token, may be asking himself or herself, 'Who have I especially got to keep an eye on here?' A thorough subject knowledge is taken as read in teaching, but survival in the class wars requires intuitive levels of alertness. When introducing myself to a new class, I would explain a particular habit that I'd acquired: whenever I focused my gaze specifically in one direction of the classroom, I was more than likely to be concentrating my attention in the opposite direction. This strategy was more than useful when assessing students' speaking and listening contributions in group work.

Not every teacher can be a charismatic role model, but if pupils feel secure in your company you're well on the way to being accepted. A keen eye and composure under pressure are essential qualities. A teacher seeks to be respected, not to be liked, and respect has to be earned.

Children are extremely astute when it comes to identifying those who reveal even the most casual antipathy towards them. Although it's not a requirement to like children to be a teacher, there are many Mrs Rudds ('*King Street Junior*') in the profession who would be better occupied beyond the school gates. These are professionals whose own achievements will always be more important than those of their students. The professional most likely to gain their attention and, consequently, respect is the one who demonstrates a sincere interest in the academic progress of each and every child in the room. This teacher will never be deflected from the focus on ability and performance, however indolent, uncooperative, disobedient, or even confrontational individuals may appear to be. All pupils, of whatever ability, invariably recognise and respond to the consistent application of this principle. It was not uncommon for me to have a 'run-in' with a student one day, then to witness him demonstrating genuine industry the next.

Children have the right to be temperamental and awkward at times because they are children. Teachers, on the other hand, should strive to be stone-cold unflustered, whatever arises. My main criticism of the steadfastly authoritarian approach is the denial of childhood, the refusal to acknowledge what it is to be a child.

Despite any ideas about children you may have formed from reading the 'Beano', most of them are highly agreeable. They'll fetch the register for you, give out photocopied sheets, collect in exercise books, and leave as quickly as they can when lessons end. They may even want to hang around when you are on playground duty and chew the fat with you. In my final year before I retired, two friendly fourteen-year-old boys regularly searched me out for a daily chat. They were keen to find out why Portsmouth F.C. had lost again at the weekend, how much I earned, what I did in the evenings and when I was going to change my car. They were very considerate, taking into account that they were talking to an old guy who really ought to be put out to grass. Once, I gingerly bent down to pick up a crisp packet that had blown at my feet, taking every precaution to protect my back by bending slowly at the knees and lowering myself gently. One of them commented in what seemed to be genuine concern, 'That's a long way down there, sir, isn't it?' I thought to myself, what a compassionate little bugger!

The one constant with children generally is that they are bursting with energy. They are far livelier than adults, and they'll be especially lively when it's windy. This isn't an old wives' tale. They really do become more difficult to handle. The age-old quandary every teacher faces is that the thirty bodies in the classroom won't be absolutely silent on every occasion one needs them to be. This doesn't mean that they are inherently disobedient or that they don't like you. Being even more sociable than adults, in my view, they simply need to interact with those around them from time to time. Those entering the profession need to familiarise themselves with this fact of school life. Idle chatter is sometimes irresistible, even for adolescents. Children are stimulating company.

Every experienced teacher knows that the best-planned lesson may fail to go according to plan and become a tedious experience for everyone, the teacher included. On such occasions a mini-break could prove useful – a thirty-second interlude to lighten the grind, a time to go with the flow momentarily when you can, for example, respond thoughtfully to an off-the-cuff pupil comment, or make an observation about somebody's creative input.

A lesson won't be derailed so long as the teacher ensures that input is relevant and constructive. Natural breaks, or pauses for reflection, can be especially useful when the subject matter is particularly challenging. I made time to encourage the capacity for reflection. It is mistakenly claimed that curiosity killed the cat, but intellectual curiosity is, to me, humankind's greatest driving force. Whilst reading

'Frankenstein' with a Year 10 class, a student suddenly interrupted. He argued that the book was 'rubbish' because Frankenstein said he'd discovered the 'secret of creating life' but then said he couldn't reveal this dangerous knowledge. This was just Mary Shelley trying to cover up the fact that there is no secret. These comments instigated a thoughtful class discussion that encompassed topics as wide-ranging as authorial licence, cloning and the evolution of the science fiction genre.

For anyone considering a teaching career, promoting intellectual curiosity in children is as fulfilling an experience as can be imagined.

Inspiring

Whenever I tell anyone that I'm a retired secondary school teacher, a typical eye-rolling response is, 'I could never have been a teacher because I wouldn't have been able to keep my hands off the kids.' I admit that there were one or two I'd felt needed a dose of their own medicine, although there were also countless souls I'd wanted to hug because I felt so desperately sorry for them. But you can't touch children, whatever your impulse. This statement needs qualification: a teacher can touch children emotionally and spiritually. You can tell children things, for example, that their parents don't always take the trouble to tell them. The big thing you have to make clear to them is 'You have special talents and you could do special things with your life.' Many children grow up never realising these facts of life. Any professional can supervise a cramming course. Real teaching is about inspiring self-confidence, convincing children of their unique abilities and inculcating the desire to develop them. These considerations were powerful factors in my choosing to remain in the profession for as long as I could.

Growing up, I'd formed the mistaken impression that the facts of life were just about willies, sex and making babies. They're also about accepting responsibility for trying to do the best with the life and talents one's been given. Children need constant encouragement by adults if they are to become responsible guardians of their lives.

There is the blinkered viewpoint amongst some in the profession that organising relevant syllabus information is all that ultimately matters. The logic follows that if one is able to deliver perfect three-part lessons, then it's up to the students whether or not they can be bothered to do the work to guarantee good end-of-course results. Anybody who's not up to the challenge can simply be withdrawn from the examination. Such a focus on test scores and league tables results in student casualties. Teachers who become browbeaten by preoccupations with predicted grades and performance data can lose sight of the individuals and personalities before them. Each one of them is special, whatever their academic potential.

The word 'education' derives from the Latin word 'ducere', meaning 'to lead', a concept carrying with it an obligation for moral and philosophical improvement. Whatever subject one teaches, there's no avoiding these imperatives. Teaching with examination performance as the only valid criterion for success is little better than animal training. I worked alongside animal trainers for four decades, some of whom told me that I was an unambitious dinosaur.

I qualify the opinion stated above by pointing out that being special has nothing to do with being famous and making lots of money. Getting an audition for 'X-Factor' isn't the most valuable gauge of self-worth. However, I want children to believe in their individuality and to retain that belief throughout their lives. This isn't sentimental twaddle – it's one of the tools a teacher should have in her or his armoury to keep young people interested in their existence. Compulsory education has always had a job to do to protect children from the disease of disaffection.

Advising students who are experiencing learning difficulties is a far from straightforward task. Studying has become more problematical because there are so many more distractions for children to cope with than was ever the case when I was young. There is so much more information to process from so many different sources. Young minds must have a capacity for reflection, which means offering them opportunities during the school day to stop and assess the diversity of beliefs and attitudes in response to life's daily round. I never had any qualms about stopping mid-flow in a lesson if a student asked a telling question that probed a grey moral area. This tended to happen regularly in English lessons as a direct result of their introduction to good literature.

Guidance

Being in a position to offer guidance to young people in every aspect of their lives makes teaching an exceptionally rewarding career.

I would urge youngsters not to be slaves to computer screens in their free time. My argument to deter them would be that passive lifestyles make for passive minds. In messianic tones, I would declare that all children have a duty to guard against technology monopolising their lives. I surveyed a class once to find out how many hours per week each child spent in front of a screen. The majority disclosed that they were regularly clocking up in excess of forty hours a week with television, PCs, computer games, mobile phones and tablets. I worry that young people's need for constant sensory stimulation of this kind is a form of addiction, a habit that is difficult to break.

I enjoyed playing devil's advocate as a teacher by promoting the heretical point of view that 99% of everything is rubbish. I could guarantee a lively debate if I encouraged children to focus on the vacuous and superfluous in their lives. This debate raised hackles to the extent that even shy, retiring pupils would find themselves shaking off their complacency. You can't beat the exhilaration of a good argument.

Children need to grow up sifting out the quality from the dross in every area of life, and this is another of the teacher's prime responsibilities. Listening to children attempting to discriminate between what is worthwhile and what is worthless is a fascinating experience for any teacher. Guiding them towards intellectual autonomy is both wonderful and humbling.

The 99%-of-everything-is-rubbish conversation was always one of my favourites with older teenagers. The novelty of the concept engendered genuine passion, setting them thinking in ways that many had not considered. Young people are vulnerable in that they are at greater risk than adults of absorbing information unthinkingly. The ability to be discriminating and selective requires high-level cognitive thinking. For most teenagers, the notion that adults perceive young people's behaviour and tastes as being seriously proscribed by their peers comes as a shock to them. I only have to remind them that on mufti days at school the majority continues to conform to a strict dress code of hoodies, jeans and trainers, when not required to wear formal school uniform.

I liked to get classes on the topic of 'vulgar pleasures'. Adopting the contentious viewpoint that much of what is of interest to them has little value and is, indeed, a waste of their time does wonders for children's critical faculties. This activity was great fun, whether considering computer games, fiction books, television programmes, popular music, footballers, or cinema films (or 'movies' as students would insist on calling them). I enjoyed the cut and thrust of our conversations immensely, admiring their attempts to articulate complex value judgements. I could always come up with a counter to any opinion put to me, but the boys' determination to pursue apparently lost causes in argument genuinely impressed me.

My intention was for students seriously to address the question 'How should I live my life?' I had to think fast and present objective reasons in support of my position, whatever topic we covered. It did surprise me how astutely they latched on to some of the more outlandish statements I made that were intentionally unreasonable. There was universal disbelief that I should consider the sitcom *Friends* to be tedious in the extreme, and *The Royle Family* to be vastly superior entertainment. "How can you say that?" they would ask, smiling as if I were a simpleton. "I don't find sitcoms that are merely vehicles for tired one-liners to be at all entertaining", I might say as a starter. "But nothing happens in *The Royle Family*!" somebody would interject. "Exactly!" I'd respond. "This is the profound point that the sitcom is making. For most people, nothing much happens in their lives." I'd then introduce Becket's *Waiting for Godot* into the conversation and we'd read a few sections from the copies I had. Discussion of the existential dimensions of Estragon's gloomy comment 'Another day done with' could occupy us for a whole lesson.

Children must acquire the ability to contemplate and appreciate the minutiae of life in the world around us. One of my favourite starters for the day before taking morning registration was to ask everyone to look out of the window to marvel at the beauty of the line of tall trees outside the classroom window, whatever the season. I was jealous of my reputation for being mildly flaky, as it enabled me to make eccentric requests of this sort. Reflection is an essential prerequisite for the development of the intellect. I think, therefore I'm on the road to becoming an intellectual.

Protection

Children look to adults for protection in an uncertain world, and I found that this responsibility brought home to me the full importance of the career I'd chosen.

I find it metaphysically comforting to discover that some of the greatest literature available to us deals with inescapable truths of the human condition. Most of us are stoics: doggedly we endure in the face of the general uneventfulness of human existence. Distractions are available to occupy one's time, offering respite from this disturbing truth. Children need to be prepared for the possibility that they may be tempted to indulge in what could become addictive behaviours, such as drug dependency, alcoholism, violence, sexual promiscuity, and gambling. I would even include computer gaming. Young people nowadays are subject to far more threats to their wellbeing than I ever had to face. Every child should be made aware that the entertainment industry works hard to provide round-the-clock fun for everyone, but the effects of all fun pills are short-lived and can be damaging if taken to excess.

The case can be put that the media has a more significant influence on the spiritual, emotional and moral development of children nowadays than ever before. I, along with most, enjoy the sophisticated range of entertainment and information available from the mass media, and would welcome the prospect of all young minds being educated into the intricacies involved in the creation of media products. The argument for introducing all children to study of the media is reinforced when considering the negative influences to which young people may be exposed. The impressionable need some protection from hidden persuaders on the one hand and the more blatant forms of exploitation on the other, from the sexual to the political. I was pleased when it was eventually decided to ban alcohol advertising on television, but am now troubled by the explosion in the promotion of online gambling. I don't share the viewpoint of many in the education world that Media Studies is a Mickey-Mouse subject.

Enlightenment (The Meaning of Life)

My father's limited career advice to me was that I had two options: a horse-racing jockey or a bookmaker. I, meanwhile, had been for an unsuccessful interview at Marks and Spencer, and applied for the civil service. Mr Booth, my History teacher and form tutor, enlightened me as to the world of teaching. I was completely out of my depth with this suggestion, but he was convinced that I had the qualities required. He provided reading materials explaining every angle of the job, recommended training colleges, and helped me fill out application forms. With his help, I found my niche in life.

I was fortunate in that I studied classical literature. I particularly enjoyed the tragedies of Aeschylus, Euripedes and Sophocles. These studies developed within me a keener awareness of life's deeper secrets that I wanted to share with those I taught. But I had to be subtle in my approach to ensure that children wouldn't switch off if I simply referred generally to the wonders of ancient Greece.

Discussion of film genres enabled me to introduce my topic with a lively debate. I would argue that I far preferred superhero films to the action adventure, 'slasher', and sci-fi genres they enjoyed. I'd justify my comment by informing them of the parallels between modern-day superheroes and the heroes of Greek mythology. I'd start with Spiderman and ask if his super power were a boon or a curse to him. Then I'd explain how a superhero is permanently set apart from the rest of humanity, ordinary mortals, by his special power, just like the heroes of Greek myth.

On that topic, students were always incredulous to hear of the reasons that drove Oedipus to put out his eyes, the background details of the Minotaur's conception, and the madness induced by the gods that drove Agavé to tear her own son, Pentheus, limb from limb. The news that these stories were written three thousand years ago only added to their amazement. My closing statement after introducing them to the wonders of Greek mythology, was to make the point that there are no new stories, only old ones that have been rehashed. The argument that this observation generated was always heated.

I can only trust that you will believe me when I describe the thrill of engaging in deep philosophical discussion with formative minds searching for truth and meaning in life.

Fun versus Boredom

Throughout my teacher training, nobody ever told me that I would need to be an entertainer. Others may have got through their careers without ever considering this facet of the job, but to me it was essential. Teaching, for me, was fun. Thus, I placed a high priority on learning being fun in my lessons. However, I must be honest here and spend a little time elaborating on the new realities that threaten the extinction of this essential teaching and learning concept. I offer my apologies in advance if any sections of the remainder of this chapter bear resemblance to a rant.

Any job working with children has to be enjoyable. Teaching used to have a strong fun component. However, three decades of sustained teacher sledging from above and a mounting workload has diminished teaching's fun factor significantly.

Whenever anybody asks me now about my career, my answer is, 'The job is tough, but the students are great.' I use the word 'tough' to indicate that one mustn't underestimate the reserves of stamina that are required. Every lesson is a performance if one teaches properly, and performing daily for forty weeks a year is a demanding physical and mental challenge. The great compensation, of course, is that one has the privilege of being able to work with children. Regular interaction with young minds is hugely rewarding and entertaining. It's a desperately sad state of affairs that teaching within the state school system now generates ever-increasing levels of anxiety, resulting in reduced job satisfaction and lower morale across the profession.

In an age where there are so many competing elements for children's attention, schools should be exciting learning environments. My impression is that they are increasingly becoming intellectually confining. The development of the imagination is now low on the education establishment's list of priorities, however strongly arguments to the contrary are presented, particularly with regard to the academically less able. State schools are being forced into becoming educationally claustrophobic and, thus, guilty of stifling talent and initiative. If a child shows limitations of cognitive ability, below average intelligence is assumed. Ability in areas beyond the parameters of hypothetical and deductive reasoning tends to be accorded lower status or be overlooked altogether.

One of the great injustices of the national curriculum was the devaluing of subjects such as art, music and drama as foundation subjects, not considered worthy to be accorded the same status as the core subjects of English, Mathematics and Science. The fact that many people make a comfortable living in music, the arts and sport, doing what they consider to be fun, continues to make me wonder at the wisdom of this gross misjudgement.

Despite the best efforts of teachers to encourage the exploration of ideas and information, the acquisition of facts and analysis of data have become the currency of 'intelligence'. There are reams of minutely detailed and idiot-proof criteria for success at every level in each subject area, from SATs to GCSEs to A-Levels. Such criteria are 'useful' because they facilitate the identification and quantification of failure. In a system dominated by the nation's fixation with league tables, success equates to bald percentage scores. League tables reflect one facet of a school's performance, but there are many others that count for little in our sound-bite culture. Few would admit to the fact, but these have second-class status or worse.

Failing teachers can be quickly identified and cannot be countenanced. They can be summarily dealt with thanks to the short-term contract culture, enabling them to move on and take their 'failure' elsewhere. External staff support, that used to be a regular facet of teaching in the days of education advisers who made regular visits to trainee teachers' lessons, has all but disappeared.

The imposition of ruthless top-down initiatives and assessment systems risks giving rise to ruthless management strategies. Teacher turnover has never been so high in state schools. Creativity, individuality and initiative are, dispiritingly, supplementary and risky luxuries in such a culture. Those who aren't prepared to wed themselves body and soul to the educational delusions of autocratic politicians will not last long on Animal Farm.

State education in its present form requires remedial attention. Schools are creaking because the fun of learning and the joy of teaching are being squeezed out of the educational landscape.

Children benefit best from individual attention. This approach is even more essential in the twenty-first century. The world is one in which academy children, sorry schoolchildren, are assimilating more information than I could have imagined when I first started teaching. They are also required to demonstrate social awareness in areas that would have been inconceivable a few decades ago. I heard recently of an Ofsted inspector who threatened to judge a school as being 'an unsafe environment' because children he had spoken to casually in the playground had never heard of female genital mutilation. An inhuman practice, it need not be said, but basing a school-safety judgement on this sole criterion is madness.

We persist with a system where, on all but a few occasions, we cram thirty or so individuals into a single room for every timetabled lesson. I was never entirely confident with the arrangement of having no other choice but to communicate to thirty individuals at the same time, but I committed myself to the 'class system' and did my best. An example of one cause of frustration I regularly experienced involved having to explain an important point three or four times, employing different phrasing on each occasion, to ensure that everyone eventually had an understanding of what I was trying to impart to them. Setting or streaming pupils according to ability does not, as you may think, eliminate this problem.

Class teaching now relies heavily on pupils' acquisition of what are called 'basic skills'. It's a system designed to organise knowledge in such a way that it can be transferred to large groups of children in specially-processed chunks. Knowledge is a consumer commodity that is handily-packaged to enable it to be absorbed as easily and as quickly as possible. The time constraints on teachers to get through the full syllabus in any subject area nowadays are so great that there is little time for children to discriminate on the quality or usefulness of what they are being fed. The encouragement of imaginative engagement with material can be sidelined by busy teachers constantly under pressure to cover packed course content. An education system that pays only token attention to high-level intellectual processes, such as lateral thinking and complex problem-solving exercises, needs a re-think.

Coping with large groups of children every lesson of every day can become a fairly tortuous process in the current climate, for children and teachers. Ofsted now recommends that a teacher set aside time at the end of each lesson to ask a class quality-control questions. Whenever I followed this teaching protocol and asked my students what they had learned from my teaching, I could guarantee that some wag would reply, 'If you don't know, sir, how do you expect us to?'

This tedious industrial-model technique is one that both amuses and infuriates intelligent consumers. Soon after my car has been serviced, I receive an email that will 'only take ten minutes of your time to complete, sir', asking me to respond to unintentionally hilarious questions:

Were you happy with the conduct of the driver who collected your car from your home? Were you taken through the invoice for work carried out to your vehicle when your car was returned to your home? Did the driver smile deferentially and tug his forelock as he left your premises? Would you be happy for members of our staff to see your responses to this questionnaire?

Whatever the condition of my car or the exorbitant cost of repairs, I respond to every question by pressing the 'completely satisfied' option if I can even be bothered to reply to the online quiz. There's no way I want to risk the possibility of a revenge sabotage job when my car next goes into the garage by expressing any dissatisfaction whatsoever.

I once tried an alternative end-of-lesson assessment, asking one bright spark, 'Can you tell me anything you forgot from my lesson?'

'Yes, sir,' he replied. 'I forgot to ask if I could go to the toilet.'

This was praise indeed. If you're currently teaching and you want to know how enthralling (euphemism for 'effective') your lessons are, there's no need to wind things up by asking for and anticipating positive feedback. Simply keep a record of how many pupils asked to be excused whilst you were teaching. Three or more means you should investigate other career options. Experienced teachers quickly discover the urinating regulars – these do not have bladder problems but serious issues with tolerating boredom. I sympathise.

It really is a notable achievement to get through a lesson without one of your regulars needing to take a leak. Children's acute bullshit sensors never failed to give me a lift when the tedium of teaching weakened my resolve. I suppose I must acknowledge, at this point, the irony that incorporating a significant boredom element into children's educational experience is a necessary preparation for many of the career openings available to them in the twenty-first century. If it appears that I am promoting an inappropriately negative message about the world of work, consider the prospect of, for example, working in a call centre. (I can hear Marlon Brando again – 'The horror! The horror!')

I constantly struggled to combat the ever-present threat of boredom in the classroom that is becoming increasingly unavoidable. A significant minority of children, now accustomed to instant entertainment at the touch of a multiplicity of buttons at their disposal, don't do boredom.

These pupils can destroy any lesson if not handled sympathetically.

I learned not to be afraid of spontaneous outbursts of fun, but to embrace them as they lifted my spirits. In my early days as a teacher, at the start of a class reading lesson with one particular group, I would hand out the fiction books and invite someone to read aloud. I'd give the nominated reader the page number from which he should start at the top, adding the instruction, 'Top of!' This initially prompted one boy to add the words, 'The monkey'. The first time this happened I was unaware that there was a pre-school children's programme called *Pipkins*, and one of the main characters was a monkey called Topov. From then on, I was required to wait for the class to chorus the words 'The monkey!' whenever I instructed them to turn to the top of a particular page.

Children really enjoy set routines of this kind, as they help to restore a semblance of sanity to lessons in which students are subjected to excruciating levels of tedium. Older students can be just as playful. I remember a sixth former arriving late for a lesson a quarter of a century ago, giving me the excuse that he had been delayed watching *Poddington Peas* on television. The excuse generated a ripple of laughter because this was a cartoon series again targeting pre-school children. There were wonderful moments from then on when my A-Level students took me by surprise during a pause in a lesson by spontaneously breaking out into a tuneless rendition of the programme's theme tune:

'♫ Down at the bottom of the garden ♫…' Pure fun!

Thirty years ago, English teaching was possibly the most exciting curriculum subject to teach. Now, even this subject is at risk. It's being repackaged as a service subject, a narrowing of English teaching that reduces it to focusing on the literacy requirements necessary for students to function effectively in every other subject area. The scope for experiencing joy in both teaching and learning in English lessons is diminishing.

Take the typical GCSE English syllabuses ('syllabi' if you prefer) that are now on offer. A teacher can no longer simply set students an assignment in response to studying a literature text. Exemplar essays, intended to show how candidates 'should' write about texts, are distributed and analysed in depth. These exemplars ensure that candidates are familiar with the assessment criteria and the weightings given to the different assessment objectives. The ability to respond to literature imaginatively and spontaneously becomes a casualty with this objectives-centred approach.

The promotion of such formulaic responses, relying on satisfying checklists as opposed to employing the imagination, has become the new vogue, one that risks destroying young people's interest in literature – for the rest of their lives. Not to worry, however, because the big pay-off is that we now have an examination that trained chimpanzees can mark. There is no guarantee that candidates are able to show the ability they possess or gain the marks they deserve, but the task of producing the results' tables has been much simplified.

I suffer pangs of guilt when I recall how much time I spent drilling classes on the strategy of preparing a six-point plan before completing any extended writing exercise. For a question on a literature set text, I would guiltily advocate the 'PQC' formula for success (Point – Quotation – Comment). Each paragraph begins with the making of a relevant *point* towards the construction of a concise answer to the question set. This point is then illustrated by a supporting *quotation* from the text. Finally, an explanatory *comment* on the originality of the writer's language and aptness of the quotation concludes the paragraph. This approach was useful for those students who might find it difficult to produce structured essays. I did make a point, however, of urging boys to adopt their own methods of writing about literature, rather than use the model I had introduced to them. My embarrassment was heightened when I was asked to share my scheme, using a glitzy PowerPoint presentation, at a full staff meeting. Despite explaining that a teacher using the plan could end up with thirty near-identical essays, I was thanked for coming up with an idiot's guide to essay writing.

To add insult to injury, I often found myself standing before a group of fifteen year olds with a wad of assessment objectives firmly in my grasp. It was a regular task to explain at length what these objectives meant. Apprehensively scanning the rows of wrinkling brows before me, I would try to imagine the thoughts forming behind the blank expressions: 'When is he going to shut up and let us get on with something interesting?' There were all sorts of short cuts to relative success that I employed, none of which gave me any genuine sense of fulfilment. I was simply surrendering to the pressure to guarantee acceptable examination results. In such a stifling learning environment, neither students nor teachers experience much of the enjoyment that should be at the heart of the educational process. Fun becomes the first casualty when the main focus of teaching is assessment. I would, therefore, urge prospective teachers to exploit the fun factor that children bring to learning, rather than quash it unthinkingly.

Over the course of time I found myself increasingly spouting so much skills-based drivel that my voice started to annoy me. When my wife once complained about my taciturnity at home, I excused myself by explaining that, for me, being a teacher sometimes resulted in my growing heartily sick of the sound of my own voice. In social situations outside of school, I developed a tendency to be a listener rather than talker.

Whenever there was a threat of boredom levels rising, my most valuable asset, other than my knowledge of and love of my subject, was my sense of fun. It was the strategy I used unfailingly to maintain the attention of every pupil in the room, no matter how mind-numbing the topic. I could generally rely on my ability to raise a smile in class when the going got tough. I wouldn't have survived long in the job if I hadn't known how to poke fun at myself or some of the more risible subject information I was required to pass on.

I accumulated a mental catalogue of jokes for every topic and text I covered. Some of my material was of the feeble quality expected of teachers, but I also borrowed quality humour from my favourite comedians, such as Ken Dodd and Les Dawson. When reading 'A Kestrel for a Knave' aloud to a Year 10 class, I remember encouraging them to empathize with the poverty of Billy Casper's home life. I confided to the students that, when I was a child, my parents had also been so poor that they hadn't been able to afford to buy me any clothes. Then, I told them that one day they bought me a top hat so that I could look out of the window. I anticipated chuckles all round, but hardly any one laughed. Instead, I received sympathetic glances from all corners of the room; many of the boys had taken my comical aside literally. I discovered then how even a teacher can elicit sympathy from a class by telling lame jokes.

Teaching is becoming such a stuffy science that teachers are inhibited in ways that I never was. For example, when returning marked exercise books to a class, I would spin them through the air so that each pupil's book landed on the table right in front of him, such was the accuracy I'd perfected. I can't imagine a teacher attempting such aeronautical manoeuvres in the current ultra-health-and-safety climate. Sounds dangerous to me, you may be thinking, but in thirty eight years I never took out a single eye. I appreciate the necessity for comprehensive school risk-assessment policies, but they can have an inhibiting effect on teaching styles.

I recall an unexpected and intriguing occurrence resulting from reading *Great Expectations* for twenty minutes at the end of a Year 9 lesson just before lunch. I pride myself that I could be as dynamic a reader as the best but, on this occasion, I lowered my tone as I read a wonderfully evocative descriptive section. As the lesson drew to a close, I discovered that I had sent a tired student, who must have spent the whole of the previous night playing computer games, into a doze. I resisted the temptation to wake him with a blast of my well-tuned larynx. Such cruelty was not in my nature, but mischief was.

I hushed the class theatrically and got them to leave the room as quietly as possible. I then exited, shut the door behind me and stood in the corridor. I gave the sleeper five minutes to wake up. As I'd expected, a few boys hung around to witness the outcome. When Rip Van Winkle didn't surface, I re-entered the classroom, gently woke him and told him that he ought to be hurrying off to the lunch queue. The look of combined surprise, embarrassment and amazement on the boy's face as he came to his senses was a picture to behold. I felt sure I could count on the offender making a greater effort to concentrate in class in the future.

I believe that the capacity occasionally to produce the unexpected keeps students on their toes. In the early days of my career, many of my colleagues were what one would call 'characters'. I don't use this term pejoratively; there was simply something a little 'off the wall' about them. Their teaching methodology wasn't entirely predictable and, consequently, pupils would be deterred from becoming complacent in the classroom, in the sense that they believed that they had the teacher 'sussed'. I played on this quality myself, and had a battery of personal eccentricities in my teaching arsenal.

Young people, one is led to believe, have lower boredom thresholds and shorter attention spans than was the case before the advent of personal computers; online social networking; MP3s; computer gaming; iPads, iPhones with a multiplicity of apps; and hundreds of television channels to watch from around the world. These distractions represent just a small part of the competition with which a teacher has to compete to hold a child's attention.

The first teacher in the category of characters who comes to mind is Mr F., the second Head of English under whom I served. He had the reputation of being ultra-eloquent, and was able to conjure a witty rejoinder to anyone who dared question his professionalism. At a staff meeting long ago, the headteacher, believing that he had found an opportunity to be critical of Mr F.'s lack of perspicacity, pointedly said to him, 'You should already have found out about the report deadline from the staff bulletin that was circulated last week, Mr F. Do you ever bother to read staff bulletins?' Mr. F.'s instant rejoinder was, 'Yes, I have them all neatly bound at home in natterjack toad skin.'

This was the first time I'd ever heard a teacher answer a headmaster back. Not a soul dared laugh. The head realized that a riposte of any kind would result in him sinking further into the hole he had dug for himself. It was not unusual for me to encounter students that this colourful character taught attempting to mimic his wonderfully Wildean epigrams in school corridors. His wit was legendary. Nowadays, teachers worn down by the immense workload and ever-present possibility of being unmasked as an incompetent, are inclined to buckle in the face of criticism from anyone above them in the school hierarchy. Those who display any mind of their own risk being perceived as 'blockers' or troublemakers who should be sent on their way at the earliest opportunity. Children do find it fun to be taught by characters who add an extra dimension to learning.

Mr W., an English teacher with whom I once taught, was a model of convention in every respect except that he never cut the long, wiry, grey hair that grew horizontally from the side and vertically from the top of his head. He also had a collection of vividly-coloured waistcoats that I'm sure he had tailor-made. His appearance was almost freakish, in the style of a Dickensian grotesque. Some children found the novelty of his appearance disconcerting, but few poked fun. His other-worldly appearance masked his exceptional literary knowledge. He never experienced any problems with classroom control, perhaps because his students knew better than to mess with an 'alien'.

Mr P., who taught history, was another colleague who never experienced problems in the classroom. In his case he was a martial arts black belt who had a hundred handy hints for his class members on how to respond to bullying. He never laid a finger on his pupils, but one stern glance in a boy's direction could give him whiplash. He was another masterful exponent of the evil glare. The trick with this is to create the illusion that you are looking into a child's very soul when issuing the most serious of reprimands. For this technique to work, blinking whilst glaring is a no-no. So, if you can't control your blink muscles forget this tip.

Miss M., an attractive French teacher, had the most extensive wardrobe of clothes imaginable. I was constantly surprised that adolescent boys could be so interested in ladies' fashions, such was her popularity with all year groups. During the occasional free period, when I was busy marking in the staff room, it was not unusual for one of her pupils to knock and enter, make her a cup of coffee and hurry back dutifully to her classroom with the hot brew.

'Character' has now become taboo in schools. Caution and conformity are the watchwords of teaching nowadays. By 2010 when I retired, with one exception, there were no 'characters' to speak of in the school where I taught. The exception was a hugely intelligent and highly self-deprecating science teacher, Mr O'N., who studied degree courses at break time in the staff room. To my knowledge he has eight degree qualifications under his belt at the time of writing. He bears a striking resemblance to every child's comic representation of the mad professor, one that he has always actively encouraged. My view of him was that he was both an exceptional teacher and an intellectual giant. I never tire of genius – nor do children.

I did countless hours on duty at breaks and lunch times over the years and employed a multiplicity of strategies to keep boys in order. I could usually be found patrolling the school field. At the end of the break, I would blow my whistle and shout out, 'Get your asses to your classes!' For those whose form periods were held in temporary single-storey structures, I called out a second instruction, 'Get your butts to the huts!' This went on for years and nobody ever complained. Indeed, there were days when I blew my whistle and said nothing – possibly I was in too much of a hurry. There would, however, usually be a pleading request from one or two of those in the immediate vicinity along the lines of, 'Oh, go on, sir! Say it!' It was expected of me. What could I do but oblige them.

The mindset of professionals in school life generally over the past few decades has been that everything has to be deadly serious. It doesn't. There are many ways good teachers can ensure that the school experience never becomes a rigorous, formulaic, humourless and mind-numbing process for everyone involved.

Concerns about choosing a teaching career

Optimum examination performance is the only meaningful standard in schools today. Classroom teachers are left in no doubt by school managers that this is the Holy Grail, and any other school achievements, laudable as they may be, pale into insignificance beside this reality.

Schools in inner-city areas with high levels of social deprivation will never be able to compete with those in upmarket leafy backwaters. There can be no argument about identifying 'bad schools': the truth is in the statistical evidence. In the real world, results vary considerably as a result of complex social and geographical factors. Poor areas will struggle to attract the high-achieving and experienced subject specialists that tend to be drawn to affluent areas.

We have a state-school system that fails significant numbers of enthusiastic students whose strengths are not accorded the same value as those who can sail through rigorous programmes of assessment and written examinations. For many, the pleasure of learning at secondary level is being replaced by drudgery. Our schools have a hang-up with 'standards', as opposed to embracing the concepts of individuality and difference. I place the individual child at the centre of any debate on school achievement, but our educational task masters have long since turned their backs on child-centred learning.

Successive political administrations have worked tirelessly to undermine the unity of the teaching profession by encouraging division within the ranks. The bigger picture is that the 'standards' culture sets all secondary schools against each other. On the micro level, staff in discrete subject areas may succumb to the temptation to gloat when those in others produce poor results. It's no surprise, therefore, that professionals fall prey to enmity of their colleagues, and pupils likewise succumb to the temptation to 'diss' the *boffs* on the one hand and the *dummies* on the other. This is not a healthy state of affairs for the education of the country's children. I am not setting myself up in opposition to competition, but I am opposed to competition where there is only one meaningful yardstick by which to measure success or failure. The primitive leadership philosophy of divide and rule is alive and well and resides at Sanctuary Buildings.

What follows in the succeeding chapters is a blend of fond recollection, tongue-in-cheek commentary, well-intentioned advice, and a concluding pipe dream. As

119

previously explained, I find it difficult to avoid the occasional rant – teachers are recognised as having a special expertise in ranting. It's part of the pressure of the job, so long as one doesn't rant in the hearing of a line manager. Children love to tell stories about how a teacher 'lost it' after being wound up by the students of his or her class and 'went off on one'. Children sometimes resort to creating their own fun during lessons, when it is not a feature of their learning environment. Thus, there are times when the teacher will become the object of fun.

Tolerating condescending attitudes from the general public towards teachers has always rankled with me, even more so since I retired. Whenever I hear lay people's jibes about 'thirteen weeks' holiday a year', 'only working half a day' and 'the fat pension', I can't stop myself becoming agitated. I reassess people I thought of as friends when they're unable to resist taking the standard pops at the profession. This probably explains why many teachers' close friends are also teachers. Until armchair critics try to do the job I did, they haven't earned the right to sound off with mealy-mouthed jibes.

If you're thinking of a teaching career, are already teaching, or have a morbid interest in what goes on in schools, then you may find the second half of this book to be of more than passing interest. Other than convey my enthusiasm about working with young people, despite being hamstrung by having operated exclusively within the state-school system, my wish is to entertain as well as inform. The final section of this book, in which I set out suggestions for radically alternative teaching approaches, may invite the accusation that my thinking is hopelessly idealistic. I offer no apologies for applying common sense to the thorny subject of secondary education because it is my ardent belief that the whole system needs a major shake-up. I hope that this work will be perceived as making something of a contribution to initiating such a process.

8. Teaching Style

Here I offer a summary of the idiosyncrasies of my teaching style that sustained me for almost four decades.

Personal Traits

1] Laser Eyes

Growing up in a working class area in the West Country, I became aware of the importance of watching my back. There were boys I had to avoid in the interests of self-preservation, individuals who could do serious damage if they took a dislike to me. An incident that surfaces from my memory from time to time is of being badly beaten up by an older boy to whom I replied 'Yes', when he smilingly asked me, 'Do you want a fight?' I was six at the time, and I maintain that I had no idea what a 'fight' was. I thought it was some sort of game. He took me behind what everyone called the 'power house', the small sub-power station on our prefabricated estate, and knocked seven bells out of me. When people ask if I broke my nose playing rugby, I reply, "No, I was beaten up when I was six." Nobody ever believes me.

This painful experience made me wary of new faces from then on. Friendships became difficult for me, as I was distrustful of the smiles that could hide dark intentions. I learned the importance of careful observation of acquaintances and friends at all times – searching for any warning sign that they might 'turn'. Establishing eye contact to protect myself from harm became second nature to me. I then went on to discover that staring directly at a person and not turning away could be taken as a sign of strength. The ability silently to outstare anyone displaying hostile intentions could often pre-empt a violent altercation.

Years later I found this skill invaluable as a teacher. When dealing with potentially disruptive children, a good stare can do wonders. In extreme situations, I would call a challenging pupil to the front of the class, stand facing him and talk quietly and forcefully about the need for self-control during lessons. All the while I would be staring fixedly into his eyes. Some of the boys would try to take me on, particularly if they were a little taller than me. But they were the first to turn away. To survive in the classroom, it is useful to develop a stare. It can obviate the need for energetic displays of faux anger. Laser eyes are an absolute indicator to children of a teacher's assurance and self-confidence.

Many of the boys I taught had difficult home lives and cooperative behaviour could not always be assumed. The parents who caused most trouble for schools, indirectly through their disturbed and sometimes emotionally unstable offspring, were those who were ill-equipped to rear children at all. I took the view that there was a direct correlation between bad parenting and pupil misbehaviour. It frequently amazed me how some boys ever managed to remain as biddable as they did at school, such was the emotional maelstrom they must have routinely lived through at home. Firm but fair handling of certain classroom elements was essential, particularly in the early stages of relationships with boys. My laser eyes got me out of quite a few holes with children and some of their parents throughout my career.

2] Loud voice

A loud voice isn't essential for a teacher. Don, the most accomplished mathematics teacher I ever knew was also the most modest and softly spoken colleague with whom I ever worked. His subject knowledge couldn't be faulted and his examination results were consistently exceptional. I don't think he was allowed to retire until he was seventy five. But my voice compensated to a degree for my limited stature. If necessary, I could rattle the windows of my classroom with my voice, a skill that perfectly complemented my diabolically piercing eyes. I may have been a few bales short of a rick when it came to height, but my strapping larynx compensated enormously when facing down agitated teenagers.

If you possess a unique gift, there are occasions when you would be foolish not to exploit it. I am quietly spoken generally, a characteristic that makes the noise I'm able to generate when I raise my voice to its peak even more of a shock to its unsuspecting recipient. It was this shock element that I relied on. I would describe its effect as being similar to that created by the crow scarers that farmers used on the farmland to the back of my home when I was a young boy. When one exploded, as it often did after the farmer's sowing, my bedroom walls seemed to shake, and murders of crows could be seen immediately winging away from seeded fields.

Whilst on lunch duty, I had no trouble making myself heard a hundred yards away across the school field if I spotted any skulduggery going on. In the classroom, I almost frightened myself. Don't get me wrong, I didn't bellow at students at every opportunity. I used my talent sparingly, but every pupil I ever taught soon discovered the capabilities of my awesome larynx and they weren't keen to be on the end of it. I knew that my throat would be sore if I overdid it, another practical reason why I kept this piece of heavy artillery in reserve.

When something untoward is going on anywhere in a school that requires speedy intervention from a teacher, a blast on a whistle usually puts a stop to it. But a teacher doesn't always have a whistle to hand. I always had a whistle in my jacket pocket, but if I weren't wearing my jacket I knew that my voice would be a more than adequate substitute. It even surprised me at times to see a ne'er-do-well stop in mid-stride the moment his eardrums reverberated to the crack of my vocal chords.

My daughter, who coincidentally also possesses a loud voice, enjoys recalling an incident in my career when I was a head of English. It was a Sunday evening and I was moderating some GCSE speaking and listening material. An English colleague had audio-taped students delivering individual talks. The class concerned had been reading *Of Mice and Men*, and I was in the lounge listening to one boy's attempt to describe an incident from Slim's viewpoint, whilst my teenage daughter was reading a magazine. Suddenly she looked up and said, "What was that on the tape?"

"Just a student's talk that I'm moderating," I replied.

"No," she said, "there's something else."

I rewound the tape for a few seconds and pressed the play button again. Then I heard it – my own voice clearly audible in the background bellowing "Stop clicking that pen at me!"

When the teacher had recorded the material on tape during his lesson, I had been teaching along the corridor two classrooms away. I remembered that a few days earlier I'd been conducting a class discussion, and one student had been trying to interrupt a contribution being made by another by repeatedly clicking a startlingly loud ballpoint pen. I must have been a little under the weather and not my usual patient self because I'd raised my voice to put an end to the interruptions.

My daughter found this hilarious and went into fits of uncontrollable laughter. I felt a bit shamefaced that I'd perhaps interrupted a colleague's lesson but, at the same time, I was impressed with the decibel level I'd managed to achieve. Other than not being my usual good-natured self, my only excuse is that I sometimes forget the volume my voice can generate.

Whenever I taught new Year 7 boys, I made a point of keeping my loud voice locked away as a result of an unfortunate experience, about which I feel guilty to this day. The event in question occurred when I was teaching a class of fresh-faced twelve year olds in early September. I noticed that one member of the class, a Tigger-like character, found it impossible to remain in his seat whilst I was reading one of my favourite novels to the class, *The Turbulent Term of Tyke Tiler* by Gene Kemp. He was continuously wriggling and squirming in his seat, turning this way and that to distract those around him. Unable to continue reading aloud, I paused in mid-flow.

'Sit down on that chair now!' I barked in his direction.

Imagine my horror when the whole of the front row of the class jumped visibly and the offending party spontaneously burst into tears. It often slipped my mind that I could project my voice to ultra-high level from a standing start. The effect was as if I had discharged a twelve bore in the classroom.

I apologised profusely to Tigger, and generally to the front row. My conscience punished me for the rest of that day for being so cruel.

3] Sense of humour

The chalkface can be a daunting environment and, as I have already explained, I found my sense of humour to be an essential tool throughout my teaching career. Children feel more at ease when they don't feel threatened, so much of my humour was self-deprecating. It can help to talk about your own childhood: children tend to assume that teachers all come from privileged backgrounds, and I consciously set out to show them that I hadn't. For me it was simply a case of identifying and explaining an area of commonality with those in my care. I never wanted to be perceived as a distant, aloof pedagogue, but one who was approachable and essentially sympathetic.

At the start of my career I had to decide how I intended children to take me seriously. How should I present myself? There were colleagues of much larger frame than me who imposed themselves on their classes by their sheer physical presence. I know some who got through a whole career in this way. I saw this approach as questionable professional practice. I didn't want to try to get students to like me but I didn't want them to dislike me. Children generally lose respect for any member of the teaching staff who tries too obviously to be chummy. The word 'respect' is all important. Teachers have their likes and dislikes amongst those they teach, but every child deserves respect. I drew this important distinction from the outset. I've dealt with hundreds of boys who have spent an inordinate amount of time in the classroom trying to disrupt proceedings but who, at the same time, have been capable of producing worthwhile work. It's the work that is important, particularly in this age of high teacher accountability when the results of every student in every class are analysed in detail. One of the secrets of success in this job is to respect the mind of a child and not preoccupy oneself with the behaviour. Humour can aid that process.

Children were never the targets of my humour, and I ruled out sarcasm. Childhood is, for many, a period of vulnerability and uncertainty, and my students didn't need me poking fun at them (unless they fell asleep in class).

I've already alluded to my humble origins. Owing to my father's niggardliness with his earnings, food was regularly in short supply for my two sisters, my brother and me, and our clothes had to last a long time. When I was ten, I won a top-of-the-class prize, but I was anxious about the prize-giving evening because there were holes in the seat of my grey trousers where the white lining showed through. I still remember how I knocked on the door of my friend Steven's home and asked his mother if I could borrow a pair of his trousers.

When I eventually climbed the few wooden steps to the school stage to collect my copy of Kingsley's *The Water Babies* from Mr Fellowes, the headmaster, I was so constricted by Steven's short trousers that my plump thighs bulged from beneath the cotton material and I waddled awkwardly across the stage. I used to tell this story to successive classes and nobody believed me. It was just another tall story. How could a teacher come from such a background!

Talking openly about the poverty I experienced as a child was to benefit me as a teacher. A number of the boys I taught in west London came from similar backgrounds, experiencing deprivation of various kinds, and I could establish points of contact with them that were not possible for many of my more fortunate colleagues. I understood how straitened home circumstances can militate against a young person's chances of acquiring or even desiring an education, and I made a point of lending additional support to those in greatest emotional need.

There were rare occasions when I was unable to prepare a lesson for a class I was due to teach. This situation wasn't a problem for me, as I found it relatively easy to occupy a class for an hour by improvising on the spot. This is where I think the 'performance' aspect of teaching shows itself at its best. The best teachers perform in the classroom, demonstrating a range of talents that can increase attentiveness. This range includes 'stand-up' comedy. I developed a number of routines over the years that I would pull out of the bag at the most opportune times. On mufti days, somebody would invariably ask me why I didn't come to school dressed informally, wearing the same casual clothes that they wore. This was another golden opportunity to play devil's advocate. My 'set' went as follows:

'I don't wear designer gear. Designer wear is more expensive than the clothes I can afford. If someone from a designer clothing company paid me a significant amount of money to wear an expensive shirt displaying its logo, I would probably accept the offer. But I wouldn't shell out several pounds of my own money for the privilege of advertising that company. That would be a case of exploitation, with me as

*the exploited party. In the capitalist west, nobody should fall
into the trap of false accounting: if I provide a service, I
should expect to be paid for it. Advertising is big business and
it's not good business sense to work for nothing. I would need
to be paid to advertise somebody's products.*

*It's fashionable for young people to wear expensive
designer trainers. When I buy trainers myself, I only use them
for their intended purpose – running. I don't see the point of
wearing them on a daily basis because they'd wear out too
quickly. Young people now wear them all the time, and many
of them would struggle to run for a bus, particularly as it's
now the fashion to wear trousers at half-mast...'*

After listening to this for a few minutes, the boys were
always in the mood to hit back with their take on
contemporary fashion. You often get the shrewdest reasoning
from students once they've been primed, and they were
always ready to shoot my older-generation prejudices down
in flames.

It's often the quirkiest thing that children find amusing.
In my final year of teaching, the deputy head in charge of
timetabling found herself short of a French teacher. After
trawling through the teaching profiles of the whole staff, she
discovered that I was also qualified to teach French. I'd
managed to keep this information quiet for thirty seven years,
but now it was out. After a brief you'd-be-doing-me-and-the-
school-a-great-favour conversation, I was down to teach
French for three lessons a week to a middle-ability Year 8
class. I was dreading it: MFL was not the most popular of
subject areas for our boys.

The head of faculty handed me a synopsis of the syllabus
and a copy of the textbook I'd be using. She assumed that, as

I was an assistant head, I'd have no problems with the class. My task was made more difficult by the fact that lessons were, supposedly, conducted entirely in French. I groaned aloud. Then I discovered that I would be teaching this class last thing on a Friday – in my experience the toughest lesson of the week. I groaned again – this time more loudly. I soon learned that 8B had a great capacity for fun, which I hoped I could use productively in my teaching.

Despite my doubts, I decided to be as positive as possible. I regularly praised those who had the courage to venture answers to my questions. I spoke French as much as I could, which was more than I'd imagined. My accent was fairly good, so the pupils didn't laugh at me. However, the one word that they latched on to was my bouncy pronunciation of the word 'bon' when I congratulated them. They were unaccustomed to my full-mouthed pronunciation of the 'b' consonant and the silent 'n'. Their version was more of a 'bonnn'. Every single time I said the word aloud during lessons, there would be an amused echo from the whole class – every single time.

Strangely, I found this genuinely amusing, not in the least irritating. It seemed to me a positive indicator of classroom solidarity. I decided never to take offence at it, but to use the word sparingly. The word 'excellent', the same as in English but with different pronunciation, would have to replace it on most occasions. But I knew that the class was on tenterhooks every lesson, waiting for my 'bon', their cue for the choral chime. I laughed along with them every time it happened, and our relationship was forged. I now knew I had their undivided attention.

Out and about locally at weekends in my capacity as a fully-paid-up member of the retired teachers' community, I might find myself looking in a shop window, suddenly to hear a murmured 'bon' issuing from amongst a group of passers-by.

4] Actor

Being somewhat vertically challenged, I knew that I could never play the part of a teacher tyrant, even if I'd been that way inclined. There were occasions when I felt genuinely intimidated by boys, and I relied heavily on my acting ability. In such situations, I had to remain calm and controlled, giving the impression that I was not at all anxious, when in reality I was. There was a great deal of play-acting involved in my teaching. Much of the time I spent in the classroom involved coercion, using sophisticated tricks and wiles to make young people do what they wouldn't necessarily choose to do themselves. This was a particular aspect of teaching I had to accept, but one with which I experienced difficulties.

In the early 1970s when I started out, secondary school teachers had the power to administer corporal punishment to pupils during lessons. Many of my colleagues took advantage of this disciplinary measure, but I was not a subscriber. I regularly pretended to be unbending and inflexible, if the need arose, when dealing with pupils who interrupted the education of the rest of the class. At the same time, I instinctively sympathised with individuals who genuinely found work difficult. Such children can become frustrated, demonstrating a range of unwanted behaviours covering the full spectrum from the mildly disruptive to confrontational.

I became an accomplished actor. I've spoken to men now in their forties that I used to teach, each of whom generally made some sort of comment about my lessons. I'm always pleased to hear that my displays of anger were convincing, but it was rare for me to feel the real emotion when dealing with youngsters. This was especially the case when handling children from backgrounds similar to mine and those who'd fallen into the drug-taking habit. On the few occasions when students directed four-letter tirades at me, substance abuse was usually the cause. Rather than fight fire with fire in such situations, I called on the school nurse.

On the first occasion that a student swore at me, all I had done was to ask if he had completed his homework. I sensed that the rest of the class was anticipating a spontaneous and robust response. I wouldn't advocate the ton-of-bricks approach on two counts: it creates enemies and takes a significant amount of physical effort. The recovery period on your lungs after a full-scale hair dryer is about two hours, and the likelihood of subsequently developing a sore throat increases dramatically. There's also the possibility that you will feel a little foolish afterwards. I discovered this after I once decided to go for maximum volume with a boy who was guilty of bullying. When I'd completed my full repertoire of ear-drum-blowing vocal gymnastics, the boy in question retorted with, 'Could you stop breathing your coffee breath in my face, sir?'

The sensible (and brave) option is to ignore the outburst, smile and tell the pupil that you'll talk about the misbehaviour after the lesson. This is the one I preferred, but the risk here is that other children may see it as an act of weakness on the teacher's part. Being perceived as 'soft', however, is not a problem so long as the class witnesses that incidents are followed up on every occasion. Consistency here, as in all cases of pupil indiscipline, is all-important. Far from being seen as weak, such an approach may help to establish the desired reputation of being genuinely concerned and essentially sympathetic. I avoided the immediate, horn-locking response when dealing with rare incidents of open abuse, but never took a backward step. The message I tried to give developing adolescents is that bad behaviour does not necessarily indicate a bad pupil.

In very extreme cases of a prolonged temper tantrum, there is the option of sending a reliable member of the group to the main office to call for a senior member of staff, with a view to withdrawing the pupil concerned. No teacher wants to deprive a student of learning, to which he or she has a right, but there are occasions when the rights of the twenty nine others carry greater weight. But, as every teacher soon discovers, you can't send for the 'heavies' too often because you may then be perceived as 'ineffective' by the school management team. This can be a more serious problem altogether.

I'm aware that there are many possible explanations for children unexpectedly blowing up in a teacher's face but, for me, one is the influence of television soaps. I'm concerned that they may be 'teaching' some of the more immature minds that when children and adults converse, decibel levels and tempers are often raised. This is just one of the many reasons why I wouldn't consider watching the nation's longest-running soaps. I find antipodean imports that specifically target teenagers to be particularly suspect. Script writers fixated on the idea that regular doses of adult/child confrontation make for exciting drama may need some form of counselling.

When 'acting', I was able temporarily to put my own personality to one side. This approach enabled me to smile at those displaying troublesome behaviour, when they might be anticipating a standard telling off. A smile can disarm a child, prevent bad feeling, and foster mutual respect. Class comedians are a case in point. I found many of them genuinely amusing and made a point of telling them so.

There are students who experience an intellectual awakening and blossoming under the sympathetic and encouraging gaze of the teacher, but the majority of boys I taught simply did what I told them to get a decent grade in the examination. I worked on fostering good relationships with my students and, as a consequence, was ever prepared to accept positive advice from the floor. Certainly, on more than one occasion, I can recall being told by an exasperated GCSE student, struggling to follow one of my intellectual tangents: 'Just tell us what we have to do for the exam, sir.'

I was an actor for the most part, tailoring my performances to suit the audience before me or the level of difficulty of the topic being taught. But my intention was never cynically to patronise; my concern was to bring about good long-term ends. At all times, I combined my acting with 'leading'. One can easily instruct an attentive class with what are believed to be the accepted truths or mantras of a particular subject, but it is more difficult, and ultimately more satisfying, to 'lead' pupils to assess given information and formulate their own responses.

The most difficult part of the act, as I've stated, was to give the impression that, whatever occurred, I was always in total control. Some of my most memorable lessons were often those when I felt like a tightrope walker, one lapse of concentration resulting in my undoing. But risk-taking was intrinsic to my style. I also liken the job of teaching to that of a stand-up comedian in one important respect: unwelcome interruptions have to be dealt with as coolly as possible in order to continue with the routine and get to the end of the act.

Anxiety about the possibility of potential flashpoints or outbursts from children constitutes an ever-present tension for teachers. Some classes on one's teaching timetable generate greater anxiety than others. Many was the time I remember the discomfort caused by sweat suddenly issuing from my armpits the moment I heard the approach from way down the corridor of some of my more volatile teaching groups. A valuable tip I picked up early on was to be wary of a pupil who, on arriving for a lesson, greeted me with the ominous words, 'Hello, sir, and how are you today?' The sinister implication was that, however well my day was going, things would soon change.

I found Year 9 groups to be the most unpredictable age group in this respect: when puberty takes a grip, mood swings are more prevalent. I grew accustomed to the stock responses of over-active fourteen year olds: 'Why me? What have I done?' In all likelihood, the offenders were genuinely unaware of what they had done because their rampant hormones had been responsible for their misbehaviour.

5] Eccentricity

When elaborating at any length on my teaching style, I have to mention my oddball tendencies. With the notable exceptions previously mentioned, my secondary school education had been peopled by a succession of distant, disdainful teachers with whom I was unable to identify in any way. I had no intention of conforming to this teaching caricature of bygone days. Consequently, on occasions, I adopted what my pupils might have perceived as slightly eccentric behaviour in order to capture interest. I never went too far, making sure that my behavioural deviations weren't so novel as to cause alarm in the ranks.

If I were dealing with a little minor mischief in the classroom I would pretend to be angry by baring my top teeth in an unusual way. By wiping my index finger quickly across my top row of teeth a few times, the teeth would become dry enough to prevent my top lip from covering them. I would stand quietly for several seconds with this nightmarishly sinister Lon Chaney 'Phantom' expression fixed on my face in the direction of the offenders, a scene that always created mild amusement.

It's surprising how often the verb 'to peer' appears in a text when reading aloud to a class. If I could see the word coming up, I'd occasionally drop the letter 'r'. Hearing a teacher saying 'He peed through the letter box' wasn't an everyday occurrence for most children. I would then stop and apologise for having made a gaffe whilst reading. An ulterior motive was that I could check who wasn't following the text. The boys paying attention would laugh like drains whilst one or two would be silent and po-faced. Softly, softly, catchee monkey.

I would also, very occasionally with a class that I knew well, affect a mood of boredom if a lesson's subject matter was less than inspiring. After yawning extravagantly, I'd incline forward from my standing position at the front of the class, place my hands palms down pointing towards me on a table, and lean forward until my body was supported horizontally on my hands. Holding myself in this position, I would explain that I had momentarily felt fatigued and needed to adopt a more relaxing posture. I never met one student with the strength to carry out this manoeuvre, although many tried. Since retiring from teaching, I've met countless ex-students out and about and many ask the same question, 'Can you still do that thing on the table?' I met one at the local gym recently and was once again required to perform to gasps of disbelief.

General aims

1) Making a difference

Determined to carve a permanent niche for myself within the world of education, I set out to be a teacher who made a difference. I worked on the assumption that all boys have feelings of insecurity, far greater than any I might have about being their teacher. My career was not going to be a five-minute wonder. I was adamant that I would be a permanent fixture in schools. No Bash Street Kids were going to turn me over.

When I was first led into a classroom at the age of twenty two, I was confronted by my registration group, rows of twelve-year-old boys who seemed to be aching for opportunities to create mischief. Unnerved as I was, I maintained a semblance of composure by convincing myself that, individually, each pupil would present me with no problems whatsoever. So why worry about a group of thirty?

Besides having faith in my determination to be a successful teacher, my second conviction was that I would demonstrate a genuine interest in all pupils. Whether or not I 'liked' the individuals ranged before me would be irrelevant because I was being paid to develop their intellectual potential, and everyone has potential in one or more directions. When difficult situations arose, with students seeming incapable of grasping important teaching points, there was an unusual strategy that I adopted. I would stress that, as a public servant, I was responsible for ensuring that their learning progressed satisfactorily. I even went as far as to tell some, 'I am your servant, paid for by your parents' taxes, and it's up to you to make the best use of me that you can.' This startling admission on the part of their teacher occasionally had the effect of relieving the stress caused by their apparent inability to comprehend. Some struggling students chose to take this information on board, and modified their attitude to learning accordingly.

A professional interest in child development is essential. When I studied at teacher training college, child psychology was an important element throughout the three-year course. Nowadays, by contrast, a qualified teacher can begin a career without ever encountering the topic. Perhaps Piaget's theories on concrete operational thinking are now redundant, but his work made an invaluable contribution to my interaction with children.

One activity I introduced with a number of teaching groups, of whatever age, involved inviting everyone to participate in a psychological test. I would hand out sheets of blank paper and pencils and ask each student to draw a quick sketch that had to include the following elements:

1) a tree, 2) the sun, 3) a house, and 4) water.

I would then explain that the drawings revealed important facts about personality, and offer my own potted interpretations. I hasten to add that I only made positive observations that would give the pupils a confidence boost. This activity always excited maximum attention and concentration from the class. Children and adults alike enjoy being the centre of attention, and the element of mystery ensures a captive audience.

Each of the elements supposedly corresponds to a specific concept: 1) tree – father figure; 2) sun – mother figure; 3) house – perception of the self; and 4) water – ambition. Interpretations could be based solely on the comparative sizes of the different components of the image. For example, if somebody had drawn a large house with plenty of additional detail, I would state that this was an indication of a very well-ordered and capable mind. One who drew a waterfall next to his house would be informed that he was one of the most ambitious students I'd ever taught.

One of the interesting bonuses of this activity is that children, being impressionable, can take on the positive qualities that one ascribes to them. It's the give-a-dog-a-bad-name syndrome in reverse. Primary school teachers do this all the time: 'What a kind girl you are!' and so on. Secondary school teachers need to remember that positive qualities can be imprinted on adolescents in much the same way. Regular reinforcement of notable characteristics can become a permanent feature of a child's conduct. It's a case of being persistently positive.

My experience of secondary school teachers who taught me in the 1960s was that several took a grim pleasure in focusing on my academic weaknesses and predicting less than successful examination performance. Consequently, my self-confidence suffered for long periods of time in certain areas. I fell badly behind in my first two years of studying French from age eleven, as a consequence, in my opinion, of being a target of one teacher. He took a perverse pleasure in constantly browbeating me with humiliating taunts in the classroom. Insensitive adults (my euphemism for the proud possessors of a degree in Psychological Thuggery) can do immeasurable damage to developing minds. My French teacher in my third year, who was more interested in teaching than ridiculing the least able during lessons, proved inspirationally motivating. When I gained my qualification to teach eight years later it was in two subjects – English and French.

2) The reading habit

I set out on my career wanting my classes to see me as approachable and sympathetic. I also wanted to foster an interest in literature, promoting the message that what one reads may not only be pleasurable but also help young people to shape their lives and find a place in the world.

What one reads in childhood contributes to the development of personality. At primary school, I aspired to be a cross between Roy of the Rovers and Jennings. I managed to be elected captain of my primary school football team, St Luke's, so my reading of the 'Tiger' comic bore the desired fruit. In addition, I had rigged up my own version of 'the snorkel' to enable me to read under the bedclothes when the lights were switched off. Jennings and Darbs would have been proud of me. 'Treasure Island' was also very formative: the combination of modesty and courage in Jim Hawkins' character had a compelling appeal. Children unconsciously search for role models as they develop, and these can be found in abundance in novels. I think that the teacher I have to thank for seriously exciting my interest in fiction was Miss Holmes who, as a reward for my class's good behaviour, would read from the *Milly Molly Mandy* books that held me spellbound. At the age of seven, I so wished I could be Billy Blunt.

The promotion of the reading habit became a firmly embedded component of my teaching approach. One sharp individual once asked me, 'If stories are so important, why can't we just watch films?' I answered the question by comparing the three ways that one can follow a story: 1) reading fiction; 2) listening to audio-books or the radio; and 3) watching a film. When one watches a film, one has the satisfaction of following a story, but the imagination has no work to do whatsoever as sounds and moving images are provided. Listening is a better option as one has to create images and sounds in the mind as a consequence of hearing a spoken narrative. But reading fiction is by far the most beneficial activity as one first has to decipher a written code, and then translate this code into a coherent and colourful narrative world in one's imagination.

I enjoyed asking children to talk about their personal reading that I set for homework for all sorts of reasons. One comment that always excited my particular interest would be when a pupil drew a comparison between his ideas about a character in a novel and the representation of that character in a subsequent film version. Invariably I would hear, 'The way the person in the film looked and behaved was nothing like the way that I imagined him/her from the book.' Music to my ears.

The desire to read fiction books for enjoyment is also a primary hub for the development of the intellect. I'd go further and argue that the pleasure principle early reading satisfies has a potentially healing influence on a child's state of mind. I know from personal experience the stabilising effect reading had on me in times of emotional crisis. Books provided a constant refuge during difficult periods of my childhood, unlocking the secrets of alternative worlds of experience for me. The comfort I gain from reading even now is such that, whenever I finish a novel, it's as though I'm saying goodbye to a friend. I am convinced that, had I never

142

acquired the reading habit, my personality would not have been as rounded, and I would not be the comparatively level-headed, confident person that I have become.

If the reading habit is interrupted in childhood, language acquisition and emotional development are hindered. I used to badger teenagers constantly to stick with private reading, as many lose their appetite for fiction. Keeping boys on track with personal reading can be difficult, particularly as there are now so many alternative time-occupying diversions available that didn't exist a few decades ago.

In earnest conversations with my classes, I explained that language acquisition gives one strength. I enthused over the practical benefits of word power, from being able to complete a driving licence application form accurately to grasping the arguments of political debate. Articulating the point at its simplest level, I would warn those who had chosen to stop reading in their own time that they were literally putting a cap on the number of words that they would be able to use for the rest of their lives. Scare-mongering, you may say, but it was an argument to which I often resorted.

The more one feeds the brain, the more information it absorbs, like the process of osmosis. Children were able to relate to the idea that the brain is like a huge computer hard drive, with a limitless capacity for storing information. The more language one has acquired, the more one is able to discriminate between and express complex shades of meaning. This is how I attempted to define the notion of intellect, the acquisition of which is everyone's obligation.

When *Dungeons and Dragons* game-playing came along in the mid-70s, it proved to be a hugely time-consuming adolescent pastime. I became aware of a dramatic falling off in personal reading amongst the many boys who participated in the new fad, the ominous precursor to computer games. When the games console industry got into its stride, gaming monopolised so much of my students' free time that the reading habit suffered a lethal blow. I'm sure that there are some benefits to be gained from playing electronic games for hours on end, but I'd be grateful if an expert in the field could fill me in. I couldn't resist poking fun at the addiction to what I considered repetitive and mindless activity whenever I had the chance.

Early games were played using a joystick, a device so obviously phallic in appearance and use that my mischievous nature couldn't be contained. Good sense would not permit me to say as much in the classroom. However, I would suggest that a parent walking into a son's bedroom must be a little disturbed by the sight of seeing him hunched over a glowing screen and waggling a joystick furiously.

I worry that reading will eventually become marginalised as an area of human activity. Satellite and cable television, smart phones and all the other competing paraphernalia represent, for me, a serious threat to the reading habit. The advent of the electronic book may yet save the day.

As an English teacher, I also reinforced the reading habit with a view to making it easier for children to make sense of the rules of grammar. My belief is that teaching grammar per se is of limited use to those who never read. English grammar is a complex business that makes far more sense if one reads regularly.

3) Ego suppression

I found the ploy of behaving submissively useful when interacting with 'difficult' colleagues who, you may not be surprised to hear, could be much more challenging than some of the troubled pupils I taught. Shortly after taking up a post in a secondary school as a teaching assistant, the Head of English burst into the staff room at break time one morning looking for me. I happened to be directly in his path and he bawled me out publicly for accepting a returned text book from one of his class members, when the boy in question had been specifically instructed to hand it in to him personally. A petty attitude, in my view.

The humiliation I experienced in front of most of the school staff, for no justifiable reason, made me understand how children must feel when teachers unreasonably turn on them during a lesson. Genuinely losing one's temper with a child is fraught with danger.

I learned to make every effort to suppress my ego when dealing with children. I'm as confident, opinionated and competitive as most people in life. For example, I played local club rugby until I was fifty and achieved a black belt in aiki-jutsu. I did avoid, however, behaving in a routinely overbearing and superior manner with my students. There is no future in seeking to embarrass anyone by publicly highlighting weaknesses or insecurities, as had happened in my secondary school days when I'd had to endure crashing adult egotists galore, all of them males.

I constantly told students how much more intelligent they were than I was at the same age, referring to their mastery of computers, electronics, mobile phones, and their infinitely greater knowledge of what was going on in the world around them. By comparison, I'd been a teenage Neanderthal. I encouraged all my pupils to believe that, in years to come, they possessed the capacity to become vastly superior to me in every aspect of intellectual development.

9. The Seven Pillars of Pedagogy (or 'P' Words)

This chapter focuses on those qualities that I wouldn't hesitate to recommend for prospective teachers. As the teacher with responsibility for the induction of beginner teachers in my final teaching post, I was the mystic on the mountain, the fount of sacred knowledge. (Well, one can dream.) It's an amazing coincidence that all of the qualities on which I dwell begin with the letter 'P'.

1) Passion

I was fortunate that my wife remained with me to the end of my teaching career, despite her conviction that I was a bigamist who was already married to my job. My excuse for putting so much effort into my work was that I couldn't accept the possibility of being unprepared in the classroom. As in most walks of life, it's all about the preparation. Thus, I retained the self-confidence to be passionate about my teaching.

The realisation that one is able to hold the attention of adolescents who are habitually engrossed in such monster computer gaming products as 'Assassin's Creed' is a buzz of monumental proportions. But possession of this power is both a curse and a blessing. Living up to my ideals of optimum professional performance required heart-pumping enthusiasm that left me emotionally drained at the end of each school day. I didn't always meet my high expectations, but the intention to do so was obligatory.

Besides covering all of a lesson's prepared material and presenting it in a manner that made it as palatable and engaging as possible, there was the need to be endlessly attuned to all the vagaries of pupil behaviour. Any interruption had to be dealt with as calmly and as swiftly as possible in order that it did not intrude on the 'zone' that I entered for each lesson. Children intuitively register when the person standing before them is buzzing, and this awareness can enervate and motivate them.

I liken teaching a lesson to being a jockey negotiating the Aintree course in the Grand National. Completing the ultimate racing trip requires a jockey's total concentration and the application of every scrap of professional experience. Not winning the race isn't an indicator of failure if you manage to get the best out of yourself and your horse.

Of the thirty six thousand or so lessons I taught over a long career, I'd estimate that few of them were complete failures, but in only about half of them did I meet the high standards I set myself. The reasons for this modest success rate range from going into school when you're not well enough to teach to not having had enough time to prepare every lesson in complete detail owing to other pressing administration. I was lucky never to be troubled by laziness or alcohol dependency. Experience taught me to bite my tongue before accusing those in other lines of work of not performing to my expectations. I was equally tolerant of students when they had the occasional 'off' days.

One of the worst things that could happen to me during a lesson was for someone to knock on the door and break my spell of concentration: 'Can Mr B. borrow a set of 'Of Mice and Men' please, sir?' Suppressing the urge to reply, 'Can you go back and tell Mr B. to...!' I would dutifully fetch the books. Interrupting colleagues' lessons is best avoided.

I never liked being observed whilst teaching. It wasn't that I felt I had any weaknesses that I needed to hide. It wasn't that I feared judgement being made on my ability by an inspector who'd struggle to teach a dog to sit. It wasn't that I didn't want my colleagues to witness how much nervous energy and perspiration I generated whilst holding forth. It was that I considered my classroom space to be my territory, and nobody else should be allowed to encroach if I didn't want them there. I was a professional and I had earned the right to be trusted and to be left to my own devices. Call it pig-headed pride if you like, but I didn't deserve such treatment. Are surgeons observed when they carry out a hip replacement? Are bankers observed when they dish out loans to sub-prime borrowers? Who observes the observers? For this reason, observing colleagues' teaching, part of my remit as the teacher responsible for professional development, was never enjoyable. I knew how I felt about being scrutinised, and was the most sympathetic and supportive observer it was possible to be.

Passion can't be taught at university. I was lucky enough to have had a passion muscle that made teaching more than just a job. It seemed paradoxical to me that, despite being unable to produce fiction or poetry of any merit myself, I had the ability to present language and literature study in ways that would arouse the curiosity of a sizeable percentage of those I taught. When learning is accompanied by excitement and a genuine sense of discovery, there is nothing more rewarding for a teacher. For example, asking a class to explore the imagery of 'boxes' in Philip Larkin's *Mr Bleaney* is great fun. Watching students smile with delight as they grasp the metaphorical and literal connotations of 'putting people in boxes' always gave me a tingle of pleasure. At best, teaching is as fulfilling an enterprise as I could imagine outside of family life.

2) Patience

Job's Old Testament patience is an extreme example of that quality considered essential for anyone making the leap of faith into teaching. It's a statement of the obvious to say that spadefuls of patience enable one to complete the groundwork required for children to develop strong learning roots and grow towards the light of understanding.

Unfortunately, a number of colleagues with whom I worked were notable for their impatience and often made a hell of a life for themselves and their students. I know this because lesson observation was a matter of course, even more so when the machinery of professional development was introduced in schools. Impatience is a quality that cannot survive in the pressure cooker of teaching.

The teacher with the Basil Fawlty gene is inclined to refuse children entry to the classroom until they have formed a perfectly straight line in the corridor and have stopped talking. I've witnessed colleagues in possession of a good degree pass in one or more subjects becoming enraged because a child whispered five minutes into this silent line-forming process. I'm a great advocate of starting lessons in an orderly manner, but corridor drills are a waste of everyone's time and energy. The same teachers were just as likely to be heard going into orbit once their lesson had started: "How many times have I told you not to open your books until I've instructed you to do so!" My view is that the power-trip approach to dealing with young people, the style of the clinically apoplectic, will probably shorten one's life by about twenty years.

Just as doomed to educational failure is the opposite method, the ultra-sensitive and myopically considerate. Patience taken to extremes can be equally counter-productive. The lessons of those demonstrating patience to the *n*th degree will progress at a snail's pace. Laboured lesson delivery, the result of not wishing to place undue stress on fragile brain cells, is as much of a curse as the helter-skelter switchback teaching style. The painfully-patient approach will inevitably increase the incidence of artfully-contrived time-wasting strategies.

The concept of patience does not only apply to one's dealings with pupils in the classroom. Tiptoeing around the bursting egos of some fellow classroom practitioners will also test reserves of patience. I have occasionally encountered personalities who, in their brazen pursuit of professional advancement, seek out opportunities for open confrontation. Such assertive behaviour, they believe, will stamp them as being hard-headed, no-nonsense go-getters. It never ceased to surprise me how this calibre of humanity was so often perceived to be a genuinely attractive promotion prospect when job interview time came around.

Another type of patience that is useful is that required to cope with the speed of curriculum and syllabus change. Fifty years ago, I remember enjoying project work at grammar school, long before I had to think of sitting O-Level examinations. Lessons were set aside in each subject area to

151

allow us to complete individual projects, pursuing whatever topic appealed. I've already mentioned my tour de force on 'Henry V and the French Wars' and my scientific exploration of 'The History of Flight'. I can say without fear of uttering a falsehood that I remember comparatively little about *The Stuarts* or *The Elizabethans*, two areas in which I received formal tuition during the same period, but I can still recall the battle formations and outcomes of the siege of Harfleur and the Battle of Agincourt.

I mention this most engaging method of study because it was surprisingly reintroduced as a radical new humanities course very successfully for key stage 3 pupils at my school a few years before I retired. If you have the patience to wait a while in teaching, the old may eventually be repackaged as the new; project work becomes cross-curricular learning. They'll be bringing school caps back next to protect children from the sun.

Having the patience and time to investigate why individuals are unmotivated, under-achieving or lacking concentration is time well spent. Children have personal problems, domestic issues and mind blocks just as adults do, and teachers are likely to pay a price if they choose to ignore such considerations. A growing problem throughout my career was the chemical; for example, children becoming dependent on high-energy drinks for caffeine and sugar fixes. It was easy to guess which pupils had indulged during the morning and lunch breaks because they could euphemistically be described as being 'full of beans' for their next lesson. For those who prefer hyperbole, the boys could be 'climbing the walls'. There is a case to be made for claiming that children's poor educational performance is just as likely to be the result of poor diet as poor teaching.

My advice when the going gets tough in the classroom is not necessarily to fight on regardless of any resistance. The ability to take a step back and reassess the underlying causes of any interruptions to one's teaching may result in a fresh and more fruitful approach. A busy secondary school, where everybody is working furiously to get everything done yesterday, isn't the ideal environment for reflecting and reassessing. When a teacher is in full swing, rushing hurriedly from one lesson to another, sorting out difficulties with students on the hoof requires unerring patience. Time does have to be found, nevertheless, to deal sensitively with matters relating to student cooperation and motivation before they become obstacles to learning.

I recall one muscular Year 10 boy who appeared to take devious pleasure in undermining my lessons from the back of the room. His interruptions seemed calculated to waste time, but he was never openly confrontational. When I talked through the situation with him, it transpired that he took exception to my regular correction of his faulty spelling whenever I marked a piece of his work. He admitted that he was also frustrated by his weakness with grammar, but felt that I was picking on him. He laboured under the delusion that I thought his work lacked any merit and considered him a no-hoper. After I'd reassured him that nothing could be further from the truth and that I was trying to ensure that he gained the 'B' grade in GCSE English that he deserved, he became more amenable during lessons. Non-cooperation can be an indicator of a perceived grievance that may arise from a simple misunderstanding. Children are, perhaps, more rational than teachers care to think and are likely to respond positively to frank and honest dialogue.

A final word on the theme of patience to those entertaining the prospect of teaching as a career: it is necessary to deal with political interference in educational matters more patiently than one deals with recalcitrant children, because politicians never stop.

3) Persistence

Like mountain climbers or marathon runners, teachers need to have vast reserves of endurance. Staying power is essential. Ordinary members of the public who tediously rail on about teachers' long holidays say this out of guilt. They secretly know that they couldn't hack the job and think that anyone who can is a suitable case for counselling. Parents regularly told me that they were close to breaking point by the end of the summer holiday, having been in too-close proximity to their 2.4 offspring for the six-week stretch. Ironically, parents never seem to tire of telling teachers how relieved they are when this period of imposed 'quality time' comes to an end and they no longer have their children under their feet, or wherever else it is they keep them. Parenting for many, it seems, is initially perceived as a right and then a chore.

The nature of the job required of me the commitment to sell myself completely to the calling. My wife referred to it as 'my mistress'. She was no different from most other teachers' partners when she complained bitterly that for thirty nine weeks of every year I was virtually uncontactable on any serious level.

I'm reminded of an old joke where a teacher is sitting on the sofa next to his wife. The punchline from the teacher is, "Now have you got anything serious that you want to talk about before term starts?"

154

When I did periodically surface as a husband, I often went down with some illness or other, particularly at Christmas. The sudden withdrawal of adrenalin that normally courses through a teacher's veins causes a real shock to the system when it's temporarily switched off. My favourite trick was to put my back out on Christmas Eve and to be incapacitated for the next three days. The physical and emotional intensity of the job has all kinds of unexpected side-effects.

Despite what you may read about the profession, the common-or-garden teacher is highly competent and wonderful at meeting strict deadlines. References to gasmen and estate agents consistently trip off the tongue when incompetence in the workplace is under discussion. Professional reliability seems to be becoming a thing of the past in many areas of life. Not so with teachers. They cannot miss deadlines. The daily administrative workload, other than lesson preparation, has snowballed incredibly over the past few decades. For example, a teacher's annual professional development programme alone involves copious form-filling. Keeping abreast of the administrative burden puts unnecessary pressure on one's teaching commitments. The syndrome I particularly suffered from was *exam nightmare phobia*. Every year I struggled to suppress the fear that, on the day of the first A-Level English Literature examination paper, I would discover that I had taught the wrong set texts. Fortunately it never happened.

By the time my wife had reached her mid-forties, she'd had enough of the 'other woman'. She decided (Shock! Horror!) that we would go abroad for a holiday during the two-week Easter break. This caused me to go into private-panic mode: I'd come to rely on that two-week period to sort out the Year 11 examination coursework – an inordinately time-consuming but essential process. With my school-deadlines-are-my-life hat on, I tried to calculate how I could do ten days' work in five. I couldn't, which left me with only one course of action.

A few months later, Lindsey was becoming tired of waiting for me to join her at the pool of the family-run hotel just down the hill from Taormina on the island of Sicily. The balmy late-morning heat, the aromatic smells of the garden and her relaxing sunbed were not enough. Where was her husband? She eventually decided to search me out. Imagine her surprise when she entered the apartment to find me stretched out on the bed surrounded by student papers. I'd smuggled the offending materials out of the UK at the bottom of my suitcase, never thinking that I'd get caught. All hell broke loose.

You'd think that I would have learned my lesson, but the day before Christmas Eve a few years later was another landmark moment in my marriage. We had travelled down to my wife's parents' thatched cottage to enjoy the festivities in the Dorset countryside. My father-in-law had gone to unusual lengths that year to get into the Christmas spirit. As we approached the house, a huge neon Santa and sleigh glowed on the wall. Once indoors, we were given a run-through of the seasonal timetable for the next few days – friends visiting, must-see television programmes, the church service, the Christmas meal at the local hostelry… Unfortunately, I had a stack of GCSE mock examination papers at the bottom of my weekend bag, and I was wondering how I'd find time to mark them. They took me so long I had to chip away at them for a few hours every single day over the holiday period to complete them by the return to school in early January. For me, Christmas Eve, Christmas Day and Boxing Day represented a considerable amount of marking time that couldn't be sacrificed.

It was late on Christmas Eve when Lindsey marched up the stairs to find out why I hadn't come down to watch the *Morecambe and Wise Christmas Special* that everyone was looking forward to. I'm sure some sixth sense had warned her as to what she would find. She wasn't disappointed in that respect, but I was. My red pen was flashing over an almost-completed script when she strode into the bedroom, nostrils flaring: 'I thought this would be what you were doing…!' I took my punishment like the demented teacher I was and sheepishly followed her downstairs. Some married men lead straightforward lives of undisturbed indolence but, being a teacher, I was constantly on the lookout for a spare hour or two to do some marking. To be honest, acts of God apart, nothing deterred me from the admin load. I had real stickability, probably a consequence of being a Capricorn – the goat picking its way slowly but steadily up the mountain slope.

It is impossible to describe the feeling of utter tranquillity I experienced on the first Sunday evening of my retirement. I knew that I wouldn't have to do at least three hours' marking…ever again. I'd never shirked this most arduous of chores: pupils deserve and demand speedy feedback on their efforts. But it was wonderful that marking would no longer be a part of my life. Unfortunately, strange as it may seem, I did experience withdrawal symptoms. I couldn't settle to relaxing with mindless television. I was restless and had to do something constructive. For the first time in my life I read the business section of 'The Observer'.

My wife believed that the only way I could cope with teaching was that I had a high boredom threshold. She witnessed the monotonous regularity with which I brought home piles of marking night after night, year after year. She gave up complaining about me being parked for hours on end in the same chair, red pen in hand. And then, a few years before I retired, there was a breakthrough moment. I brought home a green pen for marking because red pen marks in an exercise book were suddenly deemed to be injurious to a child's self-confidence. I'd been doing it wrong for three decades. I couldn't bear to think of the harm I'd caused to thousands of children. To complicate matters further, pupils were then required to complete a written response to my comment. A marking revolution had taken place. In all areas of teaching, any task will eventually come in for the lets-over-complicate-it makeover. Whatever was thrown at me, however, I soldiered on uncomplaining.

If only my wife had seen me performing in the classroom, she would have discovered that boredom played no part in my professional approach. I was a committed workaholic who went to any lengths to maintain the attention and interest of my students. Being a fan of early Steve Martin comedy films, I exploited opportunities for physical humour to enliven my lessons. Writing with chalk on a blackboard or, later, with a felt-tip pen on the whiteboard, I would pretend that I'd had a heavy night on the tiles. I'd give the impression that I was so tired as I moved from one side of the board to the other, buckling at the knees slightly as I did so, that each line sloped dramatically downwards. I really can't imagine that I would get away with such silliness in the current educational climate. A child would probably report me and I'd end up being sectioned.

4) Praise

Children know more about human behaviour than we credit them. In a busy school environment where one is in constant contact with hundreds of them on a daily basis, it is easy to overlook this common-sense fact. Each child in a classroom forms a different impression of the teacher. Whilst one is overcome with a sense of awe at the accumulated knowledge and wisdom on show, another will be intimidated by an authoritarian manner or aloof tone of voice. It is uncertain whether or not a teacher will ever be fully aware of the myriad perceptions every pupil has of her because the majority of them are adept at concealing their innermost feelings, just like adults. However, praise is the common currency which, with very few exceptions, all children welcome.

The attitude of a child towards a teacher will have a significant bearing on whether or not learning will take place. I once volunteered to take on two extra contact lessons a week to get a GCSE class through the last two terms of their English and English Literature courses. The class of mixed-ability students had suffered as a result of losing their regular teacher to maternity leave, and in their first term in Year 11 they had been subjected to a series of ineffectual cover teachers. I stepped in to fill the breach and was initially surprised at the simmering hostility of a number of the boys.

They knew that they had been short-changed for a full term and several feared that their examination results in this core subject would suffer. The antipathy towards me lasted for the whole of my first term with them. On numerous occasions I was tempted to castigate the class for its ingratitude at my volunteering to help them, but I resisted. Instead, I bided my time and adopted an ultra-supportive attitude, apologising and praising as opposed to berating and criticising.

On results day the following August, I was relieved to find that my optimistic predictions had come to fruition for the class. One of the parents subsequently wrote to me, thanking me for stepping up to the GCSE plate on her son's behalf. Five years after my retirement, I bumped into that boy, a primary school teacher in north London. His first instinct was to acknowledge and apologise for the antagonism he and his classmates had shown me years earlier: "You may remember me, sir. I sat at the front of the class and gave you a hard time."

The commitment to giving positive messages to every child is a teaching mindset that must become habitual. I never had any trouble knowing the characters to whom I would give a wide berth if I bumped into them outside of school, but I was also aware that these were most in need of the positivity I had to offer in the classroom.

Children generally respond positively to adult approbation, but they immediately identify and ignore insincere praise. Some teachers rarely praise, whilst others who've glutted on praise pills do nothing else. Trotting out compliments ad nauseam is redolent of obsessive compulsive disorder and can become a counter-productive condition: 'Well done, Joey! Good boy, Joey! Excellent effort, Joey! Keep it up, Joey! Nice try, Joey!' This is when praise becomes an annoyance, the sort of treatment that makes children feel uncomfortable, not rewarded. When a teacher gives praise, it should be for a specific achievement, one that sets the achiever apart from others. Observing beginner teachers, I stressed the point that for praise to be valued, it must be perceived as merited.

5) Protection

Many teachers, male and female alike, have something of the mother-hen quality about them. If you've ever bumped into a school party of infant-school age on the street, you'll know what I mean: "Come on everyone! Hold hands in a line like I showed you and follow me up these steps!" It's the protective impulse, formalised in recent years (with a view to the potential threat of litigation and/or a prison sentence in the event of professional malpractice) as *health and safety*.

At secondary level, when students are not as accommodating as tiny tots, the prospect of taking a group out of school to the theatre can be the ultimate exercise in high anxiety. I once accompanied a sixth-form group to a west-end theatre production of *Our Town* by Thornton Wilder starring Alan Alda. I was completely at ease until the interval, after which some of my students decided to sit not in their own seats but in unoccupied ones closer to the stage. Would this constitute a breach of the school's health and safety procedures that I had signed? I remembered one of the statements I had written in the section *Measures that will be taken to ensure the safety of pupils at all times when out of school*: 'Students will be seated at the theatre in pre-paid seats within close proximity to me during the entire performance.' I recall very little of the second half of the production such was my discomfort – one boy was even behind a pillar and I occasionally lost sight of him. Organising extra-curricular activities nowadays is a hazardous business.

The instinct to protect one's charges is deeply instilled in all teachers. Science teachers fear long-term health problems resulting from children inhaling noxious fumes in the lab, and domestic science teachers secretly fear unsuspecting parents/carers being poisoned by cakes taken home by happy junior patisseurs.

In addition to following the various protocols to preserve children's physical well-being, there is another protective layer at work in the classroom: the impulse to protect children from the seamier aspects of the world. Studies of the content of the internet indicate that in excess of 40 per cent of all online material is currently pornography-related. Images of extreme violence and race-hate are also too easily accessible.

Aristotle's belief that the state should be instrumental in helping individuals to achieve a good life is still sound. As a teacher, I was part of the state provision controlling and directing individual lives, and I was constantly aware of my responsibility of protection towards those in my care. If children are to receive the benefits of a rewarding or flourishing life, teachers play an important part. Children may be persuaded to adopt a generally upright lifestyle by their teachers if there is mutual trust and respect. This may sound high-flown and idealistic to the teacher preoccupied with how best to teach everyone in the class how to calculate the circumference of a circle or when to use a semicolon.

Intellectual and emotional development are prerequisites to children making important decisions about their lives. Young people reposition themselves with regard to the world on a daily basis. For many, teachers are the most important role models they will ever have. The responsibility of being a moral guardian for the tens of thousands one teaches during one's career can never be understated. As an ex-student who became a primary school teacher himself once said to me, "My pupils see more of me than they do their parents."

The requirement of being respectable and law-abiding in every aspect of life is a weighty professional obligation. I'd

162

only been teaching a few years when my wife and I found that we were struggling to pay the bills after taking on a mortgage. A friend invited me to join him doing a couple of evenings' loading work a week at Heathrow airport. I saved money by cycling to and from the airport and found that the extra few pounds a month kept us solvent. However, after only three months, I couldn't deal with the guilt I experienced moonlighting under the assumed name of James Garner. (The false names used by my workmates all tended to be those of actors in westerns – James Stewart, Randolph Scott and Clint Eastwood.) This was no way for a respectable teacher to behave, so I threw in the part-time job and returned to the life of penury. I was broke but I was able to keep up with my marking again and sleep nights.

Becoming a teacher carried with it, for me, the knowledge that there could be no criminal blemishes whatsoever on my character. Picking up hooky gear at the pub, buying bent MOT certificates and cheating the taxman may be risks worth taking for other members of the public, but not for a teacher. I could only pass myself off as a bona fide public protector of children's morals if I adopted an authentic moral disposition in my private life.

6) Physical Exercise

When I became an assistant head, one of my responsibilities was staff induction, for new members of staff and trainee teachers. In my first meeting with them, I recommended some form of exercise, anything from walking to snowboarding. I managed to survive in the job because I always had the inclination to be physically active to counter the long hours of sedentary activity. I maintained a good level of personal fitness, such that I ran the London Marathon with my daughter twice in my sixties. I don't say that every teacher has to take up a challenge as gruelling as a marathon, but I would advise doing something. From swimming to salsa dancing, there's an activity for everyone.

Throughout my career, I was content to encourage the pupil myth that I was 'fit'. It gave me value-added interest in the eyes of the students, and made my job as a teacher easier.

Unless you've attempted it, you cannot know the physical demands of standing before classes lesson after lesson, day after day. I used to have favourite shirts in my wardrobe that suddenly went missing. When I asked my wife what had happened to them, she'd say, "I had to throw them out because I couldn't get rid of the stains under the armpits." I'd only had them a few months and they were gone. But it was true: I could look outwardly calm, organised and totally in control, but I couldn't control my armpits. The perspiration would sometimes start before I left the house in the morning. It was a standing joke with Lindsey that as soon as I put on my shirt I would walk around holding my arms away from my body, armpits open, looking like a weightlifter preparing for a clean and jerk. I was trying to give my shirts a bit of extra life, but I was wasting my time.

The moment I walked into the classroom, I could feel and often hear my heartbeat. My pulse raced and my mind also ran on at a heightened rate. I would imagine that the 'rush' I experienced in the classroom was similar to the effect caused by taking artificial stimulants. At the end of my busiest teaching days, I often needed to sit down quietly for ten or fifteen minutes in my office to 'come down'. Teaching can be a very empowering experience, but I did feel that physical fitness was essential in my case.

One of the most exhausting exercises is pretending to be angry when asked to deal with a pupil's serious misbehaviour during a lesson. As an experienced teacher, I was often called into a colleague's classroom to deal with such situations. The teacher's expectation was that I should give the pupil concerned a good telling off in front of his classmates. This I found difficult, as I was dealing with a situation cold, having no grievance myself with the alleged miscreant. Shifting from the mindset of trying to keep a low profile and getting on with a mountainous backlog of work to the what-the-hell-do-you-think-you're-up-to! mode requires several energy-level gearshifts. I'd sometimes oblige and do my best to put on one of my greatest shows of offended dignity, lamenting the fact that I'd been called to deal with a student who should know the acceptable parameters of classroom behaviour. But I felt drained immediately afterwards by displays of emotional excess. With the permission of the teacher concerned, I preferred to take the child out of the classroom for a while and try, in a quiet way, to encourage a sense of contrition. That route usually resulted in him returning of his own volition to the classroom and apologising to the teacher.

7) Pride

It may seem to be a statement of the obvious to say that one should feel proud at being able to work with young people. This is not an emotion universally acknowledged within the profession. I knew colleagues early in my teaching life who felt that schools would be better places without children. They were the teeming hordes one feared, and lessons were essentially a constant struggle.

One foreign languages teacher, in particular, comes to mind. Well into middle age, she struggled to cope with high levels of anxiety from which she suffered the moment she entered the school building in the morning to departing as soon as possible after the last bell. Highly intelligent and reserved in the extreme, she never joined in with staff room small talk and rarely discussed the pupils in her care with other members of staff. My main memory is the image of her sitting in an easy chair bolt upright and staring straight ahead of her for the duration of every free lesson she had. The moment the bell sounded calling her to teach, she would snatch up her handbag, purse her lips and hurry off to her classroom. This daily performance suggested to me the actions of a Tommy, filled with trepidation, leaping out of his trench and going over the top at the fateful blast of a whistle.

On the subject of small talk, many teachers take pleasure in bad-mouthing children within the sanctuary of the staff room. This practice irritated me. To counteract the many slurs directed against the children with whom I worked, I tried to adhere to a policy of being complimentary if I ever mentioned them collectively or individually. It may be argued that I was being hyper-sensitive, or even politically correct as one alpha-male colleague once humorously suggested.

If new members of staff are to maintain a healthy attitude towards children, experienced teachers must be seen to set a positive example. If it's wrong to refer to a pupil as a 'knob head' in the classroom, it's wrong to use the term with reference to a child in the staff room.

The habit of bad-mouthing pupils to other children is too easy a habit to pick up. When I was involved in Saturday morning school sports fixtures, the temptation to refer disparagingly to a team member who failed to turn up was difficult to resist. Equally serious is the situation where a child is berated on a personal level during a lesson. If we want children to respect themselves and each other at all times, teachers must be unwavering in their positivity towards the good, the bad and the disaffected, whatever the child's perceived provocation or the teacher's mood.

There is a direct correlation between the level of pride one experiences in the job and the credibility one enjoys with one's students. I cannot imagine that 'Banger', my secondary school geography teacher, was ever bothered by the concept of professional pride at any time in his career.

10. Irritants

So the lesson starts. The class register is taken. Everybody's present, including the two at the back whose misbehaviour can be guaranteed to make the lesson difficult. The heartbeat is already raised and the perspiration generator kicks in.

Teachers are keenly aware of the priority to cover all of their prepared lesson material, but there are always irritants, interruptions that scupper one's plans to be an effective classroom practitioner. Whilst explaining that not all adverbs have an 'ly' ending, the teacher's brain pan is also calculating when would be the best time to confiscate the mobile phone that Jimmy has secretively ('ly' adverb) taken from his pocket; how to stop Ian surreptitiously stabbing the hand of the boy next to him with a pencil; and whether or not to pick up Omar for doodling on the exercise sheet that has just been handed out.

Good classroom teachers become adept at juggling a number of balls in the air at the same time. You can never afford to drop one. What follows is advice on how to deal with lesson irritants that caused me a deal of accumulated anxiety in my time.

Bad Language

The title of this book apart, profanity is an issue with me. Bad language is a hazard for which teachers should prepare, whether it occurs within the classroom or elsewhere. A stern reprimand or more may be necessary for serious breaches, but there are other ways of dealing with lower-order offences. Seriously strong four-letter words apart, I often tried to use a lighter touch when the words 'shit', 'crap' or 'bollocks' were heard from the far reaches of the classroom.

I clearly remember a conversation with one Year 9 boy who expressed genuine surprise when I told him that 'shit' is recognised by many to be a swear word. "No, it isn't," he insisted. "My mum and dad use it all the time and they don't call it swearing." There are many such relaxed households, where colourful language use is the norm. It seems unfair to sweep into punishment mode when a child is genuinely unaware of using coarse language.

Ronnie Corbett starred as Timothy, a middle-aged man constantly browbeaten by his ageing mother, in the sitcom 'Sorry'. His insignificant father also regularly fell foul of his wife's mercurial temperament. He never challenged her bad temper, but always corrected Timothy whenever an exasperated outburst escaped his son's lips. I used his catchphrase 'Language, Timothy!' for years in the classroom to correct bad language. There would be a compliant smile and little precious teaching time lost. However, I continued to use the expression long after the programme was being broadcast, when pupils had no idea who Timothy might be. They looked at me slack-jawed as though I were an eccentric but, after I'd offered a brief explanation, they usually took the point in good humour.

Bullying

Teenagers, the media reports, are more likely nowadays to experience mental instability as a result of stress-related conditions, resulting in the increased incidence of self-harming, eating disorders and teenage suicide. Teachers readily cite anxiety caused by examinations, school assessments and family break-up as causes of student stress.

I did find that one of the most common causes of bullying resulted from children failing to cope with stressful domestic situations. The temptation to arrive at the simplistic conclusion that all bullies are mindless thugs who know no better is not one to which I'd subscribe. For example, 'trolls' who engage in extreme forms of online bullying are often revealed to be troubled misfits with serious personality issues.

Bullying was probably the situation that I found most difficult to deal with. It can be a taboo issue for school managers. The official line on the subject from many headteachers is, 'Bullying, of course, never happens in my school.' The truth is that cases of bullying do occur from time to time in most schools. Whenever I was alerted to the possibility of a case, I rarely rushed in with all guns blazing: the majority of allegations that I investigated turned out to be false.

I'm no expert on the types who become bullies, but the two who seriously disturbed my own childhood are still fixed in my mind. Tony was an outsize, ham-fisted, barely literate, fourteen-year-old who practised a variety of tortures on me. A year younger than Tony, I avoided him conscientiously but there were times when our paths crossed despite my caution. I instantly recall the feeling of him massaging into my skin the squashed apple core he put down the back of my school shirt. There was no point in me telling anyone because he would only raise the pain stakes the next time if he discovered I'd snitched. I subsequently learned that he had died an alcoholic in early middle age.

Barry, an only child and again a year older than me, had been spoilt rotten by his parents. Back in 1964, he was the only boy on the estate wearing Adidas trainers and Levi jeans. He was tall, lean and his short blond hair was immaculately neat. He once cleverly duped me into accompanying him to the local woods one summer afternoon, where I discovered his penchant for prolonged emotional torment that was genuinely terrifying. Fortunately I escaped before he could put into action his plans for physically damaging me.

Interestingly, neither boy had close friends, nor did the misfits socialise with boys or girls of their own age. Whenever I saw them, they were alone, the sullen expressions on their faces only lifting when their shifty-eyed curiosity was aroused. They were isolates who couldn't engage with their peers on the easy-going terms that I took for granted.

As a teacher, I was in a dilemma once I was persuaded that I was dealing with a genuine case of bullying. Procedures for dealing with those inflicting physical or emotional violence on another, possibly over a long period of time, were never as clearly defined for me as I would have liked.

Those who bully are often themselves unfortunate victims of bullying or neglect, often by members of their own family. Thus, the reluctance to risk labelling any child a 'bully', albeit out of a sense of sympathy, may be one of the reasons why long-term physical and emotional abuse of children by their peers is not an uncommon occurrence in schools. The inclination to wait as long as possible for a troublesome situation to resolve itself is all too common. It is an explanation for a failure formally to identify aggressive anti-social behaviour, and to provide the necessary protection for the vulnerable. But procrastination, albeit employed to give troubled youngsters time and space to grow out of the bullying habit, is not a good reason for failing to intervene until a situation reaches a critical juncture.

When a case does come to light, it is, therefore, likely to be a situation that has been going on for some time. I spoke to an ex-student I met recently who, during the course of our conversation, explained at length how his brother had eventually been hospitalised following an extended period of violent treatment at the hands of fellow students. An epileptic, the fifteen year old ran away from home, leaving a note for his parents explaining that he was going to commit suicide. Fortunately he was found before he could carry out the threat. The long-term emotional scars continue to trouble him. His mother had visited the school on more than one occasion to ask that her son be protected but, whatever action was taken, he continued to suffer. The ex-student gave me to believe that his brother had been targeted for ill-treatment because his medical condition distinguished him as being 'different'.

Despite my concern for the plight of those driven to bully others, I am aware that there comes a point when any concern for his or her unfortunate circumstances has to be subordinated to concern for the victim. I recommend that schools be called to demonstrate a greater commitment to following up reported instances of extreme bullying promptly. This should involve pupils as well as teachers, with student panels being set up to investigate incidents in addition to pastoral staff.

In confirmed instances of serial bullying, offenders should be withdrawn from the school system and only returned after the completion of a full support programme.

Ideally, this would comprise off-site provision, organised centrally by the education authority and staffed by child behaviour specialists. It's not enough for a school's pastoral team simply to authorise a week's exclusion that serves no useful purpose whatsoever. During the period of withdrawal, the child concerned would continue to receive tuition. One-to-one or small group teaching may provide the 'bully' with the attention required to facilitate reform. Those with a troublesome predilection for tormenting their peers require sensitive, remedial intervention if they are to be made fully aware of the seriousness of their misconduct. A point to reinforce to them is that receiving an education in the company of one's peers is a privilege.

Whenever I dealt with a boy found guilty of bullying, the first question I asked would be: 'How would you feel if a child of your own were bullied in exactly the same way that you have been bullying your victim?' The reply was often dispiriting: if he did father children, they would never be victimised because they would be tough and able to look after themselves. On hearing this response, I would then ask, 'But what if your child were born with a genetic abnormality that made him physically weak or mentally impaired?' Preparing children for the realities of adulthood, where one cannot be guaranteed having tough-guy offspring, was one of the facts of life that I did feel a duty to pass on.

The damage inflicted on those who become the targets of bullying cannot be underestimated. If children are required to attend schools, there must be a guarantee that they will not become victims of systematic cruelty, least of all from their peers.

Before the criticism is levelled at me that I am putting forward a simplistic solution to a school issue that has complex social, psychological and even financial dimensions, I offer the following anecdote. It illustrates the kind of confused situation that can occur in the absence of clearly defined procedures for dealing effectively with those who feel that they can bully others unchecked. In this case, at a loss as to how to deal with just such a student, I literally turned my back and walked away when the tables were unexpectedly turned on him.

I was a head of sixth form at the time and my job had been made far more difficult than it should have been by a sixth-form student of average ability who was a constant annoyance and threat to everyone's wellbeing. He readily abused his peers verbally, male and female, often lashed out physically at other boys when a temper tantrum got the better of him, and was strongly suspected of supplementing his income by dealing in drugs.

Matters came to a head whilst I was on break-time playground duty. From a distance I saw the troublesome student suddenly burst through a door at the rear of the school. He turned and ran full tilt towards the staff car park, pursued by another ordinarily even-tempered youth. A last-straw situation must have occurred.

Whatever the cause, the pursuer caught up with his prey just as he'd managed to reach the rear exit. At that point, what would be described in a police report as 'an altercation' took place. The troublemaker received a very bloody nose and, from the sounds I could make out, a few other bloody bits and pieces. My reaction: I did a quick about turn, before anybody might realise that I'd heard or seen anything amiss, and headed off away from the incident as quickly as possible. I wasn't proud of my conduct, but cold common sense got the better of me. For some time after this incident, that was never brought to the headteacher's attention, sixth-form life improved for everyone.

I shouldn't have behaved in the way that I did on witnessing an assault on one student by another. I also felt that I should never have been placed in that situation. A student with unpredictable violent tendencies should not be admitted to a sixth form with no effective check having been made on his errant behaviour. In that respect I was part of the problem, having reluctantly agreed to enrol him in the first place. It was to my great relief that nothing further came of the incident.

In my workaday life as a teacher, it was difficult at times to retain a sympathetic attitude towards those who seemed to enjoy indulging in regular fits of violence. Brutish instincts have to be curbed for practical as well as moral reasons: they have a disproportionately negative impact on the educational progress of those towards whom they are directed. I've taught many students of exemplary ability who were reluctant to take any part in group or class discussion for fear of being ridiculed or humiliated by envious students of sturdy physique and lashing tongue.

I never hit on a foolproof way to put a permanent stop to violent pupil behaviour. However, using the adage so beloved of lateral thinkers that there's more than one way to skin a cat, I occasionally employed one novel method that was often effective in putting a stop to bullying tendencies, whether of the physical or psychological kind. If the usual methods for dealing with such offences failed, I sometimes employed a more devious reforming strategy.

I set upon a course of using my basic knowledge of developing teenage sexuality to thwart negative designs on weaker elements within my classes. I was aware that it was fairly common for adolescents going through puberty to develop same-sex crushes before the development of heterosexual relationships in full maturity. Thus, I considered an oblique approach to the issue in question, although it was one that might have landed me in trouble if I hadn't executed it carefully enough. With my teaching group silent following the calling of the register, I moved into gear.

"I've been informed that there may be some questionable treatment of boys in this class by others sitting at this very moment before me. You'll notice that I'm not using the word 'bullying' because I don't believe that there are any bullies here. However, one or two of you may have mistaken certain types of behaviour that you've witnessed as bullying.

"I've seen students involved in rough and tumbles in the playground when I've been on duty at lunchtimes and I know that this is perfectly natural for boys of your age. You are all officially going through what is termed puberty, the stage between childhood and adulthood. It's common for boys and, of course, girls, to experience emotional confusion during this time in your lives. As teenagers encounter awakening sexuality, they can become confused about gender issues.

"A lot of the behaviour that teachers and students mistakenly refer to as 'bullying' could possibly be called 'attraction'. When one boy aggressively manhandles another or abuses him verbally, that may be his confused way of showing his admiration or liking for that person. So, before we start to get upset that somebody is a victim of bullying, or that there are bullies in the room, we should calm down and accept that we may simply be observing one student's confused attempt to show affection for another, which is not in the least anything to be worried about."

As may be imagined, the moment I used the word 'sexuality', my audience was stunned into silence. This is a word for teachers to use with the utmost caution when talking to big, tough adolescents. By the end of my informative speech, those boys in the room I was specifically targeting would be looking at me with some concern, the phrase, 'I'm not gay!' hammering away behind their temporal lobes.

Before I am judged to have exploited teenage boys' irrational fears of homosexuality, I should say in my defence that everything I said to my classes on this topic has a theoretical basis. Indeed, children are at a disadvantage if nobody ever talks openly to them about puberty and sexual attraction generally. Same-sex attraction is one of the behavioural norms in our society to which developing minds must become accustomed, whether they like it or not. My long-term hope is that, one day in a brighter future, the word 'homosexual' will no longer be in use.

Boffs

I've witnessed many pupils who start out on their secondary school careers full of innocent enthusiasm, keenly putting up their hands to answer questions and express their views, but who have become taciturn and reserved as a result of their intelligence and enthusiasm being ridiculed by an envious and disruptive minority in the classroom. A consequence of the insidious trend of negative peer pressure is that intelligence, for some, becomes an attribute to be hidden from the public gaze.

I recall having to organise a series of conversations with a timid A-Level Physics student who was being encouraged by his teachers to apply for Oxbridge. Throughout his time at secondary school, he had been an easy target for being a 'boff' and his self-esteem had taken a battering. The fact that his hair had an auburn tinge gave his tormentors even more ammunition. I found myself in the situation of having to convince a seventeen-year-old boy that he wasn't the social leper he considered himself to be, but an exceptional young man with the highest academic potential I had ever encountered. It took several meetings with his tutor and further one-to-one contact with me before he could even begin to consider coping with an Oxbridge interview. I'm pleased to write that he eventually gained a place at Cambridge, one of the school successes that gives me particular pleasure.

One of my younger students once told me during an English lesson that the boy sitting next to him, his supposed friend, had called him a 'boff'. Always anxious to dismiss any potential for friends falling out, I assumed an expression of exaggerated delight and said to the whole class, 'I always dreamed of being called a boff, but I was never intelligent enough.'

I then talked about the fact that the 'boff' in question was, indeed, far more intelligent than I had ever been at his age and that he probably had a great future ahead of him. Young boys are as materialistic as the rest of the general population, so I went on to talk about the financial benefits that would probably come his way as an adult if he continued to develop his gifts. It was ludicrous that I felt the need to resort to presenting the extrinsic rewards of intelligence in order to put a positive slant on a boy being exceptionally able. Appeals to overt materialism do not sit happily with me, but one sometimes clutches at desperate remedies in tight situations. The reflex action of giving a detention to a pupil who unthinkingly uses the term 'boff' achieves nothing.

Cussing

Cussing, the verbal intimidation that students use against their peers appeared almost overnight in the mid-'90s in my teaching career. My colleagues and I were initially bemused when we first heard students trying to needle each other by the use of the two words 'your mum'. When I eventually found out that this was shorthand for 'Your mum's a whore', I was stunned. The sickening effect of the derogatory sexual reference is compounded by the sheer cowardice inherent in the abuse. Here were boys I thought I knew well, and respected, resorting to a form of attack that, from my perspective, was cowardly on two counts: 1) the objects of scorn were the female sex, and 2) the women in question weren't present to defend themselves. I knew many pupils' mothers who would have had no trouble administering an immediate and painful rebuke to any young boy who might have been foolhardy enough to make such a statement in their hearing.

I eventually reached a point of absolute impatience with one class in which there were a few older students who abused each other aloud across the room with a selection of cusses. After one of the boys had stated 'Your mum!' to the other, I looked at him, smiled and said, 'My mum.' I'd had enough and simply wanted to establish the pointless stupidity of this sort of language. He probably thought I was insane, but the rest of the class made the connection that I thought he was being idiotic. I experienced fewer problems from him after this intervention, but the general problem continued to escalate.

Teachers also became the victims of cussing. During my teaching career, I was told more than once by an angry youngster 'I know where you live.' I had occasionally

179

experienced students losing their tempers in the classroom and directing their anger at me personally. Typically, I was told to 'Shut up!' or 'Fuck off!' once or twice, but this new audacious phenomenon did unsettle me the first time I heard it. I'd never encountered this sinister intention to unnerve a member of staff emotionally before. My only counter to defuse the situation at the time was to invite the student to drop in for a chat any time he was passing.

Although not as openly rife as it had been by the time I retired, cussing was still in evidence. I don't know where the phenomenon originated, but I sincerely hope it will eventually disappear.

Sexuality

I was unaware of the expression 'Nancy-boy' until I heard teachers at the grammar school I attended using it to berate boys who fell short of their high expectations in the classroom, on the athletics track and on the rugby field. I can clearly recall the individual members of staff who, for example, thought nothing of directing this expression loudly from the touchline at a boy missing a tackle during a school match. Teachers may no longer be heard engaging openly in homophobia, but it continues to be a casual form of verbal abuse used by teenagers.

Homosexuality was more of an issue with boys of secondary school age than I could ever have imagined. The word 'gay', spoken with as much venom as could be mustered, was the customary means by which one boy insulted another. Nothing else they could come up with was, to them, quite as injurious. Some teachers shrugged it off but I couldn't. I was told by worldly-wise colleagues that the word meant nothing coming from the mouths of adolescents and I shouldn't be bothered by it. But it did bother me, and I felt compelled to pull up those who used this method of name-calling whenever I heard it, which was often.

Some of the pupils I corrected even told me that they didn't mean anything by it, assuming that I was taking the whole matter too seriously. It was as though they were implying I was a spoilsport for not joining in 'the fun'. I find that the hypocrisy surrounding the matter of sexual orientation will continue to be with us, unless people with adult attitudes put a lid on it. We are now well advanced into the twenty-first century, but it's still a talking point in the media when a celebrity 'comes out'.

Conversely, precocious teenage boys have to be warned off talking loosely about good old red-blooded heterosexuality, particularly if they start throwing in off-the-cuff remarks about local girls with whom they've had the pleasure. From my experience of teaching in a single-sex comprehensive school, the quality of boys' informal conversation on sexual matters deteriorates if it is allowed to run for more than about ten seconds, which is why I always put it to bed, so to speak, if it ever came up. Biology teachers, I knew, dealt with the practical aspects of reproduction without interruption because boys get very squeamish the moment they're shown footage of childbirth. There were a number of standard student conversations that had to be terminated the moment my radar detected them:

1) The physical attributes of a female member of staff;

2) Escapades with students from the secondary girls' school down the road;

3) Adult-rated films they'd recently watched;

4) The content of X-rated music videos – with frequent references to 'booties'.

Whenever I read to a class of GCSE students the passage from *Of Mice and Men* in which Lennie kills Curley's wife, you could smell the testosterone in the air. Unfortunately, my estimation of this novel's literary merit is diminished as a result. I felt genuinely uncomfortable about reading this section to teenage boys. The consensus from the more vocal element of whatever class I was teaching over the twenty years or so that Steinbeck's novel featured on the syllabus was that Curley's wife was a 'tramp' looking for sex, and there was limited success in my trying to persuade these particular pupils that she was merely lonely and looking for company.

What Lennie does to Curley's wife was what this section of my teaching group believed she deserved. Any of the more intelligent ones before me knew that to agree openly with me that Curley's wife deserves the reader's sympathy would be foolhardy. It would be better to express such a viewpoint in their writing, if pressed on the point, but on no account should they say it aloud. I knew that it was preferable to cut discussion short on this matter to prevent the more outspoken 'lads' in the classroom from voicing ignorant personal prejudice.

Deathly silence fell over a class of whatever age if I ever broached the subject of homosexuality. It came as a shock to the collective red-blooded teenage ego when I pointed out that homosexuality is now a societal norm throughout the civilised world.

I felt an obligation throughout my career to disavow adolescents of any predisposition to use sexual references as a means of disrespecting others, male or female. The zeitgeist of many amongst today's adolescent boys seems disturbingly darker and more cynical than the liberal-minded and outgoing outlook that characterised my teenage generation.

On a lighter note, I had a lot of fun when hair gel came into its own as an adolescent fashion accessory during the 1980s. I felt it my duty to advise boys against the use of this 'dangerous' product that they believed made them instantly attractive to the fairer sex. The danger of the product, I regularly pointed out, was that it caused premature baldness. I'd read this somewhere and took great enjoyment teasing those who slapped it on liberally. My constant reminders that their domes would resemble billiard balls by the time they were thirty fell on deaf ears. I was dismissed as a scaremonger universally.

However, matters came to a head at one of the annual rugby fixtures when the School XV took on the local old boys' team. I was one of the few teachers representing the School XV, comprising mainly 1st XV players with the addition of a few members of staff to add extra interest to the fixture. I discreetly pointed out to the schoolboys every member of the opposition who was deficient in the hair department. They were young men I'd taught, several of whom were in their mid to late twenties. Each time I drew the boys' attention to one of these hairless ex-students, I whispered, "He used to use hair gel." I suddenly became the man of truth, the prophet whose outpourings on the secrets of a syrup-free lifestyle must never be ignored again. What larks!

11. In Sickness and in Health

Sick Notes

The joke that teachers have three months off every year tends to grate after you've heard it for the hundredth time, but it may be one of the reasons why the profession as a whole avoids throwing 'sickies'. Those with whom I worked were invariably conscientious in the extreme when it came to attendance and time-keeping, many arriving a good hour before the start of the school day, and leaving well after the end-of-school bell. In most other job environments employees go for the sensible option when sickness strikes by taking time off to recover. But, strange as it may seem, teachers are more than likely to turn up for work when they should be nursing an illness at home. Teaching still carries the 'vocation' label for the majority. The pride associated with being in a worthwhile career is responsible for the professional reflex to struggle on when illness strikes.

As a supplement to classroom teaching, additional duties and responsibilities make the workload increasingly onerous. Being ill is a real fear for teachers. There are serious repercussions for taking time off owing to sickness. Not only do busy colleagues have to cover one's lessons, but the paper jam also builds up in one's in-tray with every day taken off. Coping with an accumulated mountain of admin alone is a major challenge on returning to the fray, especially bearing in mind that a full teaching timetable also awaits.

The 'performance' aspect of teaching means that the typical classroom teacher runs high on the 'fighting' drug adrenaline throughout the day. The high stress levels that are characteristic of the job result in the continuous production of this hormone, raising blood pressure and increasing heart rate in the process. A build-up of adrenaline is also known to trigger anxiety symptoms that can be difficult to control. Experience taught me that when the flow of this drug is interrupted through illness, or even a holiday break, physical and emotional complications are inevitable. I could be certain that I would go down with something debilitating soon after the end of a term or half term, the moment my resistance was lowered.

I once fell ill with a flu virus early in my career before I'd become fully aware of the physical demands of teaching. Lindsey tells me I was hallucinating for a few days and explaining very convincingly that I was certainly going to die. In the last ten years of my career, all staff were encouraged by the head to have a free flu jab, not a common practice in other walks of life. Aware as I now am that when teachers take time off it's often an extended absence of several days or more, the headteacher's precaution was understandable.

PCs and Health

Deadlines for the preparation of examination coursework, marking, report writing, and so on cannot be missed. I maintain that, when it comes to work-place efficiency, keeping on top of every aspect of the job, teachers are an exceptional breed. Administration doesn't wait in schools; the 'mañana' attitude practised by many business

185

organisations with which I've had dealings would not be tolerated in teaching; there is a constant stream of 'paperwork' to be completed – now! The personal computer, a wonderfully creative tool in the right environment, has become the greatest threat to teachers' sanity. It's impossible to escape the laptop. It has to be loaded up daily with classroom lessons, taken to the staff room during breaks and lunch times, and accompany one home to do an additional two or three hours in the evening. When it packs up from time to time, as mine often did, the teacher becomes a gibbering half-wit, unable to do anything in the school day until it's been repaired by one of the 'tekkies'.

I once kept a record of time spent on my laptop during a typical school day. I discovered that I'd spent five hours teaching children, using my laptop in each lesson, and an additional five hours outside of contact time. Mental fatigue through screen strain is as prevalent amongst staff as physical wear and tear. The irony is that we advise children not to spend hours on end sitting in front of a computer or games console screen because it's unhealthy.

As has proved to be the case in most areas of life, the invention of the personal computer has not resulted in employees spending less time on record-keeping tasks, freeing them up to be more hands-on. It has increased workload by the creation of more and more data records. Computers have the capacity to store every aspect of children's performance and behaviour. Thus, this is the level of detail that the nation's teaching force is required to record. The only information missing is blood group.

I'm unable to see the justification for storing data in such detail. Fifty years ago there was nothing like the record keeping on children because there were no computers, but most children came through the system comparatively undamaged. I've spent a lot of time in hospitals over the past ten years visiting ailing family members, and have seen how nurses have caught the same PC disease that teachers have been suffering from for the past twenty. Much of the time nursing staff used to spend with patients, they are now spending at the nurses' 'station', hammering away at keypads. Accountability is replacing approachability everywhere. Teachers have to satisfy the insatiable appetites of school intranets on a daily basis, and feeding time is usually every spare moment that can be found.

I suffer from a medical condition called labyrinthitis, a problem with the inner ear mechanism. When it strikes, I suffer from acute nausea, identical to sea sickness, even when stationary. In my case it's induced by, amongst other things, stress resulting from concentrating on small screens for long periods. I was a regular sufferer whilst teaching, and only coped thanks to medication being permanently to hand. Since retiring, I haven't had a single bout.

Let me offer you just one example of record keeping that has become de rigueur in the world of secondary education. Fifteen years ago or more, a computer package was bought by my school to record good (merit mark) and bad (demerit mark) lesson behaviour and performance. All staff members were encouraged to reward pupils as often as possible and to enter details of merit and demerit awards on the school database. (I'd like to tell you what it was called, but it's a rule of mine to avoid the possibility of litigatory action wherever possible.) Now this all sounds wonderfully positive. Unfortunately it was hugely time-consuming. The necessary fields to complete per entry included the date of the award/incident; subject area; award details; teacher's name;

187

etc. At the end of the year, the thousands of merits and demerits for each of the school's 'houses' would be totted up and one house would be declared the overall winner. Cue wild celebrations during assembly.

One could spend an additional hour or more a day at a laptop recording information from every contact lesson. The 'advice' to reward as often as possible to keep children motivated had to be followed, or questions would be asked of those staff who were failing to 'encourage', as per instructions. One trod a dangerous path if one failed to meet an appropriate half-termly merit quota. The excuse 'I am smoking a fag!' always fell on deaf ears. I'm certainly not against the idea of extrinsic rewards for achievement. But when such a system described above assumes monumental-task proportions for hard-pressed teachers, common sense would suggest that an alternative be found. It was always an awkward moment in a lesson when a pupil's reaction to being complimented for answering a question correctly was, 'Can I have a merit, then?' Next stop teacher apoplexy.

Software companies constantly target schools for all sorts of 'essential' packages. Whether or not class teachers want the latest all-singing, all-dancing, new improved record-keeping and information packages, school management teams feel obliged to introduce them to keep pace with the competition – i.e. every other school in the country. Accountability casts a long shadow in education, and the more detailed the breakdown of school performance that an institution can produce the better, so I was regularly told.

Teaching now requires high-level computing skills, whatever subject one teaches. In my own experience, colleagues reliably kept pace with providing whatever raw data was required, often with minimal training in whatever

188

program they were obliged to use. I concede that I bent accountability rules to a certain extent when I was running my own English department in order to rationalise the workload for those in my department. Since that time, however, the software deluge has hit the education world, and there is no way of evading the packages bought in their bucketloads by schools.

The serious point I'm making here is that teachers in the state sector have been the butt of untold criticism as a profession for decades, but the truth is that the workforce maintains an exemplary approach, whatever duties are required of them. However much individual workload increases, the expectation is that everything will be done immaculately, and it usually is. The physical demands on one's stamina to complete tasks outside of contact time are now equal to or exceed those required to get through one's teaching timetable.

Sick Children

The classroom is a highly contagious environment. By my calculation, there were at least a dozen different bugs or viruses in my room at any one time. Parents have to get to work just as badly as teachers, with the result that children in varying degrees of sickness find themselves being sent to school. It's one of the facts of a teacher's life that parents believe they have the right to scream blue murder at you if you treat their offspring with anything other than the utmost respect, whatever the situation. But they'll invariably send their children to school when they're fit to drop. I've also found myself having to manage children who turn up for the school day as high as kites. When a giggling fifteen-year-old student slapped my face whilst I was on playground duty, I suggested that he was under the influence of a class 'A' drug. His parents were called in and made angry denials that he had taken any mind-altering substance. They were in no mood to give me an apology.

I would take as many precautions as possible to keep myself germ-free. Much as I had every sympathy for children who lack the hygiene standards in which my wife has trained me, I avoided contact with their viruses. I tried wearing latex gloves once when marking a pile of exercise books at home. It seemed a good idea on two counts: 1) protection from germs that are hiding inside the pages as well as those posing brazenly on the covers, and 2) eliminating the temptation to put a finger anywhere near the mouth. It's a pity you can't take a box of these gloves to school, but people talk. It didn't work because my hands sweated and it takes a lot of soap to get rid of the smell of rubber.

There are all sorts of signs to look out for if you wish to protect yourself from children's ailments. Vomiting is usually a pretty good one, especially the projectile variety. Many's the student I've had to send to the little boys' room to wash off the diced carrot stuck to the back of his head. If a student throws up whilst you are teaching, find another classroom tout de suite. However tempted you may be to clear up the mess with your whiteboard rubber, resist it. Leave it to the experts. Caretakers are still equipped with mop buckets and disinfectant by the tankload.

What I used to call the 'death mask' is another giveaway. The child who arrives at your classroom door deathly white and shivering is most definitely ill. Arrange for another pupil to accompany the death-mask casualty to the nurse. But resist any temptation you may have to put a consoling arm around the patient's shoulder – remain at arm's length or further.

Sneezing repeatedly or barking like a dog are symptoms that are more difficult to deal with. We have come to accept that everyone develops colds and hacking coughs, but they are not deemed worthy of specialist medical help. As a result, from mid-October to the end of April, a teacher can assume that a minimum of three children sitting in the classroom are suffering from a cold or flu at any one time. I wasn't allowed to teach with a builder's protective face mask, so I had to adopt an alternative autumn/winter survival policy. I sucked little brown throat sweets that fishermen apparently swear by. They have the effect of creating what I can only describe as a furnace effect in the mouth that, I believe, will incinerate 99% of juvenile germs. After the initial two-year period of acclimatising your mouth to the heat generated by these innocent-looking tablets, you'll never look back.

A Sick Story

Nevertheless, sickness inevitably strikes a teacher once or twice during the winter months, and I, like many others, regularly arrived for work feeling rough. The favourite was a sore throat that occasionally developed into a chest infection. I was a physically healthy sort throughout my career, but these conditions hit me from time to time – drawbacks of the trade. A teacher who turns up for work feeling ill is still expected to perform to the usual high standard. There is no opportunity to keep a low profile for a few days in this job until relatively good health returns. At such times, when energy and patience levels are low, the likelihood of doing something you regret is increased.

I used to tell my classes when I was feeling under the weather, in the hope that they would sympathise and cut me a bit of slack by behaving impeccably. I felt particularly confident that my form group could be relied upon to take pity on me. My first strategy for eliciting sympathy would be to put the following message up on the blackboard (pre-1995) or the whiteboard (post-1995): 'I'm not feeling well today. My throat hurts when I speak so don't do anything that may require me to speak to you.' This, of course, was like a red rag to a bull to the more vocal smart Alecs in the group who would take great pleasure in baiting me: 'What exactly is it you're suffering from, sir?'/'What illness is it this time, sir?'/'Do you want me to take over the lesson for you today, sir?' and so on. Such playfulness I could take, but illness does reduce one's capacity for patience. Sooner or later I'd say or do something I regretted when, normally, I would just laugh it off. Pubescent teenagers are outwardly resilient, but inwardly they are more vulnerable than we assume and wound easily.

A sick teacher is an unpredictable and, sometimes, dangerous animal, and I was no exception. I've bawled out pupils for very little reason when the balance of my mind was impaired by a high temperature or constant pain.

I made a serious mistake once when I had two wisdom teeth removed one morning and insisted on returning to school in the afternoon. My wife told me I was mad, and she was proved right. I'd chosen local anaesthetic for the extractions as I wanted to be fully conscious for my two classes after lunch. Besides taking my GCSE class through a vital practice paper, I had an important meeting to attend after school.

Experiencing little pain after the thirty-minute operation, and paying strict attention to the dentist's advice not to chew the inside of my mouth whilst my jaw was numb, I hurried off to school, armed with a box of painkillers. Ten minutes later I was pulling into the car park, feeling a little light-headed but determined to cope. I went straight to the staff room and took a double dose of the painkillers I'd been prescribed with a little water. By the time I was due to take my form group for afternoon registration both sides of my upper jaw were aching. I popped another couple of painkillers into my mouth and swallowed hard.

My GCSE class arrived in dribs and drabs, but I was in no state to hurry them along. Getting into teacher mode proved to be more difficult than I'd imagined. When I raised myself out of my seat the room swayed. Eventually I had a full class before me, but I realised that teaching them would be beyond me. The front row looked at me quizzically, waiting for some instruction.

I asked two boys to hand out the practice papers I'd placed on the edge of my desk, and gave instructions for the students to answer an essay question we'd previously planned. Something rose in my craw as I went to my walk-in cupboard at the front of the classroom to fetch some spare ball pens. Without warning, I vomited all over my tidy cupboard floor. It was mostly fluid and splattered on to packs of green exercise books wrapped in transparent plastic. I steadied myself on a book rack, then doubled over as I threw up again, this time in the direction of a pile of shabby dictionaries.

Leaning against a bookshelf, I pulled a tissue from my pocket and wiped my mouth. Dizziness was getting the better of me, but I couldn't allow myself to pass out whilst in charge of a class. I hauled myself upright and straightened my tie. I broke out into a cold sweat as I exited the store room and shuffled towards the chair at my desk. One or two class members looked up from their work and regarded me through narrowed eyes. I smiled weakly and managed to mutter 'Oh, forgot the spare pens'. My chest began to heave again and I hurtled back into the cupboard. The dictionaries received another splattering. I could only think that I'd overdosed on the painkillers and my stomach was in revolt. The cold sweat came again, but the room at least stopped swaying.

After a minute of resting with my head on my arms, I knew that I had to venture back into the classroom. I vowed that I would never go near a dentist again. As I slumped into my chair, a voice piped up from the front, 'You all right, sir?'

'Yes thanks, Asif,' I replied. 'Just an attack of wind.'

'Do you want me to go to the nurse for you?' he enquired, sensing that he was on to a bullet-proof work-evasion strategy.

'That's kind of you,' I replied, forcing a weak I-know-your-game smile. 'If I lose consciousness, could you be the one to go to the school office to order an ambulance? For now we'll all just soldier on.'

I don't remember anything further about that particular lesson, other than the fact that I did survive it. Curiously, I don't remember cleaning up my cupboard, but I certainly did because I wouldn't have dreamt of anyone else finding out about the only lesson I ever taught having OD'd on drugs.

The point of recounting this episode is that I'm not unusual: teachers in general have the same professional mindset. They're accustomed to being top of the list when it comes to receiving flak from parents, the press and politicians, but their instinct is to turn up for work unless there is the threat of imminent collapse. The demands of the job continue to increase, but teachers take every additional responsibility on board, not always uncomplaining, and do the very best they can.

The jokes about long holidays never made any impression on my conscience: nobody who hasn't taught can have any idea of the levels of exhaustion resulting from teaching. Every lesson is a performance, which has to be supported by written plans, and no two lessons are ever the same. In my case, as an English teacher with full KS3, KS4 and KS5 workloads, I could reckon on adding another thirty to forty hours a week with marking and other additional responsibilities. This is the price teachers have been prepared to pay in order to have the privilege of working with children. Unfortunately, the workload is now such that, for many, the prospect of a lifelong vocation has lost some of its gloss.

In ancient Greece, teachers were revered, but in the UK today teachers are more likely to be reviled. My explanation for this harsh assessment: philistine Britain is the wrong time and place to be respected as a teacher. I'm optimistic enough to hope that attitudes will improve. If you are intending to teach, screw your courage to the sticking place, stiffen your backbone and sign up. Pay no attention to the brickbats hurled by philistines. Sick or not, children deserve your enthusiasm and commitment.

12. Distractions

Teaching children is a wonderful vocation, but wonder is becoming an unaffordable luxury in schools in the twenty-first century. The expression 'school shit' sums up for me the hapless tinkering with the education system by successive education ministers between 1973 and 2010 whilst I was teaching. I need to elaborate here. I never railed on publicly about the downward slide that state education was taking whilst teaching, deluding myself that I, and like-minded others, could change the system from within. But people change. It's time for me to take the advice of Dylan Thomas: a bit of rage can't do any harm at this stage in my life and will be good therapy for me.

The Demise of Team Sports in Secondary Schools

Margaret Thatcher, the education minister at the start of my career, had already made a name for herself in 1970 as 'the milk snatcher' by scrapping free school milk for seven to eleven year olds. It's also likely that she had as little interest in sport as in the milk of human kindness because, when she came to power as Prime Minister, she gave education authorities the right to sell off surplus land, with the result that approximately 5,000 school playing fields are reported to have disappeared during her time in office.

This development was a mortal blow to the many teachers who put in a lot of unpaid time at weekends to foster participation in sport. I willingly turned out on Saturday mornings in order to assist the PE department with school football and rugby teams. I enjoyed the out-of-classroom interaction enormously. However, opposition teams suddenly started to disappear.

Thatcher's short-sighted policy resulted in a significant proportion of a generation of children no longer having the facilities available at school to enable them to exploit their many and varied sporting talents. It may have been one of the reasons why substantial numbers of secondary school pupils, unable to play football at school, started throwing basketballs into nets that subsequently began to appear in playgrounds. I'm all for varied physical exercise, but watching a boy trying to lob a basketball into a hoop non-stop for fifteen minutes whilst I was on break duty did strike me as being a rather minimalist approach to attaining sporting proficiency. Witnessing the boys' low success rates, I often used to stand directly under a basket during my playground duty. The reason I gave to NBA draft aspirants was that, with basketballs flying around in all directions in the playground, I felt it the safest place to position myself.

The chancellor's budget of March 2016 struck an ironic chord when I heard the announcement of a new sugar tax on the soft drinks industry to be introduced a few years down the line. The proceeds, in excess of £500 million a year, were to go towards financing more sporting activities in schools. An image of bolting horses springs to mind.

The Folly of the Core Curriculum

In the 1980s, Sir Keith Joseph started the ball rolling to introduce the National Curriculum, an opus completed by Kenneth Baker. The consequence, in the opinion of many people, myself included, was to generate a largely content-based curriculum. The if-you-can't-measure-it-ditch-it approach to the curriculum has blighted children's education for the past twenty five years. I was a Head of English at this time and had to spend hours drawing up the most unwieldy school document that I've ever had to produce: The National Curriculum English Handbook.

I'm sure that fellow subject heads in state schools up and down the country suffered with me. No intelligent person, surely, could have enjoyed what proved to be one of the most mind-numbing exercises I have ever been required to undertake. The process involved breaking down every single English classroom activity for all age groups into a range of tasks that could be assessed. The idea was that teachers could then start each lesson with a handy checklist of graded tasks, enabling them to enter countless ticks during lessons against pupils' names. Thus, as a department, we would be able to provide evidence (education's Holy Grail) of what each pupil could 'do' in each area of the 'curriculum'. Teachers could no longer comment on an individual pupil's performance, or levels of ability one should say, without providing evidence; i.e. ticks. National Curriculum levels, the poisoned chalice of teaching, were with us to stay. In addition to producing my own department's document, I also assisted a Drama teacher with the completion of his handbook during countless after-school get-togethers, which he appositely referred to as 'treacle-bending sessions'.

Paper Chases

The handbook I worked on also had to include a stack of policy statements on everything that went on in my department. I had to cover every topic from pupil self-assessment to marking. The only way that I could retain my sanity whilst flogging through the interminable task was to throw in a few spurious inclusions. I drew up the English Department Policy on Students Sticking Chewing Gum Under the Table, and another on Strategies to Eliminate Sizeism in the Classroom.

Treacle bending would probably have been easier than this level of record keeping. I had the shameful responsibility of producing thousands upon thousands of pupil evidence sheets ('bullshine' sheets) for a decade or more. This unfortunate period in my career resulted in me developing a deep-seated distrust of any document that purports to include 'evidence'. I'm no longer a great believer in evidence in any area of human activity.

Every teacher needed a laptop to store the vast banks of evidence, information that could be called up at the drop of a Christmas party hat to bamboozle some poor unsuspecting Ofsted inspector when the need arose. It gave a whole new twist to the expression Random Access Memory. In practice, I advised my English colleagues to try their hardest to carry on as normal in the classroom, paying lip service only to National Curriculum English where humanly possible. So long as we had the smoke screen of a two-hundred page handbook with which to misdirect inspectors, we could continue ploughing our own furrows – i.e. teaching English.

I hasten to add that we didn't behave irresponsibly as a department. Fortified by our sense of professionalism, we maintained our positive work ethic, and our SAT and GCSE results regularly compared favourably with other secondary schools in the area.

Resistance

I have to explain that in the first year that the key stage 3 tests were introduced, they were not compulsory. As I was ideologically opposed to them, and my fellow English-teaching colleagues shared the same view, my first job was to inform the school head that we wouldn't be taking part in the new assessment scheme. Tony was a likeable, large-framed, loud-voiced, heavily-bearded man who put me in mind of Brian Blessed. However, the fact that he was about a foot taller than 'P.C. 'Fancy' Smith made him an even more intimidating prospect, should one ever get on the wrong side of his good nature.

Tony's cheery and avuncular personality belied his shrewd, no-nonsense management style. I knew the sign to look out for if he intended to give me short shrift. He had a habit of turning his head to one side, and looking sidelong at one with wide eyes, just as Robert Newton frequently did in his television role as Long John Silver. If he did this, I knew that I might as well get my coat. My decision would be putting him in an awkward position, as he was always keen to maintain as professional a stance as possible in the eyes of parents and governors. Putting him on a potential collision course with parents, who idolised him, was not what I would wish for him. The fact that the Mathematics and Science departments had decided that they did want the tests for Year 9 increased my unease. But I trusted in Tony being a fair man.

I was mightily relieved when he agreed that the English department would be free to do as we wished. However, there was a proviso: I had to attend a special evening meeting with the Year 9 boys' parents, that he would organise, in order to explain my reasons for opting out of the English SAT. This was a headmaster stroke by Tony; I think he imagined that I might reverse my decision when faced with this sort of situation. However, I was a man on an educational mission. I stuck to my guns and duly turned up to face the music on the designated evening.

The turnout of parents was unexpectedly high, and I suddenly realised all too clearly that this meeting would be no formality and I could be in for quite a grilling. With my cheery-faced head sitting next to me, I stood and said my piece, with all the dignity I could muster. I then invited questions from the floor. What a response! I'd never seen so many hands waving to attract my attention. It was as though I'd asked the assembled audience if anybody wanted a tenner. With very few exceptions, most of the parents were hostile to the position that my department and I had taken up. One irate gentleman even accused me of being 'a coward', adding that I was frightened of the new tests.

Any nervousness I was experiencing up to this point evaporated and my blood rose. I raised my right arm, pointed at the individual and was about to express my ire when an even brawnier arm brushed me to one side. Tony hastily stood up, thanked the parents for coming along and expressing their views and closed the meeting. He was always very astute when dealing with difficult pupils, and he showed here that he was just as adept at dealing with their difficult parents. He probably saved my career in that one moment. I was no hothead by any means, but the low blow of the accusation of cowardice had seriously disturbed my emotional equilibrium.

The confrontation taught me a valuable lesson. Never underestimate the power of the test. Most parents, it seemed, loved formal assessment because it not only enabled them to check up on the progress of their children, but also, more important, provided an opportunity to check up on the teachers' performance – apparently. How could I have been so naïve to assume that anyone in their right mind would oppose my considered and professional judgement!

Teaching to the Test

Every professional instinct told me to avoid teaching exclusively to the test at all costs. And there were plenty of tests – oral tests, practice tests, timed tests, end-of-year tests, formal tests – resulting in less teaching. However, in the surreal national-curriculum world, it often proved unavoidable.

I still cling to the belief that introducing children to complete works of worthwhile literature is the best starting point for teaching any aspect of English. The National Curriculum left English teachers with precious little time to enjoy studying complete novels, plays, or poetry anthologies with classes. National Curriculum English, from my vantage point, comprised a compendium of codswallop that teachers had to wade through, and which elicited minimal emotional or intellectual engagement from pupils or, indeed, teachers. The experience of comparing and contrasting the openings of three classic children's novels can never compare with the excitement of reading, for example, 'Treasure Island' in full with a class. My department and I believed in the value of reading whole books, as opposed to recommended extracts, so we had to steal time from national-curriculum time. This meant that it was even more important to maintain our colour-coded collation of record sheets that nobody took seriously until the Ofsted inspectors arrived. (My apologies to those educational professionals who are offended by the idea that a teacher is like a road sweeper without a broom if s/he isn't equipped with detailed documentation on everything from "What to look for in a piece of GCSE homework to indicate if it's a grade 'C-' or 'D+'" to "Departmental policy on the protocols of conducting a classroom discussion".)

The Teacher as Aunt Sally

Governments of whatever persuasion instinctively don't trust teachers, so our deception was doing no serious harm to anyone. I had complete faith in the professionalism of my department, but I knew that, by official standards, we were fifth columnists.

As a profession, teachers have long become accustomed to being on the receiving end of criticism and abuse from politicians who have temporarily taken on the education portfolio. Michael Gove's description of so-called 'politically-motivated' teachers as 'Marxists' and 'enemies of promise' reinforced the profession's tacit understanding that the government of whatever day perceives the everyday state-school teacher as an Aunt Sally. When one takes up a teaching post in a state school, one joins the whipping boys and girls of the professional world. Political administrations down through the decades have done their damnedest to ensure that public respect for this branch of the public service is permanently maintained at a low regulo.

Whenever anybody tried to goad me into a robust response to their, sometimes playful, vilification and denunciation of the teaching profession, which happened frequently, I learned that it was best to remain silent and composed. This unexpectedly muted reaction was usually followed by frank admissions from the loud-mouthed lay person in question that 1) 'Anyone choosing to teach as a career must be mad,' and 2) 'If I had to teach some of these - ------ (expletive noun in the plural form withheld) I see on the streets, I'd end up throttling them.' The inescapable implication is that teachers are people who have a low marble count. The other acknowledged truism is that the thickest of skins is vital for survival as a teacher.

I have a message for those members of the general public who have been brainwashed into believing in the absolute incompetence of teachers. Those claiming to be the proud possessors of wit, the appreciation of the incongruous, like to trot out the following tired old assertion from George Bernard Shaw's *Man and Superman*: 'Those who can, do; those can't, teach.' My immediate rejoinder to this attempt at cleverness is 'Those who can't teach become Ofsted inspectors.' To my knowledge there are limitations to the system of quality control checks on the appointment of inspectors. Indeed, David Lowe, a former headteacher wrote in the 'Times Educational Supplement' on the 17th March 2014 that 'some headteachers who have been dismissed or resigned following a poor inspection are being hired as inspectors'. Inconsistencies in Ofsted's lesson observation criteria are also worrying; for example, teacher-led classroom activities (Heaven forbid!) may be criticised in one school observation yet found to be acceptable in another.

Classroom teachers should not be the first port of call when management teams go gunning for those apparently responsible for the failure consistently to produce top-end exam results. Poorly-performing pedagogues walk in fear during the September examination review, sweating on their short- or long-term employment prospects. This is the main reason why so many teachers are on short-term contracts –

they're eminently disposable during the autumn cull. I've known bad teachers who should never have got beyond the school gates, but I've known many more good teachers who have been beaten down by a narrowing of the curriculum and a consequently flawed assessment system.

Teacher Morale

The morale of the teaching profession suffered a major setback when the 1265 hours of directed time was put in place. The total may initially have seemed reasonable, but the requirement that teachers make themselves available for this minimum number of hours annually for 'directed' duties created widespread confusion and dissension. The irony was that the agreement was part of a policy to reduce teacher workload. For me, the figure was irrelevant: it took no account of the fact that I would have to work at least an additional 1265 hours a year to carry out my non-directed duties effectively. Arguments about tasks that teachers should and should not be doing as 'directed time 'resulted in widespread dissipation of genuine teacher goodwill, that impulse to volunteer for a host of extra-curricular activities. As previously stated, it was common for many state-school non-PE specialist teachers, in addition to PE staff, to supervise weekend sports fixtures, but much of this goodwill was lost overnight. When I retired, the comprehensive where I had taught for thirty one years was one of only a handful in the London area to provide a full programme of weekend and after-school sports fixtures for its students. Opposition teams were almost entirely from the private sector.

The logical conclusion of many in the profession to the absurdity of directed time became obvious: 'If I'm contracted to work for 1,265 hours a year, 1,265 hours is what they'll get.' Nowadays, it's not a good idea to put labels on things unnecessarily.

Hammering teachers' pensions was another policy that further stiffened the resolve of the majority of my colleagues effectively to do no more than what was demanded of them. National strikes by teaching unions are no longer the rare occurrences they once were. It is unjust to label one a 'militant' if that person decides to strike for one day because the pension terms set out at the start of one's employment are turned on their head several years down the line.

Teachers were the subject of shock-horror newspaper revelations when the press reported in October 2015 that a record number of 49,120 teachers had left the profession in a single year, between November 2013 and November 2014. I define 'shock-horror' news stories as items that cause one to gasp with dismay, but are forgotten within twenty four hours. The news that more of our teachers are now choosing to find work abroad is understandable, given the promises of lower income tax, increased benefits and more favourable conditions of service. It was further reported in November 2015 that one in six of those recruited to fill the gaps in the workforce were overseas applicants. Michael Gove was named as the villain of the piece for this calamitous state of affairs by the shadow education secretary, as a result of his denigration of the profession during his period in office as education secretary. Much as I would accept that he played a part, I believe that the causes run deeper.

Linked to the reality of the ever-increasing workload, there is another reason why morale within the profession has steadily worsened, one that may have been overlooked. It is that teachers do not enjoy behaving in ways where volunteering readily for any and every activity outside of timetabled lessons to help children learn is no longer the norm within the school culture. It's unseemly for people who wish to help young people to develop intellectually, socially and spiritually to be operating within a system of regulated cooperation. There is an increasingly prevalent attitude that withdrawing goodwill is the necessary option in the face of naked mistrust and the onerous burden of work. This stance, however, is not one that teachers enjoy adopting.

Safety

Another unanticipated factor contributing to the lowering of morale in the profession is that secondary school teachers can no longer assume that the classroom is a safe environment. All are now aware that, however remote the possibility, a violent outburst could occur whilst one is teaching, resulting in a serious physical threat. I was occasionally anxious about the possibility of a parent making an unwelcome visit during the school day. I remember this being the case when I knew that a pupil in my class was the subject of a court order, where there was a legal ban on a father making contact with his child. Physical assaults on teachers are no longer uncommon. However, I could never have envisaged that a teacher could be killed by a pupil during a lesson.

Fact and Fancy

The range of abilities and strategies for engaging pupils' interest that I developed, relied upon and valued over several years gradually became redundant. My greatest pleasure as an English teacher had been to present children with selections of literature and to discover where the students' responses led us. I had the knowledge to feed in relevant background detail and theory, but I favoured inquiry-based learning. Nevertheless, I eventually succumbed to the obligation to dangle the course syllabus in front of a class and say, 'This is one of the skills in which you have to demonstrate competence and that's what we're doing today. You've got to know how to do this because it gains you marks in the examination. If you don't do exactly what I tell you, you can't be awarded full marks.'

With older classes, it wasn't unusual for me to apologise for particular approaches I found myself adopting. The very nature of learning changed for me over four decades. Initially English courses had been broad, all-encompassing and genuinely enriching for developing minds; forty years on they have become narrow, proscribed and tedious. Fact has steamrollered fancy.

Misty-eyed sentimentalist, you may be thinking. My reply would be that the power of the imagination has been subjugated by the forces of rigour, not just in education, but in all walks of life. Just take a look at the record of the English national football team over five decades since 1966 if you want to start looking for 'evidence'. The English are suckers for rules, regulations, over-training and systems, even when they don't work. Similarly, a premium is now set on perspiration instead of inspiration in present-day education. If evidence is needed, my shirts bear testament to that fact.

Prescription

Much of what I perceived to be 'the magic' went out of English teaching for me from my late thirties. I found, however, that younger teachers coming into the profession, who had never known any system other than rigid direction, weren't overly worried about what I perceived to be unproductive and unhealthy levels of prescription. Like a dinosaur feeling the first chill of the ice age, I became vaguely aware of the threat of my own extinction.

The reduction of teaching methodology to systems that appeared to be tailored with teacher accountability to the fore and to 'guarantee' good examination results led to another unwelcome consequence. If the recording of pupil performance can be formalised, then report writing could follow suit. Thus, statement banks were produced for every area of pupil performance. One was no longer required to compose a personal report for each student, there was only the task of jotting down a sequence of numbers and/or letters and the computer would do the rest.

Students have developed a nose for the artificiality of 'modern' teaching, or teaching to the test. They see examinations essentially as tests of learned information. Thus, formulaic three-part lessons follow a predictable pattern for them in most subject areas. The reduction of subject knowledge to key facts further reinforces for them the sterility of the learning process. Most secondary school children are not as gullible as politicians imagine.

I would occasionally put to one side the dispiritingly constant focus on the assessment criteria for discrete examination grades in GCSE English and English Literature and A-Level examinations, and try to emphasise the importance of eliciting an imaginative aesthetic response to a piece of literature. With the more street-savvy, examination-blinkered students I could only go so far with this strategy. The impatiently-issued instruction from the floor of "Just tell us what we need to know for the exam, sir!" was one to which I became accustomed, but it always made me flinch. The twenty-first-century breed of hard-nosed fifteen and sixteen year olds will not be deceived by 'frilly irrelevance' when it comes to examination preparation.

Examination Failure

Radical new methods for improving SAT and GCSE performance in all subject areas were being tried by desperate teaching staff throughout my school as I approached retirement. My intention here is not to direct particular criticism at the last school at which I taught. Secondary schools nationally were going through the same hand-wringing processes.

The pressure on us all in the department to achieve a high GCSE pass rate of students with grade 'C' and above in my core subject area of English was immense. Framing structures for essay writing, for example, became the vogue. Instead of setting an essay topic and leaving the students to complete the work entirely independently, essay plans would be distributed indicating the minimum number of sections that children should consider including, with accompanying prompts and technical advice for each section. For English literature essays, I was even providing details of the pages in set texts where relevant quotation could be gleaned to support the arguments that needed to be developed. I did this, along with the rest of my subject colleagues, but always with the major misgiving that I was effectively doing half of the students' work myself. Parents considered this an excellent approach because, for them, it had the whiff of the foolproof and the fail-safe – a wonderfully infallible strategy that all but ensured examination success.

For me, though, the result would be thirty essays that were remarkably similar in terms of content, organisation, and length. GCSE courses were being reduced to the point where they no longer did the job of developing independent inquiry, intellect and imagination. Any short-cut to examination success was worthy of consideration. Examination papers were certainly easier to mark, but training children to adopt such practices was a critical movement away from what I termed education.

Coaching students to adopt any standardised essay format has only a tenuous connection with education. A subject syllabus designed to suit every child of a certain age patronises both the gifted and the less able, and does a grave disservice to the concept of learning.

Examiners at secondary level are very hard to find: the work is poorly paid and occupies a vast amount of time, especially during the six-week summer break when most sensible teachers are looking to recharge their batteries. Consequently, they do not have the time or the energy to read every word of every script of every candidate. Examiners I've spoken to have told me so. The task of marking hundreds of near-identical papers is what makes the job so mind-numbingly excruciating. They have also told me that, when marking examination essays, the subtext of their instructions had been to tick the use of 'key words' by candidates and to add up the ticks at the end of an answer. The number of ticks indicates the mark to be awarded. The flaw in this practice is that the accuracy and eloquence of a candidate's expression are less mark-worthy than the mere inclusion of tick-worthy key words.

Thus, when teaching any subject component, a teacher's priority is to provide lists of key words and phrases, for each examination area, that must be included in a written response on that topic. This is another reason for my questioning the value of written examinations in their current form They are not an adequate preparation for the demands of study at key stage 5 and beyond or, indeed, for the development of learning itself.

The fact that GCSE syllabuses change so frequently supports my conviction that it is all but impossible to produce a perfect examination format for all sixteen year olds. In addition to lacking enthusiasm for the courses themselves, I learned not to have complete faith in the final grades awarded. That was no consolation for those of my students who found themselves on the receiving end of inconsistent examination marking. Increasingly, the media focuses on marking 'horror stories' every summer. In many such cases, schools are reluctant to request a re-mark because the process is so unwieldy and time-consuming. There is also the knowledge that, historically, it is exceptional for examination grades to be changed upwards.

My firm belief is that, as far as children's learning at any age is concerned, how one studies is as important as what one studies. In this context, I regarded the faith placed by Nicky Morgan, Michael Gove's successor, in 'our new, world-class GCSEs' to be misplaced in the extreme. Politicians specialise in bombast.

I don't have a problem with children sitting examinations, but I would want some of them, at least, to be individually-tailored for students. Students working in a specific subject area do not all need to cover entirely the same content. There should be the freedom for young people to pursue topics of their own choosing, with teachers providing regular one-to-one guidance and support for the duration of the course, whether it be a term, a year or longer.

Such a change would obviate the need constantly to teach to the test, and overcome concerns about the downloading of prepared online material, often in the form of complete essays. In my preferred educational vision, classroom teaching would be a complementary activity, one element within a variety of learning contexts. Not all areas of teaching and learning lend themselves to formal class teaching arrangements.

Individual ownership of secondary education examination courses is an area to be explored. It works for those in higher education and there is no reason why it shouldn't work for younger students. The 'rigour' of the conventional examination process would continue to be a feature of secondary education, but some examination components would involve teacher/student negotiation, with the focus on more open-ended and extended study. Thus, children could be presented with opportunities to write lengthy and insightful responses on topics that they had chosen, making learning meaningful and relevant.

To take the case I mentioned earlier of my own illuminating experience of reading and writing about three Graham Greene novels, a GCSE English Literature examination question could easily be devised that would satisfy the intellectual requirements of any examination board; for example: *Referring to at least three works by a twentieth-century writer of your choice, discuss the treatment of the novels' major themes.* I see a value in students having some freedom to set their own examination questions, following a period of negotiation with a subject tutor. The fly in the ointment for the DfE would, of course, be that schools would need to be given a degree of examination autonomy at every level.

213

Hey, Kid, Leave Them Teachers Alone!

There is a line in Pink Floyd's *Another Brick in the Wall* that is now anachronistic: 'Hey, teacher, leave them kids alone!' It's only a pop song so I can overlook Roger Waters' double negatives in the opening lines, misuse of demonstrative adjectives, and whatever else might be expected to irritate an English teacher about pop lyrics. What is powerfully ironic is the fact that, from my experience as a teacher, the 'kids' are currently more likely to be taking verbal pot shots at the teachers in the classroom, rather than teachers making children's lives miserable by poking fun at them. If Roger were penning the lyrics to a song about everyday life in a state school today, he might be tempted to include the line, 'Hey, kid, leave them teachers alone!'

Waters' lyrics about teachers victimising pupils are more than likely to have had some basis in fact in connection with his unhappy time at Cambridge and County School for Boys, but the tables have been turning over the past fifty years. Teachers have to take a lot on the chin from their students these days.

Dealing with adolescents who know their rights and are less inhibited about expressing them can result in teachers feeling intimidated. But it's the price to be paid for the reasonable and fair treatment of children by adults in schools. It's rare these days to hear of bad-tempered teachers throwing heavy objects at pupils in the classroom or exerting their authority by routinely resorting to physical violence. This was the school world I knew as a pupil, but today's generation of children is less likely to be cowed by a despot – if there are still any around. The majority of secondary-school pupils know that such conduct is illegal, whereas I unquestioningly accepted teacher cruelty as par for the course in my school days.

It's certainly not my intention to be critical of young people here. I'm simply making an observation on significant changes that have taken place over time in the ways that children and teachers interact. Ideally, tolerance, empathy, and sympathy underpin the teaching force's ethos. This overtly caring approach, however, does make increasing demands in terms of time and emotional investment. I recall a few exceptional occasions when a badly-behaved pupil who refused to be escorted out of the classroom caused me to decamp with the rest of the students to another empty classroom some distance away in the school building. This strategy required me to send for the school's welfare officer to deal with the troubled pupil. She presumably implemented a thorough health check before returning him to the classroom. Batting a miscreant around the head or bellowing a tirade of inflammatory threats were speedy solutions to lesson interruptions fifty years ago. Dealing with behaviour issues now requires time, and time in the teacher's working day is in short supply.

I don't envy young people growing up in a world that I see as being so much more complex and fraught with pitfalls compared with that of my teenage world. I have every sympathy for the young and feel fortunate that I never had to cope with adolescent angst against a backdrop of global warming; international terrorism; the breakdown of the family unit; post-code gang culture; cyber-bullying; ballooning university tuition fees; and the difficulty of finding permanent full-time employment in a zero-hours culture. I lived in blissful ignorance of much of what was

215

going on in the world around me compared with young people today.

Many secondary schools, as institutions, are guilty of double thinking in their attempts to eliminate pupil misconduct: on the one hand staff are encouraged to be sympathetic in their dealings with children but, on the other, zero-tolerance behaviour policies are introduced by management teams to enforce student discipline. The teacher is caught betwixt and between these contradictory and competing impulses. Zero-tolerance policies are difficult to enforce. I repeat my conviction that a more fruitful course for headteachers, governors and education ministers would be to undertake an in-depth analysis of the organisation of teaching and learning in our schools.

I quickly learned never to take it personally when a child blew up in my face. Frustrations that become uncontrollable for some can have more to do with learning constraints placed upon them than with a teacher's attitude towards them. When children lose their tempers, they need to be given time to cool down and then, whatever penalty they may subsequently be required to pay, they should be given the chance to explain exactly what caused them to lose control of themselves. Some children make valid criticisms of their school learning experiences in a more unconventional manner than by popping a slip of paper into a suggestion box.

As a senior member of staff, one of my responsibilities was to organise school council meetings. The council comprised pupil representatives of all ages, the head of sixth form as chair, and me sitting on the sidelines. One of the main student grievances, besides the cost and temperature of school lunches, was pupil misbehaviour. Children are more troubled by the misconduct of their peers than one might imagine, and some of the solutions put forward to deal with the issue were less than compassionate: security guards patrolling corridors; the strategic installation of metal detectors; and immediate expulsion for a range of 'crimes' were fairly common suggestions. I always made sure that informal references to tear gas, rubber bullets and stun grenades were never minuted. Children generally want a quiet life, just like teachers. I believe that curricular coercion creates more student dissatisfaction and frustration than educators care to admit.

Cajoling or forcing young people to follow a number of compulsory courses, in which they have little or no interest, is not only counter-productive in terms of motivation but also results in classroom control issues. Children should have the freedom to 'specialise' in certain areas at an earlier age, and there is no reason why alternative and relevant studies should be any less challenging than the 'tried and trusted' subject offerings.

A young person with a particular interest in, say, astronomy could be encouraged to produce a written report on a specific topic, and then complete a class presentation or discuss the study in a viva with two or more teachers. The default setting for teaching is that the teacher is the expert who knows significantly more than the student, whatever the subject area. However, there is no reason why educational institutions shouldn't embrace the concept of students being able to teach their teachers.

An established English teacher of twenty years, I was asked to teach media studies at GCSE and A-Level. I'd had no formal training in the subject but took on the responsibility as I had an interest in film. I found myself reading up on the topics I had to teach a day or so before lessons, which meant that I was only a few hours ahead of the students in terms of my subject knowledge. There were occasions when I became aware that one or two pupils sensed that I was inexperienced but were prepared to be patient with me. In the early days, one very able boy came out with a comment about the 'facts of life' relating to the comparatively new computer technology we had started using that shook me sideways. He said, 'Sir, do you realise that an image of a dog just passed through your body?' He made the statement in a matter-of-fact tone, but the apparently simple observation struck me as profoundly insightful.

Within a few years, the pressure seemed to be off as I'd become generally competent and confident in my ability to deliver all aspects of the KS4 and KS5 courses. A major problem arose when all the members of my Year 12 group agreed that they wanted to take the film production option as the practical component of their course. Previously I'd selected for my classes the less ambitious advertising campaign option that required the creation of still images only. I had no experience of film production, but made enquiries at the borough's media centre to see if any training could be provided to facilitate my group's request.

The staff kindly offered not only a series of training days in the use of the software and hardware available at the centre, but also a term's free use of the film laboratory for one whole morning per week. I duly took the class along for their training, to discover that I was unable to grasp all of the detail that the students took in their stride. As a result, when they had been divided into groups of four and were working on their films, I knew less than they did about the multiplicity of procedures for manipulating the equipment available to them. I had no alternative but to admit to knowing less than they did and to being little more than an interested observer as they went about their work. In truth, my only 'skill' area was my ability to assess the final products. I need not have been worried as the completed films were of a generally high standard. They were awarded high marks in the examination and were given a public showing at a parents evening. Teachers should sometimes have the humility to accept that there are lessons that they can learn from their students.

Much of the poor pupil conduct at secondary level is a direct consequence of the ways that children are taught, and this problem is exacerbated the older they become. Thirty twelve year olds may respond uncomplaining to being taught in airless rooms five days a week at the height of summer, but sixteen year olds are not nearly so amenable. The battery-hen method of cramming children together into large and unwieldy teaching groups is inefficient. A varied range of learning arrangements will increase student motivation and engender a sense of education 'ownership'.

Parent Power

With one or two exceptions, I generally enjoyed good relationships with parents during my career. I was a teacher representative on the school's PTA for several years, helping to organise fund-raising events and social evenings. Besides the sense of fulfilment one gains from helping children along the road to academic success in life, the satisfaction to be gained from the genuine gratitude of parents also makes the job rewarding, compensating in no small way for the comparatively modest salaries teachers earn. No teacher is ever likely to become materially wealthy, but the emotional rewards are enormous.

Free Schools, introduced by the Conservative and Liberal Democrat coalition following the 2010 general election, enable parents, should they so wish, to set up their own schools. One of my personal prejudices about politicians is that the job attracts many who are not, in my opinion, suited to the requirements of the job: the pursuit of power and public advancement too often takes precedence over the desire to serve the public. On the second occasion that I ran the London Marathon with my daughter, Lucy, just before the 2015 general election, I experienced the firm conviction that all those fund raisers around me should be running the country in place of the government of the day. I mention my antipathy to politicians in general because I am equally suspicious of the motives of parents who may wish to become involved in setting up schools.

My suspicions are twofold. First, religious division is increasing in society and religious diversity is no longer celebrated as enthusiastically as in former times. It troubles me that the number of faith schools is on the increase as a result of parents wishing to exploit the potential for educational exclusivity. Second, the gulf between the rich and the poor is growing insidiously, with the result that the financially secure are more likely to be in a position to involve themselves in the practice of setting up schools, with the support of businesses or charities.

Schools are now operating in a climate in which teachers are automatically considered to be at fault for children's poor academic performance. At the sharp end of 'parent power', parents have even been known to take out lawsuits against schools in which they believe that their offspring have 'under-achieved'. The stereotypical scene at a parents' evening where frustrated mums and dads vented their spleens at their failing son or daughter after listening to the teacher's report are long gone. Now the teacher is just as likely to cop it from parents if a student is performing badly.

Just as increasing numbers of children are not intimidated by authority figures, so it is becoming the case with their parents. It does a great deal of harm to a teacher's self-confidence to be on the receiving end of belittling comments and open contempt from parents, particularly when their child is sitting next to them. Children cannot be blamed for taking an example from the poor one demonstrated by such parents. The subsequent ridiculing of beleaguered teaching staff on social networking sites further undermines the authority of both individuals and schools. I have known personally of cases where ordinary teachers have become the victims of snigger campaigns. There are positive aspects to social-networking sites of which I'm only too aware, but there are also the disturbing influences of online poison at work directed at professionals doing their best in trying online times.

Many parents give their time and financial support to schools in a range of supportive capacities, for which schools have always been and continue to be grateful. However, although I'm in favour of parents home-educating their own children, as I explain later, I'm wary of them being offered the power to form and run schools.

13. Facts of a Teacher's Life

The newly-qualified teacher stands optimistically before a room crammed full of children all waiting for the show to start. In addition to the advice offered in previous chapters to aspiring Miss Honeys or Professor Keatings, there are a few other realities that I'd like to share, the facts of a teacher's life that one rarely hears about. It's better to be prepared for as many professional scenarios as possible.

It's difficult to believe but many young people have no interest whatsoever in learning the difference between a colon and a semicolon. The minority of children whose imaginations are not inspired by language, literature or the arts are often creative in wholly different directions, about which teachers in the school are likely to have limited knowledge.

There are also children for whom it is a supreme effort to behave in class. One should not leap to the easy assumption that the least able are the most badly behaved. Gifted children, particularly those who are bored rigid by conventional teaching methods, can be just as difficult to manage as those who are struggling. Being an effective teacher, capable of engaging every child in a class of thirty simultaneously can be an onerous business.

Self-Doubt

There was never a time in my career that I didn't encounter classes that made me constantly apprehensive every time I taught them. Feeling one's heart pounding and physically breaking into a sweat whilst standing still is something few people experience. Decades into the job, I still quaked when confronted by classes with a selection of genuinely challenging pupils.

The strange fact was that a significant number of those pupils who seriously managed to unsettle my equilibrium during lessons would probably not have perceived themselves as 'difficult', quite the contrary. Teachers regularly encounter gifted individuals who are not easy to accommodate during lessons because they deserve more than the traditional classroom experience. Such students may try hard to contain their boredom, but experienced professionals can sense when a rogue intellect is on the loose.

The student leaning back in his chair, hands behind his head and legs stretched in front of him was the one who worried me. I was often correct in my assessment that this was the relaxed posture of a confident temperament and an exceptional mind. The instruction to such boys to sit up straight seemed crass in the extreme. The 'gifted and talented' presented me with challenges that I could not always meet in the classroom. I wonder how many children are best served by the conventional school experience I'd taken for granted throughout my career.

Urination

Teaching is a taxing business, not just when one is standing still, but in a host of ways. For example, I now suffer with a prostate problem because I never drank enough fluid whilst working. I couldn't risk drinking what I believed I should to keep my body hydrated because I knew that I couldn't leave my classroom to go to the WC as and when I needed. Faced with four consecutive one-hour contact lessons and only a fifteen-minute break after the first two, when I had to get out on playground duty as quickly as possible, there was no time to get to the loo.

By the time I was well into my fifties at my final school, when my waterworks problem was becoming worse, it was pointedly stated that any teacher on break duty should arrive as soon as the bell sounded. The reason for this was concern for children's health and safety (not the teacher's). I was required to remain in place until the bell rang for the next lesson. I never realised at the time the damage I was doing to myself. Dealing patiently with those who would rather be anywhere than in my classroom also tended to exacerbate issues with my bladder. Attempting to maintain a composed demeanour was difficult for me at those times when my shirt was sticking to my back and I was struggling to control a desperate urge to urinate immediately.

Incarceration

Self-evident as it may seem, students seek to satisfy the pleasure principle in our schools. The vast majority has a desire to find school enjoyable. The disappointing truth is that some merely tolerate school life, the six-and-a-half-hour daily stretch seen as being little short of imprisonment. They are particularly antipathetic to the twin concepts of confinement and coercion. I had countless conversations in the classroom with restless youths who resented being contained every day by people like me. I became accustomed to comments such as, 'I'm only here because my mum and dad said they'd kick me out if I didn't come in.' Comments of this nature came from students of all shades of academic ability. I readily sympathised with such viewpoints, often telling individuals that I wished there were some other route they could follow that would enable them to enjoy a more fulfilling and useful educational experience.

During the hot summer months, suffocating heat made the classroom an intolerable environment at times. Many were the occasions I found myself flagging in a lesson and being interrupted by a pleading voice: "Sir, can we go and work outside on the school field?" At such times I was just as keen to escape with my class and teach in the open. But it was never to be. Teachers sometimes feel as imprisoned by the four walls of their teaching room as their pupils.

I was grateful for the fact that a significant number of those students who saw themselves as being present in my classroom under duress were genuinely amusing conversationalists. I used their original viewpoints on assorted topics as provocative sounding boards to stimulate the imaginations of the more reserved students. Nevertheless, I genuinely felt a sense of guilt that I was holding such characters against their will and saw myself, on occasions, as a prison warder disguised in an M&S washable suit.

There was a host of other reasons why I sometimes interpreted my role in this light. When I think of the time devoted during my career to enforcing the school uniform rule, instructing my charges to conform in every detail, I felt petty. Certain boys, who must have shared my reservations, tried all manner of means to flout the uniform rule. The style of wearing trouser waistlines below the buttocks was a constant problem. The irony of boys modelling their behaviour and appearance on prison inmates across the Atlantic on death row didn't escape me. Adolescents will always find clever ways to register a protest. On the one hand I can't say that I enjoyed seeing them studiously transforming their school uniform into attire more suited to someone in line for lethal injection. On the other, I didn't want to get caught up in conversations about clothing because I felt I was compromising the perception I had of myself as an educator. The irony that adult celebrities eventually started to adopt this bizarre fashion trend genuinely caught me unawares. I now even find myself socialising with people who wouldn't dream of tucking their shirts into anything, and wear jeans that are decidedly on the half-mast side.

Detention duty was a soul-destroying exercise. Keeping a few dozen malefactors captive in a classroom for an hour after school never sat right with me. I witnessed one or two successful escapes in my time, but I grudgingly made every effort to ensure miscreants saw out their full sentence in my custody.

My perception that there were times I was sometimes carrying out duties more akin to a prison warder was shared by other colleagues. Issuing petty punishments for petty 'crimes' is not the business of a teacher. Schools need to be freer, more democratic institutions. Teaching and learning that takes place exclusively in crowded classrooms every day of the school year is no longer working at secondary level.

Confining children physically will, to a greater or lesser degree, confine their imaginations.

Inspiration

I still hold the belief that the most important quality of a good teacher is the ability to inspire children. However, I have seen many professionals, gifted in this respect, who have been forced out of their chosen career.

Effective classroom control is clearly an important criterion for judging whether or not someone is a good teacher. Sensible, you may be thinking. I've known those who operate brilliantly with small groups or individuals, but find large classes unmanageable. Ironically, I've also worked with uninspiring professionals who exercised iron discipline over classes of any size. They built careers on their ability to train children, but were lacking in the educating department. They were generally regarded as solidly reliable members of staff. Our near-sighted system, with its emphasis on the unwavering control of groups of thirty or more children, loses many inspirational educational practitioners.

Calcification

At risk of generalising, a failing of which my wife tells me I can be guilty, I believe that secondary school populations have become accustomed to being spoon-fed. Perhaps a more accurate term would be force-fed. The current generation of schoolchildren tolerates extended periods of boredom and what amounts to training, at the hands of a hamstrung teaching profession. Enduring a compulsory education of this nature, children can be forgiven for their acceptance of passivity and being less than dynamic in their day-to-day lives. The fact that so many young people occupy a significant amount of their waking time engaged in passive pastimes, such as computer gaming or staring fixedly at nothing on their mobile phones, is evidence for me of the state of vacant consciousness that is accepted as second nature. Western society's youth is at risk of becoming calcified by inactivity. Inactivity in itself is a concern for me. What worries me even more is that, in the eyes of some professionals with whom I worked, this could be the desirable state of affairs that contributed to a 'quiet life'.

Young people no longer socialise in the ways that I did on street corners, at the local park, posing at the youth club, or playing football on the green in the middle of my housing estate. Many lead virtual lives in seclusion, rummaging through networking sites, accessing myriad contacts via tiny iPhone screens or laptops for hours at a time. The need to be 'doing' and the desire to be in the company of others, that my teenage peers and I valued, don't seem to be such priorities for young people nowadays.

I remember once playing devil's advocate by telling a GCSE class that the development of television, computing and mobile phone technology was all part of a sinister plot. I mooted the idea of subtle social forces exerting control over them by keeping them off the streets and in front of screens. The behaviour of children, passively staring at screens of one sort or another morning, noon and night, is easier to condition, especially if the screens are able to 'watch' them. Nobody took this scenario seriously. I drew the conclusion that most youngsters prefer to live much of their private lives online. Who am I to complain? Perhaps the tabloids are right and the streets aren't safe for our children. Bedrooms do have the merit of being relatively secure environments.

Preparation

When the production and checking of a teacher's lesson preparation became mandatory, I took the news as a personal affront. I'd reached a stage in my career when I could walk into a classroom, pick up the threads of the previous lesson, and develop them with minimal planning. Suddenly, I was thrown into a world where copious notes, presumably prepared in some time warp, where time stood still so that I could get them completed, were required for every lesson. Lesson planning became ultra-formulaic when the three-part format came into vogue.

It's a staggering claim, I know, but I was able to complete short-term and medium-term planning in my head. Long-term planning was no problem because men in suits in central London's Great Smith Street made themselves responsible for that. The artifice of the compulsory three-part lesson had a marked impact on staff morale whilst I was still teaching, much of it negative. A detailed written lesson plan was required for each class taught, together with accompanying photocopied teaching materials and whiteboard presentation. The amount of time required for lesson preparation became an impossible burden. I considered myself a good teacher, but I couldn't do it.

I was prepared to undertake two or three hours of marking each evening, but I was physically unable to spend a further two or three hours an evening devising and writing up ultra-detailed lesson plans for my classes. I had to sleep. I believe that education ministers determined to subject ordinary teachers to this time-consuming monotony as yet another means of establishing absolute control over them. Conspiracy theory, anyone? I saw no other reason because there was no noticeable improvement during this period of the nation's sacred 'standards'.

The only way for individual departments to cope was to generate a bank of lessons for each year group for each day of the school year. All teachers would then find themselves obliged to use this standardised bank of lessons (if the monumental task were ever competed) year after year after year – a stultifying prospect for teachers and pupils alike.

Reformation

A 'Telegraph' report in February 2016 that there had been 'a dramatic fall in grades' for sixteen year olds taking GCSEs may have come as a surprise to Nicky Morgan, but not to me. Nor was I shocked to read that the 'number of failing (state) schools has doubled in the past year as a result of an overhaul of the exams system'. I would be worried about this situation if I attached any credibility to government 'standards'. Having lost faith in school examination systems that rely heavily on the regurgitation of memorised information, I experience only qualified alarm.

If state schools aren't 'working', as the British public is constantly being led to believe, surely education ministers will be delighted to hear my suggestion for a radical overhaul of teaching and learning practices. No matter how well schools are run, in whatever run-down areas of the country, they may never be good enough for Ofsted. If there are secondary schools that aren't working, perhaps Ofsted isn't always working.

If you can operate a laptop, you can be an inspector and don't even need to go into a school to judge its effectiveness. The technology at your disposal will process the gigabytes of raw data about an institution in a millisecond and provide the one hundred per cent accurate conclusions: 'Computer says school requiring special measures. Computer says poor leadership'. You can't argue with raw data and technology. If it is the case that the inspectorate's judgements of a school are decided before the unannounced visit even gets under way, one could be forgiven for drawing the conclusion that the teacher gradings for subsequent lesson observations will have to fit these judgements, irrespective of the quality of the teaching and learning witnessed by the inspection team. Heresy!

I do wonder if, at any time since the introduction of compulsory education, any minister has ever attempted to reform school examinations and assessment in a meaningful way. I imagine a brief conversation along the following lines:

Secretary of State for Education: *Seriously though, Baldrick, how can we reform our examination system to measure creativity and initiative, instead of just hammering away at information children have to remember?*

Baldrick: *Fucked if I know, your Right Horribleness.*

Secretary of State for Education: *Oh well, suppose we'd better just bang on with what we've got then.*

Morale amongst teachers was low when I retired, and it's even lower now. The mistake the DfE made was in assuming that a browbeaten workforce wouldn't have the energy to offer any resistance, but times are changing. Teachers have found themselves with no other recourse in recent years but to step up industrial action as a result of increasing concerns about pay, pensions and conditions of service. In short, many teachers feel ill-served by their masters and are biting back, if they haven't already found another career.

Major reform of education generally is a pressing matter. If a serious effort is ever made to tackle the issue, it must be carried out by an independent body that acknowledges the teaching profession's rights to be heard and respected. Fag-packet notes and American-style assessment fixation have done too much damage to our state schools over the past four decades.

14. Tailor-Made Courses and Examinations

Teaching in many countries is apparently a straightforward process of the delivery of knowledge. The daily round of memorising information is the staple learning diet for many unfortunate schoolchildren throughout the world. However, this system has been found wanting in some advanced nations with recognition of the need for more inquiry-based learning. Ideally children engage personally with lesson content, investigate material presented to them and endeavour to generate their own meaning. Teachers operate as facilitators to learning in this context, and I see no reason why this facilitating role should not be extended.

Independent learning requires less formal teaching in large groups and relies more on individual guidance to suggest fruitful lines of inquiry. Introducing such an element formally into the school timetable would be beneficial for students and teachers alike. This is not to argue that classroom teaching be completely abandoned. Exploiting opportunities to give young people the freedom to investigate discrete areas of interest will provide children with a much-needed injection of variety to their school experience, their personal development and to the school curriculum. Classroom tuition would continue, particularly where subject instruction is called for, but need not be the only teaching method.

One aspect of coercion in secondary schooling that troubles me concerns the established procedures for the selection and regimentation of children to facilitate the delivery of curriculum content. Such strategies have for too long been unquestioningly accepted as the norm. Children are presented with restricted learning parameters and significant numbers find themselves having to follow courses for which they are unsuited. The secondary curriculum certainly attempts to offer a stimulating range of subject options, but there is limited scope for any child to go beyond it. Personal interest areas should be encouraged, with some time in the school week set aside for students to research and develop their unique gifts or topic specialisms, albeit within traditional subject areas.

The argument that it is impossible for schools to teach every subject in which students show an interest is a fair one. I would argue the case for establishing independent study sessions within the weekly timetable, during which children formulate and pursue their own supplementary studies with professional guidance. I would advocate the modification of subject syllabuses, with the inclusion of personal research components – in all examinable subjects. This step would necessitate teaching staff negotiating with and mentoring individuals on a regular basis. Regular monitoring of students would be essential for the purpose of agreeing personal learning programmes. Such an approach would militate against the wholesale plagiarism of online or textual material.

Following the introduction of independent study arrangements, teachers' contact time with large classes would be reduced. Students would spend some of their time working at home or in supervised study areas, freeing teachers to enjoy increased one-to-one contact.

The majority of colleagues and students to whom I've spoken on the subject of the optimal conditions for teaching and learning unhesitatingly agree that one-to-one contact is their favoured method. It rarely happens in state schools. Teachers and students need to be offered opportunities to cooperate in more varied and stimulating contexts.

The many parents who pay personal tutors to coach their children through difficult examinations will also testify to the benefits of personal tuition. For two years I tutored a neighbour's son who was struggling with his GCSE English and English Literature courses. He excelled in all other areas. I discovered that he had profoundly misunderstood important elements of the examination requirements as explained in class by his English teacher. I constantly reassured him that he was not failing because he lacked ability but possessed a flawed grasp of the syllabus requirements. I found that constant clarification of specific language exercises, a practice that his classroom teacher would not have had time for, in addition to working assiduously through the packed syllabus, improved his performance immeasurably. He was predicted a grade 'C' for each examination when he first came to me and eventually gained an 'A' for English and a 'B' for English Literature. Without the additional weekend help, it is unlikely that he would ever have gained a place at Bristol University and gone on to work for Deutsche Bank.

All students should have the experience of personalised learning built into their school week. Strident opponents of constructivism, or student-centred learning, tend to prefer the shut-up-button-it-copy-this-down-and-don't-make-so-much-as-a-peep-until-I-sodding-well-say-you-can-speak approach, much favoured by educationists in other parts of the world. Put another way, if the Kray twins had ever had the opportunity to try their hand at teaching, they would have been violently opposed to constructivism. Children must be given greater opportunity to construct their own knowledge, as a complement to being passive receivers of knowledge.

The first problem that occurs as a result of such a curricular innovation concerns assessment. How can a mark scheme be provided for every single topic that arises in teacher/student negotiations? The marking of any piece of extended writing can no longer be done, current practice would lead us to believe, without detailed marking criteria. The idea of assessing the quality of a piece of writing with few marking guidelines is alien to our content-heavy-syllabus culture. There was a time before the National Curriculum, when teachers' judgements were trusted – it was all the rage fifty years ago before the teaching force was collectively branded 'trendy left-wing liberals', a moniker that mysteriously is still with us. Grade boundary guides were all that was needed then to assess students' work.

Nowadays, detailed marking criteria usually come in the form of a handy booklet, that is only handy in the sense that it can be used to replace a broken armchair caster. The unfortunate teacher or examiner who is required to apply said criteria to an examination script is required to assimilate and apply innumerable quality control mechanisms before passing judgement.

The one and only occasion I weakened and blighted my whole summer by agreeing to mark GCSE examination papers was the only time in my life that I was genuinely concerned that I might have alcoholic tendencies. When marking the hundreds of English papers, I discovered first-hand how it is possible to award a candidate any grade that pops into one's head and be able to find relevant grade criteria that will support the decision. Examination marking is a can of worms and I understand why examiners can so easily get it wrong.

A second objection I would anticipate from current curriculum planners would be that children already enjoy the privilege of subject choice under existing arrangements. Unfortunately, this is not the case. Key stage 3 students have no choice whatsoever and spend three years locked into a diet which, logic should inform us, can only be sustaining for the minority. This is the period when children become conditioned to accept the reality that their own interests, preferences and talents are of limited worth compared with the demands of the oncoming secondary education juggernaut.

There is a semblance of choice for students at key stage 4 but, after the allocation of almost half the week's lessons for the core subjects, a timetable is invariably completed by adding additional subjects on what may prove to be a best-fit basis. Despite schools' best efforts to provide choice, the reality is that few are able to pick up every subject option they would wish outside of the core. The logistics of the process come first. When allocating subjects to a year group, there are 'x' subjects on offer, 'y' teachers available, and 'n' children to fit into the grid. I was involved annually in the process for many years and became accustomed to conveying disappointing news. When boys came to me complaining, for example, that they had to study French for a further two years and couldn't do History, I could only offer sympathy.

I guiltily present a selection of excuses that my colleagues and I made to Year 10 students who found themselves unable to sign up for courses they had chosen to follow from those available:

1] 'I'm sorry, but there is only one group for that subject and it's already full.'

2] 'You can't study that subject because there's a timetable clash with another subject you've chosen.'

3] 'I'm afraid the timetable only allows you to study one humanities subject/one foreign language/one arts subject.'

4] 'You can't study this subject because the teacher doesn't think that you'll be able to cope with it.'

5] 'You can't study History and Geography because they're in the same option pool.'

6] 'You can't study Business Studies and Economics because there are some similarities in the course content.'

I rarely encountered students who were entirely happy with the composition of their final timetable. Once on the KS4 treadmill, pupils cover identical material in each subject, with little scope for individual input or the opportunity to pursue topics of particular interest in greater detail.

We are now well advanced into the twenty-first century. This is surely a good time to loosen the shackles of compulsory education and offer children greater autonomy in their learning. Reducing the level of curricular coercion is a necessary step to increasing student motivation. The younger generation of this country is sophisticated enough to merit more sophisticated teaching and learning strategies. The majority of school-age children not only possess a general grasp of technology that would embarrass most adults, but they can also operate PCs, laptops, iPads, and smartphones far more quickly. They are sifters of a constant stream of complex electronic information from all parts of the world. They no longer deserve to be patronised by the one-trick teaching arrangement that still dictates how the school day is organised.

It would be both impractical and wrong-headed to recommend that all teaching should switch to the independent inquiry model. However, I strongly make the case that there is scope in all subject areas for loosening the control element intrinsic to our educational system. The personal-research component of a child's education would not be a soft option, work completed carrying as high a weighting as all other formal assessment procedures.

Curiosity and excitement, the lynchpins of learning, have been disappearing from the educational landscape for the past half century. Tailoring secondary-school courses, at all levels, to accommodate individual strengths and interests is not an impossible mission.

Some of the excitement that has been missing from the job of teaching for decades will return. Imagine the prospect of assessing a varied range of assignments on a host of different teacher/student negotiated topics. The drudgery of marking piles of near-identical scripts would become a thing of the past.

***

Much of the criticism focusing on the 'failings' of our state schools by politicians and the press is unjustified. State education has become hamstrung by state-imposed minimalist success criteria. Experienced teachers, who know a thing or two about motivating children, are sick of decades of government mistrust, top-down prescription, and victimisation.

Comparisons between our children and their Asian counterparts have become tiresome in the extreme. My heart sank when I read of the global league table that compares the academic performance of children across more than seventy countries. On discovering that the august body that produces the three-yearly education tables was the Organisation for Economic Cooperation and Development, my reaction was a combination of anger and despair. The concepts of education and economics have now become firmly intertwined. Whatever measures are used by the OECD to produce their world league tables, they cannot fail to have a financial bias. A cursory analysis of 'OECD Multilingual Summaries: Education at a Glance 2015 OECD Indicators' disclosed blindingly obvious conclusions. These included, for example, links between high levels of tertiary education, increased earning power and subsequent good health around the world. My level of yawning power was significantly raised when I also discovered that teachers' salaries worldwide had generally been frozen or cut between 2008 and 2013.

There was no mention of one piece of data that would have interested me – children's enjoyment of learning. Perhaps this criterion was neatly avoided, there being operational and logistical difficulties when it comes to measuring the unmeasurable. I must admit to raising a silent, ironic cheer when I read 'Larger classes are correlated with less time spent on teaching and learning, and more time spent on keeping order in the classroom.'

I'm not one for spouting statistical data of any kind, but I shall take a punt here and make an assertion with total and utter conviction: I am confident that, by the year 2100, there is a significantly low level of probability that all state-educated children in this country will be receiving their secondary education five days a week in stuffy classrooms of thirty plus students.

Introducing an element of freedom of choice in all study areas for our schoolchildren will go some way to raising the profile of learning enjoyment, for pupils and teachers alike, and creating learning environments where greater responsibility is placed on the individual. I am committed to the general principle that those children who are brought up with the responsibility of managing aspects of their own learning will place a higher value on the concept of education.

The government strategy to force all schools to become academies by 2022 reflects the central mindset of coercion, disguised as freedom. The breezy promise is that schools will be totally free of any local authority control. The role of local authorities as providers of education will be supplanted by the government as officers of cramming.

15. Home Education

There are parents, many of whom presumably share some of my concerns about state education, who choose to educate their children at home. This alternative to conventional schooling has the important advantage that one can have a direct impact on the quality and style of education provided for one's own children. It is a fairly easy procedure to withdraw one's child from the system, as I was informed by Anita Spillane, who lives in a small Dorset town. She educated all four of her children at home over a twenty-five year period. Jo Thompson, another home educator and qualified teacher living on Hayling Island, also experienced no obstacles when she decided to take responsibility for the education of her son and daughter.

The local authority needs to be satisfied that a child is receiving a suitable education at home, and may meet with the family to talk to the parents and look at examples of work and learning. Other than agreeing to provide a broad, balanced and relevant curriculum, parents largely have a free hand when deciding what, how and when to teach. One important consideration for Anita was that SATs and the National Curriculum are not compulsory for children educated at home. She explained to me how important the concept of freedom of educational choice is for HE parents and her commitment to children's rights:

It should just be a matter of informing the local education authority, rather than asking for permission, as every child has the right to be educated outside of the school system in the UK.

Although my awareness of the home-education movement was limited whilst teaching, I now find myself identifying closely with those who adopt this course for their children. Home educators are likely to be keenly aware that education begins from birth, personal development being as much of a priority as academic achievement. With support groups in operation throughout the country for families, there is easy access to study resources, a full range of sporting activities, educational trips, involvement in charity work, and even sports days organised in some areas. Jo enthused at length about the enormous range of opportunities available to her children:

There are so many amazing groups meeting up for home-educated children, offering the widest choice of activities from acting, animation and animal care to science clubs, sports and work experience. You can't do them all but there are certainly many opportunities. I know probably at least twenty families quite well and belong to groups that cater for hundreds of families. We don't go to as many of the social groups as some do, but could go to something different every day of the week if we wanted.

Anita summed up the advantages of HE in terms that contrast significantly with the state-school ethos:

Our style of educating is unstructured and spontaneous according to our children's individual needs, opportunities and activities available, and even the weather.

She candidly explained her reasons for eschewing the education offered locally for her sons:

Five years old felt very young for an active young boy to be embarking on a more sedentary style of learning. Secondly the local schools weren't a good advert for school education in terms of the socialisation we observed amongst the children. Also I watched some young children in our neighbourhood go from happy, confident, little folk to withdrawn, even sullen, and certainly tired little people. Thankfully there was a Home Education support group in our area so we went along, and I liked what I saw: children interacting with others regardless of age or gender, with confidence and energy intact.

Anita was of the opinion that everyday state school life would have run the risk of introducing negative influences into her efforts to raise her children in the ways that she deemed fit. Her conviction that conventional schooling arrangements have adverse effects on young people's development resulted in the decision to afford her children protection. Her impulse was to shield them from tightly-regulated teaching arrangements at every key stage, an unavoidable necessity in her opinion. Jo was in tune with Anita's feelings on this point:

I certainly feel they have been protected from some of the more harmful aspects of secondary school life and are, in many ways, more mature than some of their peers.

My experience of a career in teaching was that far too many children perceived their education to be a protracted régime of joyless tedium that they have to undergo, as opposed to a genuinely enjoyable and character-defining life experience. Despite my attempts to make school life enjoyable for all the children I taught, I carry a weight of guilt for being part of the process that too many found sterile and unrewarding.

Jo and her husband arrived at the decision to home educate their two youngest children as a natural development of the family living in Spain together for a year:

We have home educated our two youngest for the last year, since we returned from Spain. We did, however, home educate the children for about a year whilst in Spain. This was a fantastic experience for us all. We all learned so much about Catalan traditions and festivals, including how to make olive oil, preserve olives and make wine! We visited medieval towns, mountains, forests, castles, monasteries, churches, farms, wine cellars, prehistoric caves and museums galore! The children then did little projects on whatever interested them most.

Their youngest daughter had a brief spell in Year 1 of a local primary school before leaving for Spain. From the outset, her experience was negative owing to the difficulties she had with mathematics:

She had made up her mind, aged five, that she couldn't do maths and hated it! We just took her back to the start and did lots of fun, practical activities, reinforcing her knowledge of the basics and she actually began to enjoy maths! We had an inspector come to our house and Francesca told her that she loved maths and it was really fun. The inspector informed us that we must be doing a good job as Francesca was well above average for her age group.

The news that a child so young could develop an antipathy to school life was as unsettling to me as it was unexpected. Francesca never completed Year 1. Their son, Scott, started at a comprehensive at the beginning of Year 8 on returning from Spain. He soon became frustrated: he was sorry for the teachers because *'there was never silence'* during lessons, and he also sympathised with the children because his teachers generally *'were so petty about things.'*

I asked Jo if she felt that her children had missed out in any way at all with regard to not having experienced the routines of 'going to school'. I had in mind the idea that home-educated children might be lonely or solitary, but Jo pointed out that any child can experience loneliness, whether or not he or she is a school attender.

I know friends with children at secondary schools who are lonely and never see friends out of school. Scottie told me that he was lonely at the secondary school he attended and said he either had to change to fit in or be on his own.

In her teenage son's case, loneliness was a feature he associated with school life. Anita reinforced the point that the school experience is not as important to the development of self-confidence as I had imagined. Her detailed comments on the matter were illuminating:

Most schoolchildren reassure them, through their reactions to hearing that they don't go to school, or through their behaviour, that it isn't anything too enviable that they have missed. Generally they have come through, or are coming through their childhood with confidence and a zest for life and all the opportunities ahead of them as adults. The boys, who have entered the adult world, are proving to be competent and personable in the workplace to a degree that gets noticed. I think they have had a protected childhood in some respects, but contrary to popular belief, I think this has given them the strength to cope with or avoid some of the negative pressure placed on young people.

Without wishing to be impolite about the local secondary school, Anita implied that her children's natural enthusiasm and self-confidence might have suffered from the school

246

experience. She equated retaining a youthful *'zest for life'* with her children being out of the school system. Second, she is of the opinion that the 'protected childhood' her children experienced has been responsible for developing the strength to avoid *'negative pressure'*.

She was also troubled by the prospect of her children being exposed to anti-social behaviour in a school environment. Drug abuse, gang culture, and the rise in youth knife crime are disturbing features of some children's lives that now cause alarm throughout the country, in communities large and small. Such phenomena are not solely restricted to deprived inner-city areas as one might imagine. The impulse to be anxious about harmful peer influences on one's children is felt keenly by parents wherever they may live.

Jo was a little more forthright when considering state education, expressing reservations about *'the more harmful aspects of secondary school life'*. Latterly in my career, I was acutely aware of the harm that children could do to each other using online social-networking sites. Parents' fears of the physical bullying to which their children could be subjected in schools have been augmented by the disturbing development of cyber bullying.

A friend's son, whom I taught for four years, recently qualified as a secondary school teacher and took up a post locally. I was interested to find out how he was enjoying his new job. After telling me how well things were going for him personally, he confided in shocked tones, "I can't believe how awful the children can be towards each other." He was referring to the online poison to which children are subjected by their peers at school. Teachers find 'invisible' bullying of this kind difficult to identify and, therefore, control. Home educators are conscious of the fact that their children, being out of the school loop, are less likely to have to cope with this problem.

The logisitics of providing a home education present a variety of difficulties for parents wishing to take this route. Perhaps the most obvious is the financial one. One parent or carer within a family is likely to have to forego the joys of full-time employment in order to manage this lifestyle choice. Alternatively, there may be another adult family member available, such as a grandparent, who is prepared to be involved.

Home education is probably the cheapest way to get a private education for one's offspring. It could even be argued as being a more humane alternative to, for example, sending a child to an expensive boarding school – the option that parents of 7% of children in this country find they can afford. The majority of parents, I feel sure, would probably admit to desiring a privileged education for their children, presumably cherishing the belief that they are unique and deserving of the best education available. The idea of home education for my own children never occurred to me. The arrangement wouldn't have been a workable option for us on financial grounds. Lindsey and I found it a constant struggle financially to raise a family in the capital.

Educating one's own children has the potential to be hugely fulfilling for parents. There are the prerequisites of reasonable levels of intelligence and common sense, and a genuine concern for the emotional and spiritual development of one's child. It was reassuring to discover that a full home conversion is unnecessary; for example, the kitchen becoming the reprographics room or the lounge being turned into a lecture theatre. Neither should one make the mistake of assuming that home tuition will involve a parent 'teaching' for several hours a day. The concept of independent inquiry is central to the thinking of home educators. This is the seed that they particularly wish to nurture. Groups of parents and their children meet regularly at each other's homes to provide and receive support, share resources, and to enjoy the social interaction that benefits adults and children alike.

The desire to provide an education that can be tailored to an individual's needs is a common drive that motivates this group of people. The child is at the centre of the process and, to a great extent, dictates its course. Anita explained that her children had not wanted to take GCSEs or A-Levels, which would easily have been possible at an examination centre nearby. Hamstrung by the restrictive uniformity of schooling to which I had been wedded for so long, I was surprised by this heresy of choosing to opt out of the orthodox examination route entirely.

I found myself having to come to terms with the possibility that I had operated within a system in which secondary school students are perceived essentially as league-table data fodder. Schools allocate inordinate resources to bridging the 'attainment gap', at the expense of developing the individual, and I had been one of those resources. Analysing lists of English examination results year after year, one of my dominant concerns, I have to admit, had been whether or not my department and I would be perceived as 'successful'. Much as I tried to ensure that my lessons were engaging, I rarely troubled myself by agonising for any length of time over how many students had enjoyed their English courses. Jo's comments about the enjoyment factor of home education certainly set me thinking:

We had seen how happy the children were being home educated and how creative they were allowed to be and didn't

*want that to change. Schools only seem interested in results
these days and not in developing the whole child.*

This was a parent so committed to the broadest concept
of education that she had no qualms whatever in supporting
her children's wishes to forego the orthodox schooling
experience. Talking to her brought home to me the disturbing
truth that, from her perspective, I'd been a component of a
restrictive system. She naturally placed her faith in her
children's judgement to choose the education that suited
them. Teenagers so often struggle to gain public examination
grades in subjects that their parents and school teachers have
seen fit to choose for them. Here was the other side of the
coin. Jo's son and daughter, like Anita's children, were given
a free hand to specialise in directions that they themselves
decided were best suited to their individual personalities and
aspirations. They studied in whatever areas they wanted,
whenever they wanted. When it came to tertiary education,
all four of Anita's children ultimately followed the route of
self-motivated learning offered by the Open University,
whereby they could pursue specialisms within time frames of
their own choosing.

HE is effectively a horses-for-courses approach to
education, where an informed parent is able to nurture a
child's particular talents and personal preferences. Besides a
general range of intellectual aptitudes, each child possesses
unique gifts or interests that schools cannot be relied upon
either to recognise or develop. I recall the story of a close
family friend's brother who had not learned to read by the age
of eighteen. However, he demonstrated one particular ability:
he could make accurate scale-model aeroplanes out of paper.
This aptitude was disregarded by his teachers who, ironically,
saw it as an obstacle to learning. He subsequently became an

artisan, successfully turning his artistic hand to carving objects out of wood. Having made a living for himself by exploiting his flair for designing and creating, he then acquired premises and opened a shop to sell arts and crafts artefacts and antiques, becoming a millionaire in the process.

When one refers to gifted children in a school context, the assumption is that these are the most academically able students who will achieve the highest examination grades in the subjects for which they are entered. There are also gifted children who may never achieve 'pass' grades in any examinations they ever take. My contention is that greater efforts are required to ensure that the 'gifts' all children possess, other than the academic, are actively developed. A home-education context may be both more beneficial and more sympathetic in this respect than regular attendance at a state school, particularly in the case of those labelled 'low attainers'.

Caleb, one of my nephews, would have satisfied the standard school criteria for being of low academic potential throughout his time at secondary school. He has since literally carved out a successful career for himself as a stonemason. Now in his early twenties, his skills are in such demand that he is self-employed. When I asked my sister if she had ever been aware of his special talent, she showed me a piece of Bath stone that she kept as an ornament in her garden. At the age of seven, her son had inscribed his name neatly in Roman script on its surface. Throughout his school career, no teacher had ever known of his skill. Schools let some children down in their preoccupation with high-achievers who will reflect them in a strong academic light.

I am not anti-examination. Schools must continue to provide every opportunity for students to develop their academic potential to the full. However, there has to be scope in the curriculum for the encouragement of individuals' less obvious or hidden strengths.

It's one of the ironies of our education system that schools also let students down who do possess the knack of being able to pass examinations. Encouraging sixth formers en masse to apply for higher education is not in every student's best interests. University application is the next stage on the conveyor belt for as many students as a school can manage. The kudos to be gained from sending high numbers of sixth formers on to degree courses is one of the standards of a 'successful school'.

However, the currency of a degree has seen a fall in the twenty-first century. A first-class degree and a 2:1 carry real clout with employers. Lesser degree qualifications, however, may not prove to be the anticipated passport to success in the competitive jobs market. I know many students who have taken the university route, gained a degree, spent several years looking for a career opening, and ended up doing work that was both unfulfilling and poorly paid. I should know because, as a head of sixth form, I was for almost ten years the teacher responsible for UCAS applications. University study is not in every young person's best interests, particularly if a graduate comes out at the end of the process with a middling pass, an unsuccessful search for a placement in one's desired career, and the prospect of a huge loan to pay off in the event of ever being generously remunerated.

I acknowledge the importance of children being given the opportunity to pass examinations. I also accept that schools are able to develop children in a multiplicity of directions, including sport, public speaking, charity work, and so on. I would not discount these facts. But schools may fail to identify and actively suppress the idiosyncrasies in a child's personality that are symptomatic of a special talent. Parents who home educate are unlikely to miss such inclinations in their children. These tendencies may be unconnected to a child's cognitive ability. Jo spoke with pride about her children's individual accomplishments:

We do encourage their unique talents.

Her daughter Francesca, at ten years of age, has already distinguished herself:

Francesca has excelled in art and creative activities. She has learned to crochet and sew and can follow instructions on how to make garments or toys (using the sewing machine) far better than I can. She did belong to a drama group up until recently, but now plays tennis and goes horse riding regularly. She also has piano lessons and I'm teaching her the guitar. She loves writing songs and her lyrics are particularly wacky! She loves animals and nature and spends hours in the garden. She's a good little gardener and knows all her plants and trees. She also loves reading which has been great.

Schools have increasingly become data-centred, as opposed to child-centred, institutions, resulting in students being perceived as cohorts rather than as individuals. It's small wonder that staff overloaded with the detailed administrative requirements of assessment, accountability and lesson preparation have any time at all to deal with children's individual needs on a one-to-one basis.

Home education is clearly, and will remain, a minority educational venture. However, I believe that the attractions for parents of HE do highlight major weaknesses in the state sector. Children are required to make significant adjustments in their behaviour to meet school demands. It would be preferable if schools reciprocated by doing more to adjust to children's needs.

The systems in place to educate the current generation are not flexible enough to acknowledge individuality in a meaningful sense. In any subject on the secondary school curriculum, for example, there is limited scope for a student to go off and pursue a personal line of inquiry. Subject syllabuses are clearly defined, and every element has to be covered by every student. We let children down in secondary schools by offering them the illusion of choice.

16. What Has Teaching Taught Me?

Life-Changing Decisions

A few years into my career, I discovered an important fact about young people and I subsequently made a point of passing it on to everyone I taught: many teenagers have to make the most important decisions about their lives at an age when they may not be emotionally equipped to make them. My reason for confiding this disconcerting fact to them was simply to offer them existential comfort: they weren't alone in their suffering.

Parents and teachers can advise children as much as they like about subject options, for example, but the intellectual tastes and inclinations of developing minds are changeable. What seems a good course for one to study at age fourteen may not be at all enjoyable at sixteen. It's also impossible to foresee how the onset of subsequent teenage distractions and preoccupations will interfere with study levels. The problematic stage of adolescence, when one is experiencing major psychological and physical changes, is the time when life-defining educational decisions have to be made.

On examination results days at the end of each summer break, the vulnerability of teenagers often manifested itself for me. It was one of my responsibilities to be at school to help collate and distribute examination results to tremulous students. I came to anticipate an annual phenomenon, acted out by a handful of candidates, that was guaranteed to upset me. It involved witnessing those who, over the full two years, had given the impression of having minimal interest in their GCSE or A-Level progress. Strangely, they would be amongst the first to arrive at school to collect their results. It was further upsetting when these candidates demonstrated genuine surprise at being awarded the poor grades that their teachers had predicted. Children of all ages are expert at burying fears and anxieties, able to delude themselves that all is well in the various compartments of their lives.

Interestingly, I experienced a similar situation on the day when results for degree students were released at the university my daughter attended. Lucy was too anxious about going to the campus to collect her English result, choosing instead to wait for the postman to deliver it a few days later. I secretly went along to the university and queued up with those waiting to get a look at the lists posted on the results notice board. Listening to the excited chatter of those around me, my attention was arrested by one dramatic comment from a girl behind me to her friend: 'I've just realised that I've wasted three years of my life.' After hearing that, you can imagine my relief at seeing my daughter's upper second pass on the board.

Early in my stint as a head of sixth form, I came across one alpha-juvenile who had gained a deserved reputation for being a 'jack the lad'. Full of false bonhomie and surreal excuses for failing to produce homework or arriving late, he subsequently gained passes in three subjects. One pass was two grades lower than that required to secure him a place at a local university college to take up a degree course in Sports Studies.

In the privacy of my office, he dropped all pretence and pleaded emotionally for me to help him. It seemed a long shot, but I thought that trying to contact the college office was at least worth a try. Initially surprised that I could get through by phone, I was amazed when, after hearing me singing the praises of the student's sterling contributions to the school rugby team, the college agreed to accept him. The immense gratitude he expressed seemed entirely out of character with him. Intense competition for higher-education places almost twenty years on means that such a scenario couldn't be played out today. Fortunately for that individual then, an eleventh-hour decision to demonstrate genuine concern for his academic future was successful.

Behind the Mask

Possibly the most important of my head-of-sixth-form duties was guiding students through the UCAS process. As I'd previously been a head of English, I was considered the most suitable person to help all students with the preparation of the Personal Statement. This account of about 500 words, a student's attempt to justify application for the course of choice, entailed sensitive interaction with each sixth former. Probing applicants about their personal interests, pastimes and hobbies showed me other sides to those individuals that I thought I knew well. There were details that applicants would most definitely not have wanted their peers to discover. Some were regularly involved in officiating in some capacity at religious ceremonies, others helped out with community projects, and several did voluntary work at hospitals. In the hurly burly of sixth-form life, it was inadvisable for students to make public any facts about themselves that might suggest involvement in non-alpha-male pursuits.

The older boys become, the more difficult it can be to see behind the mask of casual indifference to anything other than the immediate and superficial. This may seem an outrageous generalisation, but it was the experience I gained of teaching in a Greater London boys' comprehensive. I'd been troubled by the suspicion that few amongst the generation I was teaching had any spiritual dimension to their lives. The public face that an adolescent shows to the world is often at odds with the private self. Regularly reading personal statements reassured me that the boisterousness, brashness and bravado I daily encountered often disguised the sensitive human beings with whom I interacted. I felt privileged to discover, for example, that several of those perceived as hotheads by certain colleagues were actively involved in the community, doing voluntary work to assist old people, the physically and mentally disabled, and the homeless.

The World of Work

Teaching taught me that the majority of young people appreciate the efforts of their teachers to get them successfully through their education and prepare them for the demands and responsibilities of adult life. I held a personal prejudice for a number of years early in my career that compulsory education should not be encumbered by considerations of the world of work. Being an English teacher and, therefore, a champion of literature and the arts, I was rather precious about certain aspects of everyday life, such as earning a living. The fact that students approached me on a regular basis with questions about particular forms of employment resulted in me tempering my blinkered mindset.

I learned that a rounded education should be truly all-encompassing.

I found young people to be far more focused than I ever was on choosing the right career for themselves. The more the economy creaked and job security foundered over the four decades I taught, the more hard-nosed students seemed to become about the realities of finding themselves a place in the commercial world.

In lesson down time, I regularly invited classes to share ideas with me about life, the universe and everything. I was particularly interested in pupils' visions of how they saw themselves in fifteen years' time. I began one discussion by handing out sheets of paper and asking the students to write down, anonymously, the five things they wanted out of life by the time they reached thirty. Most of them trotted out the identical formula for ultimate happiness: 1) a big house; 2) a good job; 3) a 'fit' wife; 4) a 'flash' car; and 5) a couple of kids. There was general agreement that the key to their dreams was a well-paid job.

I reached the age of eighteen before seriously addressing the topic of deciding on a suitable job. This lack of urgency may have been because there was the assumption in the 1960s of an abundance of employment, whenever one chose to venture into the jobs market. Attending a grammar school, I accepted the student party line that the task of seeking full-time employment was best put off until all examination avenues had been exhausted.

As far as setting out on my own career path was concerned, I allowed a teacher to make up my mind up for me in the upper sixth. I had a general idea that I wanted a job that involved making a useful contribution to society, but beyond that – nothing. Any specific career probes I made were at his suggestion.

I didn't know how I should 'use' the subjects I'd studied at O and A-Level to help me find a job. A-Level study had been simply a matter of continuing with subjects for which I'd shown some aptitude, with no future occupation in mind. My form tutor, Mr Booth, who was also my careers adviser, organised an interview for me with the civil service, which came to nothing, and then produced the paperwork for me to apply for teacher training. My input to the process was negligible. The advice to apply for a place at a teacher training college seemed wildly ambitious. How could anyone in their right mind consider letting me loose with children!

The situation for young people nowadays looking ahead to gainful employment, in a society where there is far greater division of labour, would appear to make their search infinitely more difficult than the one I encountered in the late 1960s.

Schools use the careers service to provide young people with ideas about the possible directions open to them. The professional advisers who visited my students on site to provide careers guidance were in constant demand. I'm wholly in favour of such collaborative arrangements, but I have to admit to being amused by other strategies I've experienced with a view to giving children insights into the working world. For example, a general recommendation was made to staff in my time as head of English to introduce careers advice into our teaching, whenever an opportunity presented itself.

This initiative struck me as an irksome and tedious waste of time, but the exercise was not without some amusement. Always prepared for the challenge of lateral thinking, I gave the suggestion some thought. I supposed that after reading the description of the cowhands at work in Steinbeck's *Of Mice and Men*, I might point out to my class, 'By the way, if you enjoyed that extract from the novel, perhaps you might give some thought to the possibility of pursuing a career in farming when you leave school. The careers advisor can give you leaflet.' Or perhaps I wouldn't.

The scheme gathered pace and was formalised into an action plan. Instructions were passed to me to devote department meeting time to discussing and drawing up a report on ways that we could link our work schemes for Years 7 to 11 to the world of work. I don't remember how we eventually managed to satisfy the management team member's request with an actual written document, but I do remember some of the hilarious possibilities my colleagues devised in response to this curricular mandate. We investigated, amongst other topics, planning an appropriate menu for the visiting dignitaries to Macbeth's castle at Inverness for the banquet. The scene when Macbeth seeks out the three witches at their haunt on the heath also had potential for a careers project: Discuss how pharmacy has developed as a career path from the earliest times to the present day. Barry Hynes' *A Kestrel for a Knave* threw up a cornucopia of careers and crafts, from turf accounting to teaching. There were also valuable pointers in the novel for running a chip shop.

Secondary schools incorporate work experience programmes to provide tasters of the working world, year 10 students typically spending a few weeks in local work placements. These can be a genuine eye opener for those involved, the negative experiences sometimes being as important as the positive. For example, the office environment that some opted for occasionally proved to be entirely unsuitable. Learning such a lesson whilst still at school is a valuable one. There were also workplace environments that initially appeared to school staff to hold no attraction whatsoever. But what do teachers know! I remember visiting a boy who was in his element working at a mucky car-breaking yard. I found myself back at the site fifteen years later because I was looking for a second-hand replacement wing mirror for my daughter's VW Polo. I approached the office, an old static caravan, to be greeted by the same boy I'd visited on work experience. There he was, but on this occasion, as he informed me, he was the owner of the operation.

From age fourteen, I would recommend students to be encouraged to undertake their own careers research programme. This would involve exploring employment areas generally and making direct enquiries with businesses or organisations in which they showed an interest. Children should routinely carry out independent research into career opportunities. Secondary students demonstrating unique talents should be proactive as far as thinking about life beyond compulsory education is concerned: investigating professions online; contacting businesses; organising formal visits, arranging voluntary work; and applying for details of apprenticeships, further or higher education courses or on-the-job training. The completion of small-scale studies into anything from employment openings to employment law could be built into the timetable. The ideal time for this work-related research would be the weekly tutorial lesson with the form tutor.

I decided in my mid-fifties that, had I not taught for a living, I would have enjoyed film animation. I remember now that in my first year of secondary school, I used to produce a hand-drawn newspaper I called 'The Hags, Crones and Fiends Mag' with my friend John Elliott. We charged school mates a penny a time to read it. We made what we considered a fortune. Besides writing copy, I enjoyed creating the zany drawings we needed. I didn't have the wit to realise a few years later that this passion could have been the springboard for a career choice. I can't blame Mr Booth for not directing me along this course. In our brief conversations, I shyly uttered monosyllabic responses to his inquiries. I went along with what he suggested and am grateful, of course, that he took the time to advise me as best he could. But I do wonder what I might have done if I'd been clearer in those conversations about the activities I particularly enjoyed and the talents that I'd modestly kept to myself.

Role Models

Young people need role models and teachers need to be aware that they may be selected, without their knowledge, to fulfil such a responsibility. Teachers cannot help but become important to children because they spend so much time together. Mr Pembroke, a geography teacher as well as my early rugby coach, was a significant influence on me in my early secondary school days, though he would never have known it.

I secretly admired his easy manner in the classroom and his all-round rugby skill. He selected me to play at fly half in the Year 7 rugby team, when my knowledge of the game was limited. Just before our opening match against arch rivals West Hill School, he had the team in a huddle for the pre-match chat. I was thrilled when he said to the rest of the team, "Harry (my nickname then) here is faster than anybody over that first ten yards, so if he makes a break try and keep up with him." I'd had no idea that he rated me so highly. From that moment on, any time spent in Mr Pembroke's company was good time. He had a greater influence on my developing attitudes and tastes than my own father, whom I didn't see much of in my childhood. There is a team photograph I still have from that time, and it's interesting to note the similarity of our facial expressions as I sit there next to him.

There were times in my career when I suspected individual children of being more interested in me as a person than was customary in pupil/teacher relationships. This being the case, I felt an even greater responsibility on my part never to betray negative behaviour traits of any kind that an impressionable mind might pick up. On the contrary, I would sow seeds of positivity that I hoped the pupil would try to emulate. This would include attitudinal as well as behavioural mannerisms, from adopting an open-minded stance on all racial and religious matters, real problem areas in the district in which I taught, to picking up others' litter in the classroom. If one or two pupils in every class I taught looked upon me as a role model, there was a chance they might become role models for their peers.

Education Overhaul

Writing about my career from a distance, I regret the coercion that I constantly found myself using to control children, just as I regret the levels of coercion to which ordinary classroom teachers were subjected by education administrators and managers hooked on top-down management styles. Many of the formal school 'punishments' I administered left me feeling devalued as an educator. A utopian learning environment should involve as few punishments as possible, if any. Similarly, I resent the thousands of hours I spent producing reams of facile documentation. The main purpose of much of it seemed to me to secure careerists' ascent of educational or political ladders.

A secondary school teacher's workload has increased enormously over the past forty years. There are far more administrative duties to be carried out, in copious detail, and many more additional tasks, ranging from supervising breakfast duty in the canteen to 'riot control' – sitting in the withdrawal room with misbehaving pupils who have, for one reason or another, been removed from their classrooms for a specified period of time. These were often the children of struggling single-parent families, broken homes, and unstable domestic backgrounds. It was disturbing to sit in the same room as a dozen or more of these children. Some had become disillusioned with all school authority figures, adults in general and, it seemed, the very world around them. These boys needed positive examples even more than the able children.

The 'punishment' of being withdrawn from classes was the last thing they needed. Special needs departments do their best to support these children on a day-to-day basis, but a totally different, and mutually beneficial, school experience is necessary for them.

For teachers to keep headteachers, school governors and politicians happy, the focus is on getting the best academic results possible from all students in their subject areas. From this perspective, children could represent a potential obstacle to success, not the means of success. Disciplinary issues in the classroom are more prevalent with professionals who allow their careers to be dominated by consideration of assessment outcomes. Frustrated children occasionally ask teachers, "Why do we have to do all this boring stuff?" The response could well be, "Stop complaining and just get on with it." I often found myself answering, "It's nothing to do with me, I'm afraid. Unfortunately I wasn't invited to help plan this course."

I never found it did any harm being frank with children, especially given some of the mind-numbing lesson content I was responsible for passing on. Honesty and respect for children's opinions made it easier to handle some of the more challenging pupils I taught. I would have obviously preferred to be offering them a completely different learning experience, but this wasn't possible. Nevertheless, I am optimistic that I may see improvements in this respect in my lifetime.

A corollary of creeping incrementation, adding to the ever-increasing burden of responsibilities that the profession has to shoulder as a matter of course, has been that parents and carers are provided with ready-made opportunities for having less and less to do with important areas of their children's upbringing. Parents could be excused for asking themselves, for example, 'Why give my child breakfast when, if he arrives at school early enough, staff will be supervising a breakfast club in the canteen, with hot food and drink ready and waiting?' Schools even make arrangements for children to stay on site long after the end of the school day until their parents are able to pick them up after work.

Many of those employed as teachers in today's state schools fulfil the functions of surrogate parents, social workers and educators. There is a seriously limited grasp of the extent of a teacher's extra-curricular responsibilities and duties in the twenty-first century.

Knowledge and Difference

Perhaps the most important discovery teaching taught me is that the world of knowledge is changing and evolving more rapidly than it has ever done before. The clearest example to me of this phenomenon was the sudden appearance of Forensic Science as a degree study course at certain higher education institutions. 'CSI' inspired widespread curiosity amongst television audiences, and this specialist field of criminal detection is now deemed worthy of study to degree level. Thanks to the success of the many cooking and baking television programmes, it's now possible to study Baking and Confectionery Technology at university. Traditional degree courses continue to flourish, but they are being supplemented by subject options with a direct practical relevance to the commercial world. Universities are taking an important lead in the twenty-first century by attaching intellectual credibility to areas that I had previously considered unlikely ever to be accorded degree status.

I'm aware that vocational degree courses, such as Yacht Construction, provide ammunition for those who believe that we are living in an idiocracy. However, the realities of living in an advanced capitalist society are that the range of highly technical, specialist career opportunities is expanding apace.

A few decades ago, heads of sixth form were advised to encourage more university applicants to apply for a general engineering degree, to meet a national shortfall. I'm sure my efforts would have been more successful had I been able to refer specifically to exciting areas of study, such as yacht construction.

Many in the business world have been making the point for decades that our education system does not produce individuals with the 'skills' they need. Forward-thinking organisations are setting up post-graduate institutions to develop potential employees with the specialist qualities they require. Some are also undertaking major investment by reviving the apprenticeship system for sixteen to nineteen year olds. Stronger links with industry will encourage the diversity of provision our education system needs. However, it's not enough for schools to rely solely on the business world to increase the range of technical-vocational opportunities for the 14-19 age group. Government leadership in this area is vital.

Schools today tend to be hung up on imitating those institutions that gain reputations for being successful, mainly in terms of the academic achievements of their students. This trend promotes conformity of school branding, curriculum delivery and teaching priorities, as opposed to the concepts of individuality and difference. As a free thinker, I want children in schools to be given time and freedom to follow independent avenues of inquiry. Curriculum time for pursuing personal interest studies should be introduced in primary schools and built into courses at secondary level. What children are required to learn must not totally preclude opportunities for satisfying their own intellectual curiosity.

Secondary schools are tightly-run organisations claiming to provide children with the knowledge and skills to lead fulfilling lives. Formal education has traditionally emphasised the value of theoretical knowledge. I place the highest premium on the cognitive development of children in our education system. Indeed, the older I get, the more I enjoy basking in the complexities of higher order thinking and reflection. These are the greatest gifts a broad and balanced education can confer. But it is blinkered thinking to persist in the belief that subject areas with a practical bent be patronized as lower status.

Young people would be better served if they were given the opportunity to spend some of their time in compulsory education pursuing special interests. For some this may be time devoted to further theoretical exploration, whilst others may be inclined towards more practical pursuits.

Knowledge changes. Fifty years ago at school I was led to believe that the Duke of Wellington was a thoroughly good bloke; that the smallest unit of matter was the atom; that the novels of W.C. Johns were jolly good reads for developing children; and that homosexuality was an abomination. Fifty years on I smile at some of the now redundant information it was thought fit I should learn, and the crude disciplinary measures employed to force me to learn. Fifty years from now, when I'm long gone, people my age will smile at much of what was taught and how children were organised in state schools early in the twenty-first century. Knowledge may change, but one educational constant is that every child possesses individual strengths that schools should be obliged to develop. The political zeitgeist of a preoccupation with standards obscures this logic.

There are three particular areas I would identify as requiring urgent attention:

1] The need to adopt a teaching model that incorporates formalised one-to-one interaction between teacher and learner.

2] A greater emphasis on independent learning at all stages of secondary education.

3] The inclusion of a moral/philosophical education component.

Our current system is too rigid and prescriptive, and will produce a generation that 'needs' close direction because spoon-feeding is so commonplace in schools. It is no coincidence that in their private lives, conformity is what the majority of teenagers craves.

Young people in our culture who express an inclination to do or say anything that doesn't conform to the expectations of the herd run a serious risk of being considered odd. The impulse to ridicule 'oddness' is one of the main causes of bullying in our schools. It can be so ferocious that some victims resort to suicide as the only means of escape. One of the greatest threats to the peace of mind of many teenagers is that of being singled out as 'different' from the herd. Difference is stigmatized. Social networking sites can transform a child from a secure personality enjoying the anonymity of the group into a social pariah within minutes.

Education has a job to do to promote and celebrate difference, a quality that is under serious threat in our secondary education system.

17. Troubling Times

Anxiety Culture

State schools are now dominated by a culture of anxiety. Terminally-terrified teachers are constantly in fear of being brought to book for unacceptable student performance in public tests and examinations. The prevalence of the fear factor facilitates the practice of headteachers maintaining a distance between themselves and their staff. Before the days of league tables, I found it was easier for heads to remain on friendly terms with every member of staff. Current arrangements exploit the potential for friction between school managers and the main teaching body. Our state education arrangements covertly encourage divisiveness within schools. The decision to give Ofsted inspection teams the power to turn up at a school for an inspection with little notice was confirmation for me that fear is the key for the DfE.

The supportive function of LEAs is a thing of the past. Absolute power is now in the hands of Ofsted. One sneak peek from an inspection team can damn a school and does irreparable damage to the culture of education in this country. Teaching has never been a more stressful career. The announcement in February 2016 that the government had missed its teacher recruitment targets for four consecutive years came as no surprise to me. Teaching is now losing its vocational appeal.

One may argue that the focus on results and inspection is only right and proper if teachers are to be truly accountable. I would argue that a preponderance of anxiety in the staffroom does not make for a healthy classroom or, indeed, a healthy school. To add further pressure to the profession, it is no longer good enough to produce results that correspond to each student's potential. Introducing the concept of *value-added* represented a move to crank the pressure up yet another notch. Teachers are now judged on how much higher performance can be raised over and above the anticipated level of success for all examination candidates. It would be wonderful if every professional were able to produce countless silk purses every summer, but it's not humanly possible.

Disaffection

The majority of children who are disaffected with school generally are following the wrong courses. There are few viable alternatives to GCSE subjects at key stage 4 in the majority of secondary schools, and GCSEs do not suit every student. An alternative pathway should be available nationwide that has a more practical base for those struggling generally with the traditional timetable offerings.

Lack of success at any level can give rise to disaffection and resentment. I encountered numerous difficult situations where students, and their parents, were under the impression that there was almost an entitlement to success once a child had been admitted on to a course.

In extreme cases I found myself struggling with the scenario where a disaffected student systematically tried to undermine not only his own learning experience but also, cynically, that of his peers. This strategy has a twofold 'benefit' for a disruptive pupil: he won't be seen to fail alone, and he will be instrumental in undermining a teacher's reputation. The student's failure is deflected on to others. These were situations I encountered, the result of children being required to follow courses for which they were unsuited and in which they would only achieve the lowest examination grades at best.

According to Ofsted in September 2014, low-level classroom disruption results in children losing up to an hour a day of teaching. Pupil misbehaviour was one of the reasons why Jo's son Scottie was unable to tolerate everyday school life. Constantly dealing with petty disciplinary issues is probably the most dispiriting feature of teaching.

I understand the argument that every teacher should be held to account for their students' progress. But the pressure on teachers is increased enormously if a significant minority in every class is pursuing courses for which these students are unsuited. I have lost faith in the quality of the whole teaching/learning/examining process. Our 'world-class examination system', dominated by spoon-feeding and cramming to get every child in a class across the 'pass' line, does little to develop genuine creativity and intellectual curiosity.

Gone are the days when a young, keen, fresh-faced teacher would be given a pat on the head for coping with the Mathematics bottom set that nobody else in the department wanted to teach. I've taught such classes and been told that keeping the boys out of trouble would, in itself, be considered a great achievement. The regular crop of GCSE courses has been with us for over three decades. Now is the time to extend key stage 4 provision.

Frustration

Caught up in my commitment to the comprehensive ideal, I was pleased to be working in a school that I saw as being closer to the egalitarian model that, in my opinion, was right for children. The idea of teaching in a grammar school, the like of which I attended as a child, was anathema to me. A comprehensive school was surely the fairest model, and the right place to be if you were a teacher with democratic inclinations. It was only towards the end of my career that I understood why I had become disillusioned with what I had trusted would be a fulfilling public role. Teaching in a successful comprehensive for the last two decades of my career proved much more frustrating than I could have imagined in so many respects.

The difficulties that persistently troubled me centred around the fact that many of those educational activities that I valued, and that I hoped to develop when I became head of an English department, were perceived by the educational élite as having limited value. I repeat the point I made earlier that finding the time to read a complete novel with a key stage 3 English class was not straightforward. When the national curriculum tightened its grip on schools, I found myself having to justify my department's ethos with management colleagues. I also had to contend with the amateur viewpoints of educational professionals in central government offices who had limited contact with children but who knew what was best for them and, coincidentally, for their own careers.

The major flaw inherent in democracy eventually became evident to me: the people selected to fill positions of authority tend to be those who actively seek influence and power. These can be the people least able to make impartial decisions when it comes to deciding on and implementing policy. The trap of allowing extrinsic considerations linked to self-advancement to determine decision making can prove too tempting to resist.

Leadership

My aversion to high horses stems from my problem with 'leadership'. Despite eventually retiring as an assistant head, I never sought to be a leader. There were occasions I recall when I was advised to submit an application for a specific post, either because I supposedly possessed certain qualities or abilities that made me a safe bet, or to reduce the chances of an unfavourable candidate gaining the position. I was not overtly ambitious.

I have always equated leadership with protection, protecting those I am 'leading' from red tape and tedium. I listened to those in my teams in order to find ways to make their jobs as rewarding and worthwhile as possible. My interpretation of the term 'leadership' doesn't have time for the nonsense of getting those below me to toe every line going. I became dogged by the nagging doubt that any educational initiative from on high stemmed from a politician's desire to ascend a greasy pole, rather than promoting informed debate.

I'm also averse to knocking people into different shapes. A superior's instruction to knock him or her 'into shape' was the general response whenever colleagues made the foolhardy decision to express and act on viewpoints that ran counter to 'perceived wisdom'. After suffering a period of extended misbehaviour and provocation at the hands of one particularly difficult pupil, an accomplished member of my English department eventually decided that her only recourse was to resign from her post when her refusal to have the boy in her classroom was rejected. I still carry a weight of guilt for failing to prevent that teacher from taking such an extreme course of action.

My belief is that every teacher should be valued for her or his strengths and talents, whatever their position in the school hierarchy. The temptation to adopt a safety-first approach to teaching dominates the formulaic three-part lesson initiative that prevailed in class teaching when I retired. The 'characters' who inspired me in the early years of my career, who could be guaranteed to excite and arouse curiosity in students, would have had no truck with the doctrinaire approaches to teaching that now set time limits for each sub-divided section of a lesson.

Those with positions of responsibility in schools face an inescapable leadership imperative: they are required to demonstrate that individuality must not get in the way of conformity. Praise for individual strengths is a luxury in this culture. There is little time for sincere praise in an environment of constant checking and balancing. It was once explained to me that every teacher in my school had to adopt the three-part lesson régime so that 'children knew what to expect in each subject area'. It was sheer coincidence that I was reading Solzhenitsyn's *A Day in the Life of Ivan Denisovich* at the time.

I once went up to Russell Square for an INSET session that was run to prepare teaching staff for middle management. Those of us in attendance were given a role-play to undertake in pairs, requiring us to improvise a conversation between a head of English and a member of the department, with a less than perfect attendance record, who wanted time off for a doctor's appointment. Playing the part of the department head, I immediately granted the request. If a colleague is asking to see a doctor, what right had I to deny that request? I could not be tempted to be heavy-handed or craftily cajoling during the exercise that in my case lasted less than a minute. The big stick is an overrated management tool in any walk of life.

The Basics

I felt increasingly alienated by the changing face of state education as my career drew to a close. The National Curriculum had done its worst. It had been introduced with a triumphal fanfare as an educational 'entitlement' for all children. The irony of this claim, from my perspective, was that the new curriculum had imposed serious limitations on my entitlement to teach. I broached my reservations about the job to a fellow professional who explained to me that I was at fault: I was inflexible, not the system, and I was stuck in the past. My response was that I was an idealist with little left to idealise about. This cut no ice with my colleague because older teachers, apparently, simply become 'tired and reactionary'.

I continue to lack confidence in the direction state education has taken. There is too much focus on compulsory elements, for both students and their teachers. In practice, students do not have the wealth of choice I would wish for them at any stage of secondary education.

Sir Michael Wilshaw, delivering Ofsted's annual report in December 2014, issued a warning that secondary schools in England were not making sufficient progress, with up to a third judged to be not good enough. He argued that 170,000 pupils are now in inadequate secondary schools that need 'to concentrate on the basics'. Let's not be disingenuous, Sir Michael: secondary schools have been concentrating to death on 'the basics' and the policy hasn't worked.

There is a grudging acceptance that it's not only 'trendy left-wing teachers' who are to blame, but that disruptive student elements in schools have become an increasing problem. Let's be honest enough to admit that significant numbers of our secondary school populations are bored rigid much of the time they're at school. When students told me this to my face, which many of them did, I sometimes found myself at a loss and made the lame joke that coping with high levels of boredom was good preparation for life.

Reading the situation with my idealist's spectacles, the only solution is to liberate students' imaginations by root and branch reform of the secondary school curriculum. When members of any government use the word 'reform', the intention is to make the curriculum and assessment more 'rigorous' (a euphemism for 'boring'). If we were looking at a corresponding 'failing' area of performance in the private sector, astute businessmen would be calling for bankruptcy procedures to be set in motion. Sir Alan Sugar would pull the plug on the whole operation, and I'd agree with him. Primary schools place a higher premium on varied and imaginative learning experiences, but things fall apart at secondary level. The main reason, apparently, is that teachers do not stamp on low-level disruption. The low-level disruption that inspectors and educationists increasingly talk about is frequently a result of students reacting against the forces of coercion, conformity and curricular drudgery.

The majority of today's adolescents desires to be sociable in the classroom, and do not naturally perceive this impulse to be what teachers might call 'misbehaviour'. They're not the comparatively timid, retiring types that my peers and I were back in the 1960s. Teenagers have moved on, and why not? They are far more worldly wise than many imagine. A number of those I taught had no reservations about telling me how 'silly' they found the content of certain syllabus components.

Teenagers know their rights and, apparently, they are to be encouraged to have a positive sense of self-worth. A behavioural feature of which I developed a growing awareness is the absolute refusal by some to be embarrassed, cowed, humiliated, and/or victimised by an authority figure. This tendency can be threatening for a teacher but, in certain contexts, it is not a bad thing. Those my pals and I used to call 'strict' teachers in the mid-twentieth century, stamped on misconduct in ways that would be inconceivable now. A typical *I-don'tknow-how-you've-got-thebrass-neck-to-behave-in-thisway-in-my-classroom* rant would more than likely have been greeted by an ironic round of applause from the kind of classes I taught.

Young people 'grow up' quickly these days. They're 'savvy' in a host of ways that I wasn't when I was a teenager almost fifty years ago. The world-wide web provides near-spontaneous access to limitless information, ranging from the heights of human achievement to the depths of mankind's sordid underworld. Information and images from which children were protected when I was young, are now readily available to all who know which keys to press on a PC, whatever one's age.

Children want and need to be treated in a mature manner. Teachers who ignore this fact do so at their peril, as they will be in danger of pupils' efforts to turn the tables on them in the classroom. A not uncommon occurrence when attempting to discipline a student for speaking out of turn is to be greeted with the response, 'You can't control us because you're not a good teacher.' I would never have had the nerve to speak in such terms to a teacher, but it's one of the facts of teaching life in the twenty-first century, when relationships with certain children turn sour.

The pressure-cooker educational atmosphere in which teachers find themselves, dealing on a daily basis with large groups in enclosed spaces is not conducive to fostering easy relationships with children. Add the ingredients of a claustrophobic curriculum and we have a recipe that no right-minded educationist would wittingly cook up.

Guilt

After spending over ten years in charge of an English department, during the period when the bureaucrats ensured that the job suddenly became a poisoned chalice, I was asked to apply for the position of Head of Sixth Form. I did so and suddenly became my own boss in my own little world, and I enjoyed the change. I was still teaching English, which enabled me to continue working with young people in the classroom, but I also relished the task of guiding sixth formers through the arduous tasks of sixth-form course selection and applying for places in further and higher education.

The gloss was taken off the job for me when, a few years later, I eventually realised that some of those I'd directed to apply for university places should never have done so. Many found the financial hardships crippling, and some of those who completed their courses achieved only modest passes. I would feel happier now had there also been a broad range of nationally recognised vocational qualifications or apprenticeships from which certain students could have chosen.

With the chancellor of the exchequer pleased that the economy was 'motoring along' in the summer of 2015, he placed his faith in the commercial world to fill the gap in the provision of vocational education. The forming of educational policy on the hoof is a strategy that is guaranteed to activate my bullshit sensor. Businesses may, indeed, be in a strong enough position soon to flood the educational map with apprenticeships, thus extending badly-needed vocational opportunities. But, being a cautious person, I would prefer to see the speedy introduction of a coordinated government policy that gives every child of secondary school age entitlement to a wide spectrum of learning opportunities as an alternative to purely academic study.

18. Signposts

I offer a final chapter on new directions that I envisage for schools that would include consideration of the following priorities. I do so as a teacher who saw the light much later than should have been the case.

The Case for Students Spending Less Time in Classrooms

HMCI's Annual Report for 2012/13 refers to the phenomenon of 'low level but persistent disruptive behaviour in primary and secondary schools in England', and adds that 'teachers are frustrated by this behaviour'. In 2014, Ofsted chief Sir Michael Wilshaw, speaking on BBC Radio 4's 'Today' programme, said that inspectors would be "toughening up judgement on behaviour and it is in our children's interest that we do". My interpretation of Sir Michael's comments is that teachers are at fault for this worsening of children's behaviour in our state schools.

Undesirable pupil behaviour patterns and anti-social habits are serious concerns for teachers, school governors and parents. I share Sir Michael's concern for the cooperative majority of children in our schools. The effect of persistent misbehaviour, Ofsted tells us, results in some pupils in state schools losing up to an hour's learning a day, or thirty-eight days per year.

There are other dangerous anti-social practices that are increasingly exercising Ofsted; for example, the bullying of young people by their peers. Although it's discomfiting to find myself in accordance with an Ofsted judgement, it's reassuring that I am not alone in my concern. A 2015 survey by the anti-bullying pressure group *Ditch the Label* indicated that one in ten teenagers who had experienced bullying at school had attempted suicide. If true, this is a staggering statistic. Physical appearance was reported to be the main reason for the bullying. Schools do their best to deal with incidents of physical bullying, but the equally damaging psychological bullying is more difficult to pick up as the outward signs of abuse are not as obviously apparent.

Increasingly I am persuaded by the argument that, if schools are to continue to provide genuinely supportive educational environments, children need to feel and to be 'protected' from too close regular contact with the undesirable school 'behaviours' of those who are given to the casual victimisation of others. I use the word 'casual' pointedly, as my perception was that many of those engaging in anti-social conduct did not intend the psychological damage they were causing: they were simply conforming to a behavioural adolescent norm.

I found that, with few exceptions, children were even-tempered and cooperative in one-to-one situations with an adult. A worryingly significant proportion of them, however, become less manageable and even oppositional when spoken to by an adult when there was a peer-group audience. In this circumstance, the issue of offended dignity can become more important for the child than considerations of whether or not the behaviour in question is seriously at fault. It is easier to deal with a situation involving just two children, where one is physically abusing another. However, when there is a group observing the abuse, encouraging the oppressor with the chant of 'Fight! Fight! Fight!' the situation becomes more difficult to manage. The perpetrator of the violence, typically, dare not be seen to lose face to a teacher, whatever he or she may be doing.

The possibility of individuals filming such incidents with their mobile phones and uploading the material on to social networking sites further undermines a teacher's attempts to maintain order and ensure that good sense prevails when confrontational situations develop. The bane of networking sites is that they can encourage children who are immature and inexperienced in the ways of the world to dramatise themselves and their experiences in a reckless manner, with little regard for others' welfare. It's a case of a sizeable minority of unsophisticated minds in control of sophisticated technology.

The increasing incidence of graphic images of violence being uploaded by young people on to YouTube can have devastating consequences. One young person's morbid gratification at observing somebody he knows being beaten senseless is another's reason for self-harming out of a sense of blinding humiliation. The relatively sudden acquisition of high testosterone levels in adolescence can prove difficult to control for the developing mind. Unfortunately, it merely seems to some adults that children need the slightest excuse to demonstrate violent behaviour. Most worrying is the premeditated aggression that suggests an obsessive relationship with violence, as in the case of juvenile knife crime.

It would clearly be wrong to give the impression that instances of extreme misbehaviour are a feature of all secondary schools. Equally, it would be unrealistic to state that teachers never have to resolve unruly disputes between students. My reason for stating this self-evident fact is to give weight to my conviction that schools would be quieter and less stressful environments if fewer students were on site at any one time. Disciplinary problems, that waste so much valuable time in schools, would be significantly reduced if schools were not bursting at the seams with every child on the school roll in attendance every day of the week.

Besides the practical reasons outlined above, there is a more important reason still for reducing the amount of time that older students spend in formal lessons. They should be encouraged to take greater personal responsibility for their learning. Self-motivation and self-regulation are important elements of learning that must be actively developed. Children nowadays spend more time learning in all subject areas by the use of interactive computer software, and there is no reason why they shouldn't be doing some components of their work at home or, if they or their parents prefer, in supervised private study areas within school.

Consequently, if teachers spent a little less time class teaching, they could spend more working with individuals. The aim of incorporating such a system in schools would be to open the way to genuine negotiation between teacher and pupil in areas ranging from subject choice, independent study topics and general support. Lessons for large groups of students would no longer be the rule for all learning experiences. The value of one-to-one tuition, built into the structure of the timetable, would be incalculable, in my opinion.

Personalised timetables could be devised for each student, who would be attached to a specific tutor. Each tutor would be responsible for the progress of, say, ten 'clients' from Years 9 to Year 13, two from each year group, with whom weekly contact meetings would be arranged. When they are not being taught formally in small or large teaching groups, or receiving one-to-one guidance from a tutor, students would be engaged in agreed independent study programmes.

The older a child becomes, the less time needs to be spent studying at school. The majority of homes contain the equipment necessary for home study. With iPads as affordable as the obligatory pair of designer trainers, teenagers have information at their fingertips that I could not have dreamt of twenty years ago. Gone are the days when it was impossible to undertake work at home in certain areas for want of drawing equipment, ordnance-survey maps, or history text books. A written subject assignment can now be provided on a memory stick the size of one's little finger. It was a source of amusement to me and to my students when, in the last few years of my career, I collected in homework essays from students in Years 10 and above. I would invariably have a sheaf of papers and a dozen or so memory sticks. 'Saving the planet, sir!' was the refrain from those who appeared to have developed an allergy to paper.

Just as pressure is increasing for employees in certain areas of the commercial world to be allowed to work at home, I firmly believe the same arrangement should be made available to students once they enter their teens. From my experience, the serious business of producing extended pieces of English coursework was always done as homework assignments. Class teaching involves covering the groundwork on a topic that is the preparation for the important business of students producing their own writing or creative work at home. Besides the practical benefits of easing congestion on transport systems, the policy of allowing teenagers to spend periods during their school week working off site, will also ease congestion in school corridors, playgrounds and classrooms.

There is the argument that some will choose not to do any work at home at all. I accept that this may be the case for a small minority, and point out that these are the individuals who could not be relied upon to work at school either. I would offer them activity options more suited to their abilities that do not solely comprise the generally academic diet prescribed at present for all students. If the option of working at home were seen as a privilege, it's one that could be withdrawn in the event of misconduct at school or failure to complete set work. Alternative provision of year or key-stage study areas would be made for those preferring to study on site and students unable to work at home for whatever reason.

I imagine this proposal prompting hollow laughter from many amongst those directly involved in the world of education. My response is that they should get used to the idea. It will happen.

Open Study

The primary school timetable should include an open-study component as preparation for my suggested changes to the secondary school curriculum. As children of primary-school age gain confidence in spoken and written language use, independent inquiry should be introduced. Giving younger children greater freedom to research personal topics in school is an educational priority. With one-to-one guidance, children should be supported in the development of individual projects. These can be shared with the rest of the class on completion, either in written form or as an oral presentation. Innate curiosity about the world in which children find themselves is all too soon lost in our state schools, to be quickly replaced by slavish devotion to multiple schemes of work. State education in this country is currently stricken with a paralysis of the imagination at DfE level.

There would be no prescription here and no list of suggested topics from which a choice had to be made. Where one child decides to work on the production of a poetry anthology, another might choose astronomical research. Children in this age group will already be demonstrating special interests in the world around them. The possibilities would be limitless and the educational value incalculable. At secondary level, independent studies in discrete areas would be built into subject syllabuses and the timetable. I can imagine that for some children this might be the most rewarding time in their school week.

Details of all work completed independently would be recorded and given official accreditation throughout a child's school career.

Einstein didn't formulate his ground-shaking hypotheses in the hope that someone in a position of scientific authority would award him a mark of one hundred per cent for his efforts. Knowledge can be exciting and of interest in itself. In recent years, unfortunately, knowledge has become simply a quantifiable commodity, the principle use of which is to judge the 'effectiveness' of an educational institution. The value of discovery learning cannot be underestimated.

I imagine the main criticism against relaxing the policy of constantly 'policing' children in schools would have nothing to do with the threat it poses to academic rigour, but a concern for practical considerations: 'You can't have children roaming around the school willy-nilly, doing whatever they want!' This will be one predictable objection from an educational culture bound to the suffocating principles of uniformity and control. It is time to dispense with the ball-and-chain curriculum.

From the moment an infant sets foot in school, the default procedures are for the child to sit still, stay in one place and be quiet. This form of educational conditioning essentially extends to the end of one's period of compulsory education, with occasional exceptions. The fact that these arrangements have become de rigueur for all children does not make them right for future generations. Children need to express themselves independently, and the corollary of acknowledging this truth is that the classroom door must be open at certain times in the school day.

The state-education mindset of applying sophisticated controls to condition children's behaviour, learning and unique creative impulses is counter-productive. A child who finds it difficult to sit still in one classroom after another for between twenty or thirty lessons a week is not necessarily an intentionally disruptive or naughty child. But that is what may be recorded on the subject's educational report card. Some children are able to conform happily to a sedentary learning experience, but many can't. Times have moved on and traditional school practices need to be reviewed. If you have any doubts, ask a teacher you know if the following instruction is still being used to gain total control over a class of children of any age: "Hands on heads, everyone!" You'll be unpleasantly surprised.

Apprenticeships

The stigma traditionally associated with vocational education will take some time to disappear. The attitude that those students who can't cope with an academic curriculum should be offered an easy option enabling them to work with their hands needs to be reviewed. Visiting Year 10 boys at their various work-experience locations during the summer term was a regular reminder for me that the words 'vocational' and 'easy' are not synonymous.

Given a taste of working as a car mechanic, one of my academically able students found it a constant challenge juggling with the awkward practical applications of physics concepts, as in bleeding car braking systems and adjusting carburettors. When asked at the end of his three weeks in a garage whether or not he'd miss the world of work, his immediate response was, 'School's a lot easier than this. Everything here has to be done so quickly and teachers don't lose their temper with you.' Interacting intelligently, sympathetically, and willingly with others in the workplace, is an essential feature of vocational placements. Schools make token efforts to try to encourage pupils to work together, for example in pair and small-group work, but ultimately the emphasis is always on individual performance.

New apprenticeships will need to include aesthetical, mathematical and scientific content if they are to be valid additions to the secondary curriculum. The blurring of distinctions between the academic and the vocational has been with us for some time already.

All students should be required to undertake vocational studies from well before the start of key stage 4. When I visited small businesses or companies that had taken one or more of our students for the Trident Programme, as we used to call three weeks of work experience, managers would often generalise with some impatience that teenagers lacked 1) social skills; 2) the ability to use their initiative in work-place contexts; 3) a basic grasp of the 3-Rs; and 4) the ability to apply common sense to work-place problems and scenarios. After listening to comments of this nature over three decades, I formed the opinion that there is a job to be done.

It follows that youngsters are more likely to satisfy employers in the four critical areas mentioned above if they are provided with a regular vocational diet, and where better to acquire it than in the commercial world. I'm not advocating that the least able should be sifted out of mainstream education and placed on a vocationally-intensive conveyor belt with the long-term prospect of them becoming trapped in low-income jobs. Every young person has to leave formal education at some point and, hopefully, find gainful employment. Therefore, I'm for an inclusive system that entails every child receiving vocational education strands in their studies throughout their secondary education.

Moral Education

Moral and philosophical studies would be included in any educational reform if I were given a voice. Many young people fall prey to living lives in which they are constantly encouraged by the media and social-networking sites to engage in potentially addictive activities. Obsessive dependency on drugs, alcohol, sex, violence, music from rock to rap, and social networking can monopolise young adults' minds in ways that I find alarming.

The world now offers young people limitless capacity to find metaphysical refuge in an ever-increasing range of mindless activities. The unthinking descent into media-centred nihilism needs a balancing mechanism, a moral/philosophical extension to secondary education. Young people go to the internet for spontaneous fixes in all manner of experiences. Technological phenomena exercise a primal formative influence on young minds, and responsible adults have limited ability to exercise control over what is consumed by their offspring.

The church has traditionally been identified as carrying the burden of responsibility for the moral health of British society, but church-going is not a way of life for the majority of our schoolchildren.

There is a strong case for including moral education in the school syllabus. I once wrote a few thousand words on the subject and passed them to my then head for his consideration. His wry chuckle masked his effort to respond politely. He told me that it was a good read but insisted that the timetable was packed solid already. There was no room for it. I am aware that I could be hoist by my own petard here, advocating yet further prescription to a densely-packed curriculum. My defence is that I put forward my suggestion in 1979 before the National Curriculum ever saw the light of day.

Headteachers have limited scope for being educationally innovative, and they do have my sympathy. The day-to-day practicalities of running a school, with a heavy emphasis on the financial, and effecting the latest national policy whims and fashions leave them little time for thinking imaginatively about the school curriculum. The top-down approach to curriculum 'planning' preferred by politicians is now rigidly in place, with the so-called professionals left to operate on the policy fringes.

Heads and governors share a determination to present their schools as civilised environments to outsiders, and they achieve remarkable degrees of success. The school where I completed my teaching career after a stay of thirty one years is a case in point. I survived as long as I did because I enjoyed my teaching at the school, where I respected the students and staff.

Inspectors go into countless schools which they praise as being 'civilised communities'. However, even in civilised communities, one would be surprised at the levels of homophobia, sexism, racism and religious intolerance that can be heard from children during a fifteen-minute stint on any playground duty. The gap between the publicly-demonstrated good conduct of children on best behaviour and the prejudicial attitudes demonstrated by youngsters when not under adult supervision needs to be addressed. Society does have a problem in this respect. For example, the national press currently focuses many column inches on accounts of articulate school and university students who are being radicalised by religious extremists.

I am not suggesting that there is a moral vacuum at the heart of western culture. However, examples of morally bankrupt behaviour by leading public figures in the country who conceal the greater part of their wealth in offshore accounts to avoid taxation suggest that immoral conduct that can be concealed from public view is rife at every level of society. Presumably, most wealthy tax evaders went to exclusive schools where the school motto may have been some variation or other of 'Pecunia enim omnia'. Teachers must be at fault, as they are always the first port of call when serious social problems arise, so we must make a start by addressing moral issues within state education.

At regular intervals during my career, I would put a variety of questions to pupils of all ages as a means of gauging their moral health. The old chestnuts were:

1] If you found a wallet containing a hundred pounds, would you take it to your local police station?

2] If a friend approached you and offered you a new MP3/iPod/smartphone for a very small sum of money, would you buy it?

I would insist on students answering honestly and anonymously. The results were consistently disturbing, the majority putting self-interest before considerations of the public good.

There are many other examples I could cite that made me concerned about the moral health of the children I taught. If ever a fight started whilst I was on playground duty, shouts of 'Fight! Fight!' would immediately be heard. Boys responding to the herd instinct would rush to the scene as quickly as possible to shout encouragement to one or other of the boys. Fighting was a topic I used to tackle in class. I would ask why it was rare for any student to step in to stop a physical confrontation between two children. I could, perhaps, understand excuses that nobody wanted to get involved, but could not understand the only possible alternative of mindless encouragement.

Equally frustrating for me was the code of 'not grassing'. There were cases of theft at school that I dealt with where it was obvious to me that one or more people knew the identity of the thief or thieves. However, as a mere teacher, I always came up against the brick wall of blank faces and silence when I questioned those I thought could name the guilty parties. This code even extended to identifying those actively disliked by individual witnesses I questioned. Moral judgement, in such circumstances, was suspended. One worthwhile course of action when dealing with such matters, I found, was to involve the headteacher. This was the one person, the deus ex machina, most likely to be able to apply sufficient pressure to prise a name out of a witness to a theft.

Teachers can't be accused of not attempting to encourage the growth of our children's moral conduct, but there are powerful oppositional forces. I'm unable to avoid implicating the internet here. A generation of young people has grown up engaging in computer theft on a habitual basis, stealing films, music and computer games as a matter of course. One might argue that any attempt to establish a link between computer theft and personal morality is a tenuous one. The internet is a grey moral backdrop to every child's life that offers far more in terms of temptation than computer piracy. Knowing what I know now of the internet, a part of me wishes it had never come into being, but it looks to be here to stay.

A moral counterpoint to immoral and amoral online activity, appended to our education system in the form of a structured course, is necessary to maintain the moral foundations of our society.

Maintenance Payments

On the subject of children's transition to the adult world, I see no reason why a small financial maintenance payment could not be paid to all students from Year 10 to the end of compulsory education. As a head of sixth form, during those few years when the Education Maintenance Allowance was payable shortly before the economic crash, I discovered how much more amenable and motivated students become on receipt of a regular monetary payment. The justification for scrapping the universal allowance in England in 2010 on the grounds that it merely provided young people with 'beer money' tells me much about the attitudes of politicians towards young people.

I appreciate that such philanthropic gestures are currently unfashionable, bearing in mind that a higher education degree costs students tens of thousands of pounds, in contrast to my experience of being awarded a grant to enter tertiary education. I disagree violently with our government's ungenerous attitude towards the student population. When our economy began to pick up after the 2008 collapse, and foreign investors with 'dirty money' were buying up huge swathes of some of the most valuable properties in the country, there must have been untold billions swilling about in all sorts of coffers.

The March 2016 revelations that the very rich benefited hugely from tax-free offshore accounts suggests a hypocritical, mean-spirited and patronising attitude by the uber-wealthy towards the younger generation. Coming on top of the scandal of huge bonuses paid to this country's bankers, despite government insistence on the necessity for continued public cuts since the 2008 crash, my sympathy goes out to hard-pressed young people.

The systematic pauperisation of a generation may produce short-term economic benefits, but the long-term prospects for a society with a significant proportion of disempowered and disaffected young adults appear bleak. The reported loss in 2015 of 18,000 UK teachers who were choosing to teach abroad suggests a teaching force having no qualms about turning their backs on their parsimonious parent nation.

Good sense may yet prevail in this country's attitude to our school student body, as it does in Wales where KS5 students can be in receipt of up to £30 a week. Scottish undergraduates also fare better than those in this country as they do not pay university tuition fees. It disturbs me that our young people in England currently seem to be the poor student relations in the UK. Much could be done financially for their benefit, in addition to the educational modifications to their learning experiences suggested above.